外贸单证实务

主　编　向彩芬
副主编　刁春玲　梁　艳　徐向慧

北京理工大学出版社
BEIJING INSTITUTE OF TECHNOLOGY PRESS

内容简介

本书以企业实际案例为背景，以外贸流程为线索，以进出口流向为模块，突出制单操作。在简单介绍单证制作基础知识后，重点分析出口环节中各种单据的具体制作，提供信用证、托收、汇付三种结算方式下制作出口议付单据的综合模拟训练。

本书分4个模块，由19个项目组成。除基本内容外，每个项目均配有项目目标、相关知识、工作任务、能力训练；每个模块添加了对应的价值引领，以体现课程思政要求。每个模块均配有模块评估，包括模块课程评价表和基本能力测评表，书后附有外贸实务中常用的中英文对照表。

本书可作为高等教育商务英语、国际贸易、物流等专业外贸单证课程或其他相关课程的教材或教学参考用书，也可供相关专业从业人员或自学者学习参考。

图书在版编目（CIP）数据

外贸单证实务：英、汉/向彩芬主编. --北京：北京理工大学出版社，2022.9

ISBN 978-7-5763-1664-3

Ⅰ.①外…　Ⅱ.①向…　Ⅲ.①进出口贸易-原始凭证-英、汉　Ⅳ.①F740.44

中国版本图书馆CIP数据核字（2022）第160905号

出版发行／北京理工大学出版社有限责任公司
社　　址／北京市海淀区中关村南大街5号
邮　　编／100081
电　　话／（010）68914775（总编室）
　　　　　（010）82562903（教材售后服务热线）
　　　　　（010）68944723（其他图书服务热线）
网　　址／http：//www.bitpress.com.cn
经　　销／全国各地新华书店
印　　刷／涿州市新华印刷有限公司
开　　本／787毫米×1092毫米　1/16
印　　张／12.5
字　　数／291千字
版　　次／2022年9月第1版　2022年9月第1次印刷
定　　价／69.00元

责任编辑／武丽娟
文案编辑／武丽娟
责任校对／刘亚男
责任印制／李志强

图书出现印装质量问题，请拨打售后服务热线，本社负责调换

前言

中国加入世界贸易组织之后，对外贸易得到了长足的发展。在外贸业蓬勃发展的今天，外贸从业人员急剧增加，正确制作外贸工作各环节所需单据是外贸从业人员应具备的基本职业能力。本书正是围绕这个目的，综合讲述制单实务，是一本理论适当、侧重操作的教材，适合应用型本科学生使用，也适合相关从业者阅读参考。

相对于市面上的《外贸单证》教材，本书具有以下特色：

1. 叙述简洁：文字精练，段与段之间不做多余叙述，节约读者阅读时间。

2. 重点突出：对制单操作的细节进行分析，在空白单据中，以灰色字体标注填写要求，方便学生自我学习，不用边看单据，边去翻书找知识点。

3. 注重实务：从实际操作要求出发，全书在不同的学习情境下展开叙述，强调制单实务。

4. 全面系统：全书分为 4 个模块，包括单证制作基础知识，单项制作出口单据，综合模拟——不同结算方式下的出口议付单据制作，制作进口单据，包含了外贸业务中所有单据的制作，全面囊括目前对外贸从业人员需掌握的单证知识。

5. 问题导向：教材从外贸从业人员的实际工作出发，提出问题，解决问题，引发学生的思考，激发学习兴趣。

6. 课程思政：每个部分添加对应的价值引领内容，引导学生培养正确的价值观、人生观，形成对本职工作的批判性思维和正确认知。

此外，本书在内容编排与设计上新颖活泼，体现原理讲授与应用相结合、中英文相结合、平面书本与电子课件相结合、学习与自我测试相结合、教学与评价相结合，这类设计有利于教师讲授、学生复习、企业读者自学。

每个项目设计了以下栏目：

【学习情境】，引发学生联想和思考，让学生熟悉相关工作环境，进入学习状态。

【项目目标】，让学生带着目标学习、思考，培养提出问题、解决问题的能力，同时进行有针对性的学习，提升学习效果。

【相关知识】，即制单要求和重点，是单据制作的指引。

【工作任务】，即在相关知识的指导下，根据实际案例情况，提出制作相关单据的目标任务，充分展示单据制作细节，有利于教师教授和学生学习。

【能力训练】，此部分提出一个全新的案例背景，学生在这个案例背景下制单，锻炼实际操作的能力，充分体现“教学做一体”的教学思想。

【模块评估】，学生学习效果如何，对教学是否满意，存在哪些问题，可通过模块评估体现，以此增强学生与老师的互动，测评学生学习的效果。

【价值引领】，注重课程思政内容的引入，体现素质教育特色。

本书出口模块后附有英汉对照表，书后附有国际贸易相关参考资料，作者可提供课件和能力训练的答案供教师参考使用。

本书由向彩芬主编并统稿，刁春玲、梁艳和徐向慧为本书编写做了大量工作，包括资料收集、各模块课程思政提炼等。本书的出版得到了经济系王灵华教授的很多帮助和支持，同时还得到了广州赛邦印铁制罐有限公司外贸部工作人员的诸多参考意见，在此谨表衷心的感谢。

全书内容参阅了相关学者的成果，参考文献仅反映了其中的主要部分，恕不能一一答谢。本书是我们集体努力的成果，但受学识所限，书中难免有不妥与疏漏之处，希望广大读者及同行多多批评指正。本书建议课时为 32 课时，独立开设外贸单证实训课程，最好在有外贸单证实训软件的机房上课。

编　者

目录

模块一 单证制作基础知识

学习情境一

刘华毕业后在一家公司做单证员，为了能更快上手，刘华在向公司同事学习的同时，重温在学校学过的知识，进一步了解和掌握外贸单证的作用和分类、工作环节与要求；熟悉单证标准化及海运进出口单证工作的流程，深入理解信用证和合同。

价值引领

新冠疫情导致了国际运费上涨、爆仓以及国外码头工人罢工等问题，本模块旨在引导学生培养协调合作、防范风险、主动应变的职业素养。

信用证在本质上是以银行的信用为交易各方进行担保的一种书面凭证。信用证的发展和广泛运用，深刻体现出“诚信”无论对个人发展，还是对世界经济贸易都有着举足轻重的作用；如果诚信缺失，无论是个人、社会或全球经济贸易，都可能承担巨大的交易成本。

项目一：国际贸易单证概述

项目目标

通过本项目，使学生了解外贸单证的作用、分类，缮制单据的基本依据，掌握制单的基本要求。

相关知识

一、国际贸易单证的作用和分类

（一）国际贸易单证的作用

1. 单证的含义

单证是国际结算中应用的单据、文件与证书，凭借这种文件处理国际货物的交付、运输、保险、商检、报关、结汇等。狭义单证指结算单证，即信用证支付方式下的结算单证；广义单证指国际贸易中使用的各种单据、文件与证书的统称。

2. 国际贸易单证的作用

（1）国际贸易单证是合同履行的必要手段。

国际贸易主要表现为单据的买卖。卖方交单意味着交付了货物，而买方付款以得到物权凭证为前提，双方都以单证为核心。所以，单证和货款对流的原则是国际贸易中商品买卖的一般原则。在信用证业务中，各有关当事人处理单据而非相关货物、服务或其他行为。

（2）国际贸易单证是对外贸易经营管理的重要工具。

进出口企业经营的好坏与单证工作组织管理的优劣紧密联系；国际贸易单证体现了一国对外贸易政策。利用国际贸易窗口、关检合一等便利化措施推广国家政策，培养学生及相关从业者的爱国情怀和贸易强国的自信心、自豪感。

（3）国际贸易单证是进出口企业提高经济效益的重要保证 。提高单证质量可减少差错率，提高工作效率，维护企业经济效益。

（4）国际贸易单证是进出口企业形象的重要内涵 。国际贸易单证是商务和法律文件，可塑造和完善进出口企业对外形象，扩大对外宣传。

（二）国际贸易单证的分类

1.《托收统一规则》（《URC522》）的分类

（1）金融单据：具有货币属性，汇票、支票、本票或其他用于取得付款资金的类似凭证。

（2）商业单据：发票、运输单证、所有权单证或其他类似单证，或者一切不属于金融单证的其他单证。

2.《跟单信用证统一惯例》（《UCP600》）的分类

（1）运输单据：海运提单，非转让海运单，租船合约提单，多式联运单据，空运单据，公路、铁路和内陆水运单据，快递和邮包收据，运输代理人的运输单据等。

（2）保险单据：保险单、保险凭证、承保证明、预保单等。

（3）商业发票。

（4）其他单据：装箱单、重量单和各种证明书等。

3. UN/EDIFACT（EDI 国际通用标准）的分类

EDI 国际通用标准将国际贸易单证分为九大类：生产单证、订购单证、销售单证、银行单证、保险单证、货运代理服务单证、运输单证、出口单证、进口和转口单证。

4. 按单证形式分类

国际贸易单证按单证形式分为纸面单证和电子单证。

二、国际贸易单证工作环节与要求

（一）国际贸易单证工作环节

国际贸易单证工作的基本环节包括制单、审单、交单和归档。如果采用信用证支付方式，制单环节前还有审证环节。

（二）制单基本要求

1. 正确

正确是单证工作的前提，也是最重要的一条，包含以下两方面的内容：

（1）各种单据必须做到“三相符”。

单证相符：单据与信用证相符，这是“三相符”中最重要的一点。

单单相符：单据与单据相符。

单同相符：单据与贸易合同相符。

（2）单据必须与有关惯例和法令规定相符。

单据要符合信用证条款中所引用的国际惯例要求，也要注意进出口国对单据或进口国对货物有无特殊规定。例如，输往加拿大、美国等国的货物，如果没有使用木质包装，要提供无木质包装证明，如使用则要进行熏蒸处理，并提供证书。

对于单据的“三相符”，银行只要求前两个相符，以及与相关国际惯例相符；而外贸企业还要求“单货相符”。

2. 完整

完整是单证工作要求的第二条，主要有以下几点：

（1）成套单证群体的完整性。在结汇时，要提供齐全的，成套的单证。如 CIF 下，至少要提供发票、提单、保险单，还有些要提供装箱单、检验证书、产地证、附属证明等。

（2）每一种单据所填内容必须完备齐全，格式、文字、签章、背书等都要注意核对，另外还要注意隐含问题。例如，如果信用证中要求所有单据显示信用证号码，则在所有的单据中都必须要注明信用证的号码，如果没有注明，就属于内容不完整。

（3）单据的份数齐全，尤其是提单的份数，如果要求一式三份，必须是一张正本加两张副本单据。如果要求一式三张正本，必须在单据上标明三张都是正本，并附有权签字人的手签或签章。信用证要求提供的单据和条款必须齐备，不能有遗漏、差错和误期等问题。

3. 及时

及时是单证工作要求的第三条，要注意以下几点：

（1）出单及时：各种单据的出单日期必须合理可行，不能超过信用证有效期或商业习惯的合理日期。其中单据和单据之间的时间应特别注意以下几点：保险单日期早于或等于提单的签发日期，提单（实际装运的日期）日期不得迟于装运期，装运通知书必须在货物装运后立即发出。

各单据日期早晚次序：发票日期<检验证书日期或保险单日期<提单装船日期<信用证最迟装运日期<汇票出票日期<信用证最迟交单日期或信用证有效期。

（2）结汇及时：向银行交单议付不能超过信用证规定的交单期。

如果信用证未规定交单期，银行将拒收迟于运输单据出单日期 21 天后提交的单据，单据的提交也不得迟于信用证到期日。

相关期限的概念如下：

有效期：《UCP600》规定，一切信用证均须规定一个到期日和一个交单付款、承兑的地点。规定的付款、承兑或议付的到期日，将被解释为信用证的有效期。

交单期：信用证还应规定，一个运输单据出单后，必须提交符合信用证条款的单据的特定期限，即“交单期”。

装运期：卖方将货物装上运往目的港的运输工具或交付给承运人的日期。信用证可以没有装运期，只有有效期，在实际业务中叫作“双到期”。

4. 简明

单据的内容应按合同、信用证要求和国际惯例填写，力求简明，切勿加列不必要的内容，以免弄巧成拙。但对于信用证所要求的文字，必须要在单据中列明。简化单证工作，不仅可以减少外贸单证员工作量，提高工作效率，而且有利于提高单证的质量和减少单证的差错率。

5. 整洁

所谓整洁，指单证表面清洁、整齐、美观、大方；单证内容清楚易认，一目了然。单证是否整洁，不但反映制单人制单的熟练程度和工作态度，还直接影响出单效果。因此，在制作单据时，单据格式的设计和缮制力求标准化和规范化，单证内容的排列要行次整齐、主次有序、重点突出、字迹清晰、语法通顺、文句流畅、简明扼要、恰如其分。制作单据时，更改处一定要盖校对章或手签，不能在一份单据上多次涂改，如涂改过多，应重新缮制单据。

（三）制单的依据

1. 买卖合同

买卖合同是制单和审单的首要依据，其范畴有广义和狭义之分。

狭义：国际贸易单证要与合同内容一致。

广义：业务函电也可作为制单和审单的依据。

2. 信用证

在信用证支付方式下，银行仅看信用证，不看合同，因此相关人员在审证环节就要核对信用证与合同的一致性问题。

3. 商品的原始资料

生产商提供的一些资料，如出厂装箱单中显示的规格、型号、数量等。

4. 相关国际惯例

《跟单信用证统一惯例》（《UCP600》）、《跟单信用证项下银行间偿付统一规则》（《URR725》）、《审核跟单信用证项下单据的国际标准银行实务》（《ISBP681》）、《国际贸易术语解释通则》（《INCOTERMS2010》）。

此外，制单依据还包括相关国家的管理规定、国外客户要求等。

（四）单证员从业要求

（1）良好的职业道德。

外贸单证员应具备以下方面的职业道德：

①热爱祖国，热爱社会主义，自觉维护国家和企业的利益，关注国内外的政治经济形势，能正确处理好国家、集体和个人之间的利益关系。

②遵纪守法、廉洁自律，不行贿、索贿、受贿。

③严守国家机密，维护商业机密，自觉遵守外事纪律，遵守企业的各项规章制度。

④对本职工作认真负责，忠于职守，努力学习，勇于实践，积极开拓，锐意进取。

（2）必要的专业知识和技能。

知识素质是指外贸单证员做好本职工作须具备的基础知识与专业知识，包括了解我国对外贸易的方针、政策、法律和法规，贸易国家（地区）的政策；了解管辖商品销往国家或地区的政治、经济、文化、地理及风俗习惯、消费水平；具备一定的文化基础知识，一般要求具有高中（包括中专、技校、职校）以上学历，具有一定的英语基础，能够读懂信用证和外贸函电；会使用计算机常用软件；掌握一定的法律知识，了解合同法、票据法、经济法、外贸法等，以及与外贸跟单员相关法律知识，能知法、懂法和用法。

（3）丰富的实践经验。

一般公司在招聘时希望员工有 1 ~ 2 年的工作经验，在校学生应充分利用时间和机会丰富自己的经验。

（4）认真的工作态度。

严谨认真，做到单证填写无误，单单、单证核对准确，避免不必要的核改。

在国际竞争中保持职业道德，体现大国风范，为对外贸易事业的发展贡献力量。

三、国际贸易单证标准化

（一）国际贸易单证标准化进程

国际贸易单证标准化工作涉及的四大要素：单证格式、贸易数据元、贸易数据元代码、标准 EDI 报文。我国国际贸易单证标准化工作由商务部主管。

（二）我国国际贸易单证主要标准

（1）单证格式标准。外贸单证有统一的标准格式，单据中的栏目基本是一致的。

（2）代码标准。在单证中，每一个代码都有特定的解释，有其固定的含义。

（三）国际贸易单证常用代码

1.《国家和地区名称代码》

国家和地区名称代码由 2 个英文字母组成，如中国 CN，英国 GB，美国 US，德国 DE，法国 FR，俄罗斯 RU，日本 JP。

2.《中华人民共和国口岸及有关地点代码》

2008 年修订的《中华人民共和国口岸及有关地点代码》采用了国际标准惯例的主要口岸两层代码的做法，由 5 个英文字母组成，前两个符号代表国名，后三个符号代表地名，如上海 CNSHG，伦敦 GBLON，纽约 USNYC。

3.《国际贸易用标准运输标志》

运输标志又称唛头，指国际运输中标在单件货物和相关单证上的标志和编号。

唛头内容包含收货人（买方）简称、参考号（合同号）、目的地、件号编号，分四行排列，每行限 17 个字母或数字，使用英文大写或数字，不允许使用几何图形或其他图案，不允许用彩色编码。

四、进出口单证工作流程

（一）出口单证工作流程图（图 1.1）

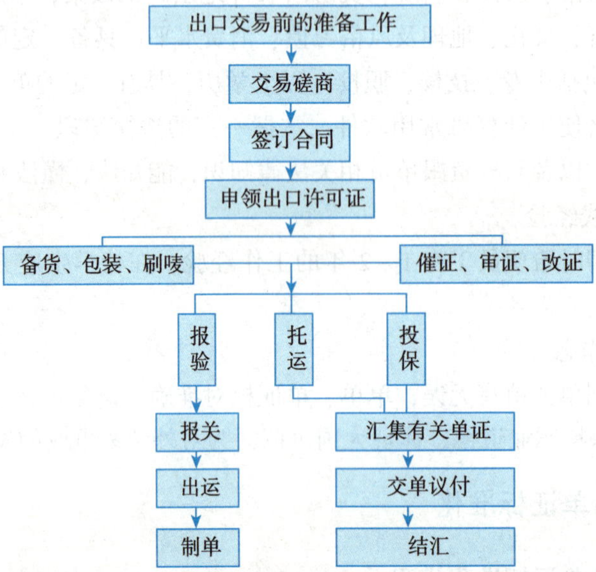

图 1.1　出口单证工作流程

1. 合同的订立

在订立合同时，一定要细致入微，审查每一处细节，包括货物的品名、数量、单价、包装、运输条款、溢短装条款、信用证到达受益人的时间、不可抗力事件等都要有详细的描述，以便后续工作的顺利完成。

2. 备货

根据合同或信用证要求，向指定工厂或储运仓库安排或催交，核实应交货物的品名、品质、数量、规格、包装及标记等情况，保证货物质量合格、包装完好、数量齐备、唛头清楚醒目。

3. 催证、审证与改证

一般在合同订立十五天内，进口方会把信用证开到出口方。在收到信用证之后，出口方要将信用证和合同进行对照，如果有不一致的地方，及时通知进口商修改信用证；尤其要注意信用证的到期日和地点，要为出口工作的落实留出足够的时间。

4. 租船订舱

如果以 FOB 贸易术语成交，就由买方租船订舱，如果买方有指定的货代出口方，也可委托其租船订舱，但一切费用和风险还是由买方来承担。如果以 CFR 和 CIF 贸易术语成交，就由卖方租船订舱。

5. 商检报验与投保

（1）商检报验。凡属法定检验的商品，以及合同或信用证规定须商检出证的商品，必须经检验机构检验，取得“出境货物通关单”或商检证书后方可出口。

（2）保险投保。凡是以 CIF 条件达成的合同，出口商在货物发运前，必须向保险公司投保货物运输险，取得保险单据。

6. 报关资料的制作

报关资料一般包括订舱委托书、装箱单、发票、核销单、报关单、报关委托书。如果商品需要检验，还要把报检的换证凭条或换证凭单以及报检委托书一起寄给货代。在报关之前一定要先进行核销单的电子口岸备案，否则，海关找不到此核销单的信息，就无法顺利报关。

7. 给进口商传通关资料

把实际出货的资料，包括箱单、发票、细码单等传给进口商，以供其通关使用。

8. 原产地证书的办理

如果信用证要求议付时需原产地证，出口商还要到商检局去办理产地证。办理产地证所需要的资料包括装箱单、发票、外销合同，要注明货物的件数、运输方式、起运港、目的港、H. S. 编码等信息。

9. 取得运输单据并发送装运通知

海关查验放行后，即在“装货单”等有关单据上加盖放行章，发货人凭之请承运人装载货物，取得运输单据。货物装运后，出口企业必须将装运情况通知买方，以便买方办理保险，并做好接货准备。

10. 使馆认证

使馆认证指一国外交机构及其授权机构在涉外文书上确认所在国公证机关或某些特殊机关的印章或该机关主管人员的签字属实。如果合同或信用证要求对出口单据进行认证，出口商还必须在各国使馆规定的时间内，按其认证的要求，尽早办理认证手续。

11. 议付资料的制作

议付资料的制作要严格按照信用证上的条款要求，保证一字不差，做到“单单一致，单证相符”，否则可能面临拒付的危险。议付的资料一般包括信用证复印件、正本箱单（盖背书章和正本章）、正本发票（盖背书章和正本章）、正本的提单、原产地证复印件、客检证等。

12. 到议付行议付

凭借制作的议付单据到议付行/通知行去交单议付。

13. 结汇

在接到通知行的结汇通知后，携带公司的公章和 IC 卡去通知行结汇；结汇完收好水单，以备后期核销。

14. 电子交单

一般在货物出口二十天后，要在电子口岸交单。

15. 催退单

在货物出口一个月后跟货代要退单，退单包括核销单、报关单、码头收据等。

16. 核销

在收到退单后，带核销单到通知行盖核销专用章，然后和核销申请书、银行水单、商业发票核销联、报关单核销联合并，到外汇管理局进行核销。

17. 退税

出口退税是指在国际贸易业务中，对我国报关出口的货物退还在国内各生产环节和流转环节按税法规定缴纳的增值税和消费税，即出口环节免税且退还以前纳税环节的已纳税款。

（二）进口流程（图 1.2）

1. 申领配额证明或进口许可证

实行关税配额以及许可证管理的限制进口商品，进口商应向相应主管部门申领配额以及许可证后方可进口。

2. 申请开立信用证

凡以信用证为支付方式进行收支的外贸活动，须申请开立信用证。申请开证至少需向银行提供合同、进口付汇核销单和购汇用汇申请书等三份文件。

3. 修改信用证

对方的改证请求与实际操作须符合国际惯例，即修改信用证应当通过开证行进行。一般情况下应尽量避免修改信用证，必须改证时要按国际惯例办事。如受益人对信用证的修改要求没有一次性提出，或者在合理时间之内没有对修改通知提出不接受等，可予以拒绝并不需承担责任。

4. 租船订舱与投保

按 FOB 术语进口，应负责安排运输，即办理租船订舱手续。按 CFR、CIF 术语进口，应办理货物的运输保险手续。

5. 审单付汇

银行通常为进口商提供一定的审单服务，但银行审核单据，仅审核其表面与信用证或托收指示书的规定是否相符，对于任何单据的形式、完整性、准确性、真实性或法律效力，以及单据上所表示的货物描述、数量、重量、质量、包装、价值等是否真实概不负责，进口商应注意分清责任。

（1）审单要点：

①审核单据的品名、规格、数量、金额、签字等内容是否符合要求。

②审核单据的种类和份数是否齐全。

③审核单据上的装运港、卸货港、目的港、装运期等是否与规定相符。

（2）对不符单据的处理：

①不符性质严重：可拒绝接受单据并拒付全部货款。

②不符性质不太严重：部分付款、部分拒付，货到检验合格付款，凭担保付款，更正单据后付款。

6. 货物的报检与通关

进口商取得全套单据后，在货物抵达国内港口时，持正本提单（大提单）至船公司换取“进口货物提货单”（小提单）提货。凡属法定检验的商品，应在报检后向海关报关，经查验无误后海关才予以放行。

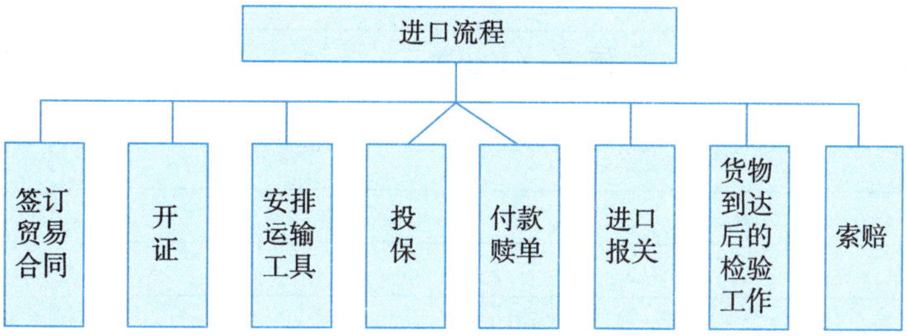

图 1.2 进口流程

工作任务

如果你是刘华，学习完上述内容，谈谈你所了解的单证工作。

项目二：分析合同条款

项目目标

通过本项目学习，使学生了解合同的基本格式和内容，掌握合同缮制中的核心项目。

相关知识

货物销售合同（英汉对照）

出口合同

SALES CONTRACT

合同编号（Contract No.）：________

签订日期（Date）：________

签订地点（Signed at）：________

买方：________

Buyer：________

地址：________

Address：________

电话（Tel）：________ 传真（Fax）：________

电子邮箱（E-mail）：________

卖方：________

Seller：________

地址：________

Address：________

电话（Tel）：________ 传真（Fax）：________

电子邮箱（E-mail）：________

买卖双方同意按照下列条款签订本合同：

The Seller and the Buyer agreed to conclude this Contract subject to the terms and conditions stated below：

1. 货物名称、规格和质量（Name, Specifications and Quality of Commodity）：________
2. 数量（Quantity）：

   允许________的溢短装（________% more or less allowed）
3. 单价（Unit Price）：________
4. 总值（Total Amount）：________
5. 交货条件（Terms of Delivery）FOB/CFR/CIF________
6. 原产地国与制造商（Country of Origin and Manufacturers）：________
7. 包装（Packing）：________

货物应具有防潮、防锈蚀、防震并适合远洋运输联运运输的包装，由于货物包装不良而造成的货物残损、灭失应由卖方负责。卖方应在每个包装箱上用不褪色的颜色标明尺码、包装箱号码、毛重、净重及“此端向上”“防潮”“小心轻放”等标记。

The packing of the goods shall be preventive from dampness, rust, shock, and shall be suitable for ocean transportation/ multiple transportation. The Seller shall be liable for any damage and loss of the goods attributable to the inadequate or improper packing. The measurement, gross weight, net weight and the cautions such as “Do not stack up side down” “Keep away from moisture” “Handle with care” shall be stenciled on the surface of each package with fadeless pigment.

8. 唛头（Shipping Marks）：________

9. 装运期限（Time of Shipment）：________

10. 装运口岸（Port of Loading）：________

11. 目的口岸（Port of Destination）：________

12. 保险（Insurance）：

由________（保险公司）按发票金额 110% 投保________险和________附加险。

Insurance shall be covered by the ________ for 110% of the invoice value against ________ Risks and ________ Additional Risks.

13. 付款条件（Terms of Payment）：

（1）信用证方式：买方应在装运期前/合同生效后____日，开出以卖方为受益人的不可撤销的议付信用证，信用证在装船完毕后____日内到期。

Letter of Credit: The Buyer shall ____ days prior to the time of shipment /after this Contract comes into effect, open an irrevocable Letter of Credit in favor of the Seller. The Letter of Credit shall expire ____ days after the completion of loading of the shipment as stipulated.

（2）付款交单：货物发运后，卖方出具以买方为付款人的付款跟单汇票，按即期付款交单（D/P）方式，通过卖方银行或________银行向买方转交单证，换取货物。

Documents against payment: After shipment, the Seller shall draw a sight bill of exchange on the Buyer and deliver the documents through Sellers bank or ________ Bank to the Buyer against payment, i. e D/P. The Buyer shall effect the payment immediately upon the first presentation of the bill (s) of exchange.

（3）承兑交单：货物发运后，卖方出具以买方为付款人的付款跟单汇票，付款期限为________后____日，按即期承兑交单（D/A____日）方式，通过卖方银行或________银行，经买方承兑后，向买方转交单证，买方在汇票期限到期时支付货款。

Documents against Acceptance: After shipment, the Seller shall draw a sight bill of exchange, payable ______ days after the Buyers delivers the document through Sellers Bank and ________ Bank to the Buyer against acceptance (D/A ____ days). The Buyer shall make the payment on date of the bill of exchange.

（4）货到付款：买方在收到货物后____天内将全部货款支付卖方（不适用于 FOB、CRF、CIF 术语）。

Cash on delivery: The Buyer shall pay to the Seller total amount within ________ days after the receipt of the goods (This clause is not applied to the Terms of FOB, CFR, CIF).

14. 单据（Documents）：

卖方应将下列单据提交银行议付/托收：

The Seller shall present the following documents to the bank for negotiation/collection:

（1）标明通知收货人/受货代理人的全套清洁的、已装船的、空白抬头、空白背书并注明运费已付/到付的海运/联运/陆运提单；

Full set of clean on board Ocean/Multiple Transportation/Land Bills of Lading and blank endorsed marked freight prepaid/ to collect;

（2）标有合同编号、信用证号（信用证支付条件下）及装运唛头的商业发票一式____份；

Signed commercial invoice in ____ copies indicating Contract No. , L/C No. (Terms of L/C) and shipping marks;

（3）由________出具的装箱或重量单一式____份；

Packing list/weight memo in ________ copies issued by ________;

（4）由________出具的质量证明书一式____份；

Certificate of Quality in ________ copies issued by ________;

（5）由________出具的数量证明书一式____份；

Certificate of Quantity in ____ copies issued by ________;

（6）保险单正本一式____份（CIF 交货条件）；

Insurance policy/certificate in ____ copies (Terms of CIF);

（7）由________签发的产地证一式____份；

Certificate of Origin in ____ copies issued by________;

（8）装运通知（Shipping advice）：卖方应在交运后________小时内以特快专递方式邮寄给买方上述第____项单据副本一式一套。

The Seller shall, within ________ hours after shipment effected, send by courier each copy of the above-mentioned documents No. ____.

15. 装运条款（Terms of Shipment）：

（1）FOB 交货方式。

卖方应在合同规定的装运日期前30天，以________方式通知买方合同号、品名、数量、金额、包装件数、毛重、尺码及装运港可装日期，以便买方安排租船/订舱。装运船只按期到达装运港后，如卖方不能按时装船，发生的空船费或滞期费由卖方负担。在货物越过船弦并脱离吊钩以前一切费用和风险由卖方负担。

The Seller shall, 30 days before the shipment date specified in the Contract, advise the Buyer by ________ of the Contract No. , commodity, quantity, amount, packages, gross weight, measurement, and the date of shipment in order that the Buyer can charter a vessel/book shipping space. In the event of the Seller's failure to effect loading when the vessel arrives duly at the loading port, all expenses including dead freight and/or demurrage charges thus incurred shall be for the Seller's account.

（2）CIF 或 CFR 交货方式。

卖方须按时在装运期限内将货物由装运港装船至目的港。在 CFR 术语下，卖方应在装船前2天以________方式通知买方合同号、品名、发票价值及开船日期，以便买方安排保险。

The Seller shall ship the goods duly within the shipping duration from the port of loading to the port of destination. Under CFR terms, the Seller shall advise the Buyer by ________ of the Contract No. , commodity, invoice value and the date of dispatch two days before the shipment for the Buyer to arrange insurance in time.

16. 装运通知（Shipping Advice）：

一旦装载完毕，卖方应在____小时内以________方式通知买方合同编号、名称、已发运数量、发票总金额、毛重、船/车/机号及启程日期等。

The Seller shall, immediately upon the completion of the loading of the goods, advise the Buyer of the Contract No. , names of commodity, loading quantity, invoice values, gross weight, name of vessel and shipment date by ________ within ________ hours.

17. 质量保证（Quality Guarantee）：

货物品质规格必须符合本合同及质量保证书之规定，品质保证期为货到目的港____个月内。在保证期限内，因制造厂商在设计制造过程中的缺陷造成的货物损害应由卖方负责赔偿。

The Seller shall guarantee that the commodity must be in conformity with the quality, specifications and quantity specified in this Contract and Letter of Quality Guarantee. The guarantee period shall be ____ months after the arrival of the goods at the port of destination, and during the period the Seller shall be responsible for the damage due to the defects in designing and manufacturing of the manufacturer.

18. 检验（Inspection）（以下两项任选一项）：

（1）卖方须在装运前____日委托________检验机构对本合同之货物进行检验并出具检验证书，货到目的港后，由买方委托________检验机构进行检验。

The Seller shall have the goods inspected by ____ days before the shipment and have the Inspection Certificate issued by ________. The Buyer may have the goods reinspected by ________ after the goods arrival at the destination.

（2）发货前，制造厂应对货物的质量、规格、性能、数量和重量进行精密全面的检验，出具检验证明书，并说明检验的技术数据和结论。货到目的港后，买方将申请中国商品检验局（以下简称“商检局”）对货物的规格、数量和重量进行检验，如发现货物残损或规格、数量与合同规定不符，除保险公司或轮船公司的责任外，买方得在货物到达目的港后____日内凭商检局出具的检验证书向卖方索赔或拒收该货。在保证期内，如货物由于设计或制造缺陷而发生损坏或品质和性能与合同规定不符时，买方将委托中国商检局进行检验。

The manufacturers shall, before delivery, make a precise and comprehensive inspection of the goods with regard to its quality, specifications, performance, quantity and weight, and issue inspection certificates certifying the technical data and conclusion of the inspection. After arrival of the goods at the port of destination, the Buyer shall apply to China Commodity Inspection Bureau (CCIB) for a further inspection as to the specifications, quantity and weight of the goods. If damages of the goods are found, or the specifications and/or quantity are not in conformity with the stipulations in this Contract, except when the responsibilities lies with Insurance Company or Shipping Company, the Buyer shall, within ____ days after arrival of the goods at the port of destination, claim against the Seller, or reject the goods according to the inspection certificate issued by CCIB. In case of damage of the goods incurred due to the design or manufacture defects and/or in case the quality and performance are not in conformity with the Contract, the Buyer shall, during the guarantee period, request CCIB to make a survey.

19. 索赔（Claim）：

买方凭委托检验机构出具的检验证明书向卖方提出索赔（包括换货），由此引起的全部费用应由卖方负担。若卖方收到上述索赔后____天未予答复，则认为卖方已接受买方索赔。

The buyer shall make a claim against the Seller (including replacement of the goods) by the further inspection certificate and all the expenses incurred therefrom shall be borne by the Seller. The claims mentioned above shall be regarded as being accepted if the Seller fail to reply within ____ days after the Seller received the Buyer's claim.

20. 迟交货与罚款（Late delivery and Penalty）：

除合同第 21 条不可抗力原因外，如卖方不能按合同规定的时间交货，买方应同意在卖方支付罚款的条件下延期交货。罚款可由议付银行在议付货款时扣除，罚款率按每____天收____%，不足____天时以____天计算。但罚款不得超过迟交货物总价的____%。如卖方延期交货超过合同规定____天时，买方有权撤销合同，此时，卖方仍应按货物不迟延的方式根据上述规定向买方支付罚款。

买方有权对因此遭受的其他损失向卖方提出索赔。

Should the Seller fail to make delivery on time as stipulated in the Contract, with the exception of Force Majeure causes specified in Clause 21 of this Contract, the Buyer shall agree to postpone the delivery on the condition that the Seller agree to pay a penalty which shall be deducted by the paying bank from the payment under negotiation. The rate of penalty is charged at ____% for every ____ days, odd days less than ____ days should be counted as ____ days. But the penalty, however, shall not exceed ____% of the total value of the goods involved in the delayed delivery. In case the Seller fail to make delivery ____ days later than the time of shipment stipulated in the Contract, the Buyer shall have the right to cancel the Contract and the Seller, in spite of the cancellation, shall nevertheless pay the aforesaid penalty to the Buyer without delay.

The buyer shall have the right to lodge a claim against the Seller for the losses sustained if any.

21. 不可抗力（Force Majeure）：

凡在制造或装船运输过程中，因不可抗力致使卖方不能或推迟交货时，卖方不负责任。在发生上述情况时，卖方应立即通知买方，并在____天内，给买方特快专递一份由当地民间商会签发的事故证明书。在此情况下，卖方仍有责任采取一切必要措施加快交货。如事故延续____天以上，买方有权撤销合同。

The Seller shall not be responsible for the delay of shipment or non-delivery of the goods due to Force Majeure, which might occur during the process of manufacturing or in the course of loading or transit. The Seller shall advise the Buyer immediately of the occurrence mentioned above and within ____ days thereafter the Seller shall send a notice by courier to the Buyer for their acceptance of a certificate of the accident issued by the local chamber of commerce under whose jurisdiction the accident occurs as evidence thereof. Under such circumstances the Seller, however, are still under the obligation to take all necessary measures to hasten the delivery of the goods. In case the accident lasts for more than ____ days, the Buyer shall have the right to cancel the Contract.

22. 争议的解决（Arbitration）：

凡因本合同引起的或与本合同有关的任何争议应协商解决。若协商不成，应提交中国国际经济贸易仲裁委员会深圳分会，按照申请时该会当时施行的仲裁规则进行仲裁。仲裁裁决是终局的，对双方均有约束力。

Any dispute arising from or in connection with the Contract shall be settled through friendly negotiation. In case no settlement is reached, the dispute shall be submitted to China International Economic and Trade Arbitration Commission (CIETAC), Shenzhen Commission, for arbitration in accordance with its rules in effect at the time of applying for arbitration. The arbitral award is final and binding upon both parties.

23. 通知（Notices）：

所有通知用________文写成，并按照如下地址用传真/电子邮件/快件送达各方。如果地址有变更，一方应在变更后____日内书面通知另一方。

All notice shall be written in ________ and served to both parties by fax/courier according to the following addresses. If any changes of the addresses occur, one party shall inform the other party of the change of address within ____ days after the change.

24. 本合同使用的 FOB、CFR、CIF 术语系根据国际商会《2010 年国际贸易术语解释通则》。

The terms of FOB, CFR, CIF in the Contract are based on INCOTERMS 2010 of the International Chamber of Commerce.

25. 附加条款（Additional Clause）：

本合同上述条款与本附加条款抵触时，以本附加条款为准。

Conflicts between Contract clause hereabove and this additional clause, if any, it is subject to this additional clause.

26. 本合同用中英文两种文字写成，两种文字具有同等效力。本合同共____份，自双方代表签字（盖章）之日起生效。

This Contract is executed in two counterparts each in Chinese and English, each of which shall deemed equally authentic. This Contract is in ____ copies, effective since being signed/sealed by both parties.

买方代表（签字）：________________________________

Representative of the Buyer

(Authorized signature)：____________________________

卖方代表（签字）：________________________________

Representative of the Seller

(Authorized signature)：____________________________

合同样单

【样单 1-1】

销货合同 SALES CONTRACT				
卖方 SELLER	LINJIANG TRADING CO. , LTD. RM2901 HUARONG MANSION, NO. 85 GUANJIAQIAO, NANJING 210005, CHINA TEL: 0086-25-4715004 FAX: 0086-25-4711363	编号 NO. 日期 DATE 地点 SIGNED IN	NEO2011026 Feb. 28,2011 NANJING, CHINA	
买方 BUYER	AFG GENERAL TRADING CO. LTD P. O. BOX 99552, RIYADH 22766, KSA TEL: 00966-1-4659220 FAX: 00966-1-4659213			
买卖双方同意以下条款达成交易： This contract is made by and agreed between the BUYER and the SELLER, in accordance with the terms and conditions stipulated below.				
1. 品名及规格 Commodity & Specification		2. 数量 Quantity	3. 单价及价格条款 Unit Price & Trade Terms	4. 金额 Amount
			CFR DAMMAM PORT, SAUDI ARABIA	
ABOUT 1 700 CARTONS CANNED MUSHROOMS PIECES & STEMS 24 TINS X 425 GRAMS NET		1, 700CARTONS	USD7. 80	USD13, 260. 00
Total		1, 700CARTONS		USD13, 260. 00
允许	溢短装，由卖方决定			
With	More or less of shipment allowed at the sellers' option			
5. 总值 Total Value	USD THIRTEEN THOUSAND TWO HUNDRED AND SIXTY ONLY.			
6. 包装 Packing	EXPORTED BROWN CARTON			
7. 唛头 Shipping Marks	ROSE BRAND 178/2011 RIYADH			
8. 装运期及运输方式 Time of Shipment & Means of Transportation		Not Later Than Apr. 30,2011 by Vessel		
9. 装运港及目的地 Port of Loading & Destination		From : SHANGHAI PORT, CHINA To : DAMMAM PORT, SAUDI ARABIA		
10. 保险 Insurance	TO be covered by the BUYER.			
11. 付款方式 Terms of Payment	The Buyers shall open through a bank acceptable to the Seller an Irrevocable Letter of Credit payable at sight of reach the seller 30 days before the month of shipment, valid for negotiation in China until the 15th day after the date of shipment.			
12. 备注 Remarks				
The Buyer		The Seller		
AFG GENERAL TRADING CO. (进口商签字盖章)		LINJIANG TRADING CO. , LTD. (出口商签字盖章)		

工作任务

如果你是刘华，看完上述合同后，请找出如下内容。

(1) 合同号与合同日期。
(2) 出口商和进口商的名址。
(3) 货物描述、数量、单位、单价、总值。
(4) 价格条款。
(5) 交货期。
(6) 运输条款。
(7) 运费和保费负担。
(8) 对信用证开证的要求。
(9) 对议付文件名称、数量、抬头的要求。
(10) 出口商与进口商签章栏。

项目三：分析信用证条款

项目目标

能看懂全英文的信用证，并理解其中的含义和要求。

相关知识

一、概述

1. 总的说明

总的说明包括信用证的编号、开证日期和地点，有效期和到期地点，交单期等。一般信用证有效期为规定的装运期后第 15 天；未规定有效期的信用证无效。

2. 信用证的种类

可否转让、是否经另一银行保兑等。

3. 信用证的当事人

开证申请人、开证行、受益人、通知行等。

4. 汇票条款

凡使用汇票的信用证，通常规定汇票的各项内容。

5. 兑付方式

兑付方式包括即期、延期、承兑、议付等。

6. 货物条款

货物条款包括货物的名称、规格、数量、包装等。

7. 价格条款

单价、总价以及使用的贸易术语。

8. 货币和信用证金额

此条款包括币别和总额。

9. 装运和保险条款

此条款包括装运的最迟期限、起运地、目的地、运输方式，可否分批装运，可否中途转运等，在 CIF 和 CIP 下，包括对保险的要求、保险的险别、投保的金额等。

10. 单据条款

信用证所要求的单据主要可分为三类：①商业发票。②运输单据，如提单，这是货物所有权的凭证。③保险单据，如保险单等。除上述三类单据外，还可能有其他单证，如包装单据、产地证、检验证书等。

11. 特殊条款

不准在某港停靠或不准在某条航线行驶、限装某船或不得装某船等。

12. 责任条款

银行保证条款等，一般为适用于《UCP600》的文句。

二、信用证常见英文详解

（一）信用证类别 Kinds of L/C

（1）revocable L/C or irrevocable L/C 可撤销信用证/不可撤销信用证。

（2）confirmed L/C or unconfirmed L/C 保兑信用证/不保兑信用证。

（3）sight L/C or usance L/C 即期信用证/远期信用证。

（4）transferable L/C or nontransferable L/C 可转让信用证/不可转让信用证。

（5）divisible L/C or undivisible L/C 可分割信用证/不可分割信用证。

（6）revolving L/C 循环信用证。

（7）L/C with T or T reimbursement clause 带电汇条款信用证。

（8）without recourse L/C or with recourse L/C 无追索权信用证/有追索权信用证。

（9）documentary L/C or clean L/C 跟单信用证/光票信用证。

（10）deferred payment L/C or anticipatory L/C 延付信用证/预支信用证。

（11）back to back L/C or reciprocal L/C 对背信用证/对开信用证。

（12）standby L/C 备用信用证。

（二）有关当事人 Names of Parties Concerned

1. opener 开证人

（1）applicant 开证人（申请开证人）。

（2）principal 开证人（委托开证人）。

（3）accountee 开证人。

（4）accreditor 开证人（委托开证人）。

（5）opener 开证人。

（6）for account of... 付（某人）账。

（7）at the request of...应（某人）请求。

（8）on behalf of...代表某人。

（9）by order of...奉（某人）之命。

（10）by order of...and for account of... 奉（某人）之命并付其账户。

（11）at the request of...and for account of... 应（某人）的要求并付其账户。

（12）in accordance with instruction received from accreditors 根据已收到的委托开证人的指示。

2. beneficiary 受益人

（1）beneficiary 受益人。

（2）in favour of...以（某人）为受益人。

（3）in one's favour 以……为受益人。

（4）favouring yourselves 以你本人为受益人。

3. drawee 付款人

（1）to drawn on（upon）以（某人）为付款人。

（2）to value on 以（某人）为付款人。

（3）to issued on 以（某人）为付款人。

4. drawer 出票人

5. advising bank 通知行

（1）advising bank 通知行。

（2）the notifying bank 通知行。

（3）advised through...bank 通过……银行通知。

6. opening bank 开证行

（1）opening bank 开证行。

（2）issuing bank 开证行。

（3）establishing bank 开证行。

7. negotiating bank 议付行

8. paying bank 付款行

9. reimbursing bank 偿付行

10. confirming bank 保兑行

（三）信用证金额 Amount of the L/C

（1）amount RMB ¥... 金额为人民币……

（2）up to an aggregate amount of Hong Kong Dollars... 累计金额最高为港币……

（3）for a sum（sums）not exceeding a total of GBP... 总金额不得超过英镑……

（4）to the extent of HKD... 总金额为港币……

（5）for the amount of USD… 金额为美元……

（6）for an amount not exceeding total of JPY… 总金额不超过日元……

（四）跟单条款 The Stipulations for the Shipping Documents

available against surrender of the following documents bearing our credit number 凭提交下列注明本证号码的单据付款

（1）drafts to be accompanied by the documents marked（×）below 汇票须随附下列注有（×）的单据。

（2）accompanied against to documents hereinafter 随附下列单据。

（3）accompanied by following documents 随附下列单据。

（4）documents required 单据要求。

（5）accompanied by the following documents marked（×）in duplicate 随附下列注有（×）的单据一式两份。

（6）drafts are to be accompanied by… 汇票要随附（指单据）……

（五）汇票 Draft Bill of Exchange

1. the kinds of drafts 汇票种类

（1）available by drafts at sight 凭即期汇票付款。

（2）draft（s）to be drawn at 30 days sight 开立 30 天的期票。

（3）sight drafs 即期汇票。

（4）term drafts 远期汇票。

2. drawn clauses 出票条款，即出具汇票的法律依据

（1）all darfts drawn under this credit must contain the clause "Drafts drawn under bank of… credit No. …dated…" 本证项下开具的汇票须注明"本汇票系凭××银行××年××月××日第××号信用证下开具"的条款。

（2）drafts are to be drawn in duplicate to our order bearing the clause "Drawn under United Malayan Banking Corp. Bhd. Irrevocable Letter of Credit No. …dated July 12, 1978" 汇票一式两份，以我行为抬头，并注明"根据马来西亚联合银行 1978 年 7 月 12 日第××号不可撤销信用证项下开立"。

（3）draft（s）drawn under this credit to be marked "Drawn under…bank L/C No. …dated (issuing date of credit)" 根据本证开出的汇票须注明"凭××银行××年××月××日（按开证日期）第××号不可撤销信用证项下开立"。

（4）drafts in duplicate at sight bearing the clauses "Drawn under…L/C No. …dated…" 即期汇票一式两份，注明"根据××银行信用证××号，××年××月××日开具"。

（5）draft（s）so drawn must be in scribed with the number and date of this L/C 开具的汇票须注上本证的号码和日期。

（6）draft（s）bearing the clause "Drawn under documentary credit No. …（shown above）of…bank" 汇票注明"根据××银行跟单信用证××号（如上所示）项下开立"。

（六）发票 Invoice

（1）signed commercial invoice 已签署的商业发票。

in duplicate 一式两份
in triplicate 一式三份
in quadruplicate 一式四份
in quintuplicate 一式五份
in sextuplicate 一式六份
in septuplicate 一式七份
in octuplicate 一式八份
in nonuplicate 一式九份
in decuplicate 一式十份

（2） beneficiary's original signed commercial invoices at least in 8 copies issued in the name of the buyer indicating (showing/evidencing/specifying/declaration of) the merchandise, country of origin and any other relevant information. 以买方的名义开具、注明商品名称、原产国及其他有关资料，并经签署受益人的商业发票正本至少一式八份。

（3） Signed attested invoice combined with certificate of origin and value in 6 copies as required for imports into Nigeria. 以签署的，连同产地证明和货物价值的，输入尼日利亚的联合发票一式六份。

（4） beneficiary must certify on the invoice...have been sent to the accountee 受益人须在发票上证明，已将××寄交开证人。

（5） 4% discount should be deducted from amount of the commercial invoice 商业发票的总金额须扣除 4% 折扣。

（6） invoice must be showed "under A/P No. ...date of expiry Jan. 19,2021" 发票须表明"根据第××号购买证，到期日为 2021 年 1 月 19 日"。

（7） documents in combined form are not acceptable 不接受联合单据。

（8） combined invoice is not acceptable 不接受联合发票。

（七）提单 Bill of Loading

（1） full set shipping (company's) clean on board bill (s) of lading marked "Freight Prepaid" to order of shipper endorsed to...Bank, notifying buyers 全套装船（公司的）洁净已装船提单应注明"运费付讫"，作为以装船人指示为抬头，背书给××银行，通知买方。

（2） bills of lading made out in negotiable form 作成可议付形式的提单。

（3） clean shipped on board ocean bills of lading to order and endorsed in blank marked "Freight Prepaid" notifying importer (openers, accountee) 洁净已装船的提单空白抬头并空白背书，注明"运费付讫"，通知进口人（开证人）。

（4） full set of clean "on board" bills of lading/cargo receipt made out to our order/to order and endorsed in blank notify buyers M/S ... Co. calling for shipment from China to Hamburg marked "Freight prepaid" "Freight Payable at Destination" 全套洁净"已装船"提单/货运收据作成以我（行）为抬头/空白抬头，空白背书，通知买方××公司，要求货物自中国运往汉堡，注明"运费付讫""运费在目的港付"。

（5） bills of lading issued in the name of... 提单以××为抬头。

（6） bills of lading must be dated not before the date of this credit and not later than Aug.

15, 2021 提单日期不得早于本证的日期，不得迟于2021年8月15日。

（7）bill of lading marked notifying buyer "Freight prepaid" "Liner terms" "received for shipment" B/L not acceptable 提单注明通知买方"运费预付"按"班轮条件"，"备运提单"不接受。

（8）non-negotiable copy of bills of lading 不可议付的提单副本。

（八）保险

the stipulations for insurance 保险条款

（1）marine insurance policy 海运保险单。

（2）specific policy 单独保险单。

（3）voyage policy 航程保险单。

（4）time policy 期限保险单。

（5）floating policy（or open policy）流动保险单。

（6）ocean marine cargo clauses 海洋运输货物保险条款。

（7）ocean marine insurance clauses（frozen products）海洋运输冷藏货物保险条款。

（8）ocean marine cargo war clauses 海洋运输货物战争险条款。

（9）ocean marine insurance clauses（wood oil in bulk）海洋运输散装桐油保险条款。

（10）overland transportation insurance clauses（train, trucks）陆上运输货物保险条款（火车、汽车）。

（11）overland transportation insurance clauses（frozen products）陆上运输冷藏货物保险条款。

（12）air transportation cargo insurance clauses 航空运输货物保险条款。

（13）air transportation cargo war risk clauses 航空运输货物战争险条款。

（14）parcel post insurance clauses 邮包保险条款。

（15）parcel post war risk insurance clauses 邮包战争保险条款。

（16）livestock、poultry insurance clauses by sea, land or air 活牲畜、家禽的海上、陆上、航空保险条款。

（17）…risks clauses of the P. I. C. C. subject to C. I. C. 根据中国人民保险公司的保险条款投保××险。

（18）marine insurance policies or certificates in negotiable form, for 110% full CIF invoice covering the risks of War & W. A. as per the People's Insurance Co., of China dated 1/1/2021. with extended cover up to Kuala Lumpur with claims payable in（at）Kuala Lumpur in the currency of draft（irrespective of percentage）作为可议付格式的海运保险单或凭证按照到岸价的发票金额110%投保中国人民保险公司1981年1月1日的战争险和基本险，负责到吉隆坡为止，按照汇票所使用的货币在吉隆坡赔付（无免赔率）。

（19）insurance policy or certificate settling agent's name is to be indicated, any additional premium to cover uplift between 10% and 17% may be drawn in excess of the credit value 保险单或凭证须表明理赔代理人的名称，保险费如增加10%～17%可在本证金额以外支付。

（20）insurance policy（certificate）… Name of Assured to be showed A. B. C. Co., Ltd. 保险单或凭证作成以A. B. C. 有限公司为被保险人。

（21） insurance policy or certificate covering W. A. （or F. P. A.） and war risks as per ocean marine cargo clause and ocean marine cargo war risk clauses of the People's Insurance Company of China dated 1/1/1981 保险单或凭证根据中国人民保险公司 1981 年 1 月 1 日的海洋运输货物保险条款和海洋运输货物战争险条款投保水渍险（或平安险）和战争险。

（22） insurance policy/certificate covering all risks, war risk, mines risk 保险单/凭证投保一切险、战争险、地雷险（注：mines 解释为地雷，属于战争险的负责范围，可以接受）。

（23） W. A. this insurance must be valid for period of 60 days after the discharge of goods 水渍险在货物卸船后 60 天有效。

（24） in triplicate covering all risks and war risks including W. A. and breakage in excess of five percent on the whole consignment and including W/W up to buyer's godown in Penang 投保一切险和战争险包括水渍险，破碎损失有 5% 绝对免赔率，按全部货物计算，包括仓至仓条款，负责到买方在槟城的仓库为止（的保险单）一式三份。

（25） insurance policy issued of endorsed to order … for the face value of invoice plus 10% covering including war with 15 days after arrival of goods at destination, only against FPA and T. P. N. D. 按发票面值加 10% 投保战争险，货物到达目的地后 15 天有效，仅负责平安险和盗窃提货不着险的保险单开给或背书给××。

（26） insurance policy or certificate issued by an insurance Co. with W. P. A. clause covering the merchandise for about 10% above the full invoice value including unlimited transhipment with claims payable at Singapore 由保险公司签发的保险单或凭证按发票总金额另加 10% 投保水渍险，包括非限定转船的损失，在新加坡赔付。

（27） covering all eventual risks 投保一切意外风险。

（28） covering all marine risks 投保一切海运风险。

（29） marine insurance policy including "both - to - blame" collision clauses and fully covering the shipment 海运保险单包括负责船舶互撞条款和全部货载。

（30） insurance including deviation clauses 保险包括绕道条款。

（31） covering overland transportation all risks as per overland transportation cargo insurance clauses（train, trucks）of the People's Insurance Company of China dated…按照中国人民保险公司××年××月××日陆上运输货物保险条款（火车、汽车）投保陆上运输一切险。

（32） covering air transportation all risk as per air transportation cargo insurance clauses of P. I. C. C. 按照中国人民保险公司航空运输货物保险条款投保航空运输一切险。

（33） insurance policy or certificate covering parcel post all risks including war risks as per parcel post insurance clauses and parcel post war risk insuracne clauses of the People's Insurance Company of China dated…保险单或凭证按照中国人民保险公司××年××月××日邮包保险条款和邮包战争险条款投保邮包一切险和邮包战争险。

（34） covering all risks including war risks as per ocean marine cargo clauses and air transportation cargo insurance clauses and ocean marine cargo war risk clauses and air transportation cargo war risk clauses of the People's Insurance Company of China dated…按照中国人民保险公司××年××月××日海洋运输货物保险条款、航空运输货物保险条款、海洋运输货物战争险条款和航空运输货物战争险条款投保海空联运一切险和战争险。

（35） covering all risks as per ocean marine cargo clauses and overland transportation cargo insurance clause (train, truck) of P. I. C. C. dated…按照中国人民保险公司××年××月××日海洋运输货物保险条款和陆上运输货物保险条款（火车、汽车）投保海陆联运一切险。

（36） covering all risks including war risks as per overland transportation cargo insurance clauses (train, truck) and air transportation cargo insurance clauses and air transportation cargo war risk clause and war clauses (for cargo transportation by rail) of the People's Insurance Company of China dated…按照中国人民保险公司××年××月××日陆运货物保险条款（火车、汽车）和空运货物保险条款以及空运货物战争险条款和铁路货运战争条款投保陆空陆联运一切险和战争险。

（37） including shortage in weight in excess of 0.5% (with 0.5% franchise) on the whole consignment 包括短量损失有0.5%绝对免赔率（0.5%相对免赔率），按全部货物计算。

（38） including risk of breaking or clashing 包括破裂或凹瘪险。

（39） including risk of chipping or denting 包括碎裂或凹弯险。

（40） including risk of bad odour 包括恶味险。

（41） including damage by hooks, oils, muds and contact with other cargo (insured value) 包括钩损、油污、泥污以及和他物接触所致的损失（以保险价值为限）。

（42） including damage caused by rain and fresh water, internal combustion (total or partial loss) 包括淡水雨淋、自燃所致的损失（包括全部或部分损失）。

（43） including loss and/or damage caused by seawater, fresh-water, acid, grease 包括海水、淡水、酸蚀、油脂所致的损失。

（44） including T. P. N. D. loss and/or damage caused by heat, ship's sweat and odour, hoop-rust, breakage of packing 包括偷窃提货不着，受热，船舱发汗、串味，铁箍锈损，包装破裂所致的损失。

（45） includingd amage caused by infestation mould 包括虫蛀霉烂的损失。

（46） including damage due to rough handling during transit subject to C. T. C. 按照中国保险条款包括运输途中操作不当所致的损失。

（47） including loss and/or damage from any external cause as per CIC 按照中国保险条款包括外来原因所致的损失。

（48） including damage by slings, stains, grease, acids 包括吊具、斑污、油脂、酸蚀造成的损失。

（49） excluding risk of breakage 不包括破碎险。

（50） including the breakage does not cover the goods remarked in the invoice as originally damage 包括破碎险，但不负责发票所示之货物的原残损失。

（51） excluding natural loss in weight 不包括途耗短量的损失。

（52） including 60 days after discharge of the goods at port of destination (or at station of destination) subject to C. T. C. 按照中国保险条款货物在目的港卸船（或在目的地车站卸车）后60天为止。

（53） including W. A. & risk of fire for 60 days in customs warehouse after discharge of the goods at port of destination subject to CIC 按照中国保险条款投保水渍险和火险，在目的港卸货后存入海关仓库60天为止。

（54） this insurance must be valid for a period of 60 days after arrival of merchandise at inland destination 本保险扩展到货物到达内地的目的地后 60 天有效。

（55） insurance policy or certificate covering F. P. A. including the risk of war and risks of S. R. C. C. as per I. C. C. dated…and institute war clauses dated…and institute S. R. C. C. clauses dated… 按照××年××月××日伦敦保险学会条款和××年××月××日学会战争险条款以及××年××月××日学会罢工、暴动、民变险条款投保平安险、战争险和罢工、暴动、民变险。

（56） the People's Insurance Company of China investment insurance (political risks) clauses 中国人民保险公司投资保险（政治风险）条款

（57） property insurance clauses 财产保险条款。

（58） the People's Insurance Company of China erection all risks clauses 中国人民保险公司安装工程一切险条款。

（59） the People's Insurance Company of China contractors all risks clauses 中国人民保险公司建筑工程一切险条款。

（九）产地证 Certificate of Origin

（1） certificate of origin of China 中国产地证明书。

（2） certificate of origin shipment of goods of … origin prohibited 产地证不允许装运××的产品。

（3） declaration of origin 产地证明书（产地声明）。

（4） certificate of origin separated 单独出具的产地证。

（5） certificate of origin "form A" 产地证明书（格式 A）。

（6） generalised system of preference certificate of origin form "A" 普惠制产地证明书（格式 A）。

（十）装箱单与重量单 Packing List and Weight List

（1） packing list detailing the complete inner packing specification and contents of each package 载明每件货物之内部包装的规格和内容的装箱单。

（2） packing list detailing… 详注××的装箱单。

（3） packing list showing in detail… 注明××细节的装箱单。

（4） weight list 重量单。

（5） weight notes 磅码单（重量单）。

（6） detailed weight list 明细重量单。

（7） weight and measurement list 重量和尺码单。

（十一）检验证书 Inspection Certificate

（1） certificate of weight 重量证明书。

（2） certificate of inspection certifying quality & quantity in triplicate issued by…由××出具的品质和数量检验证明书一式三份。

（3） phytosanitary certificate 植物检疫证明书。

（4） plant quarantine certificate 植物检疫证明书。

（5） fumigation certificate 熏蒸证明书。

（6） certificate stating that the goods are free from live weevil 无活虫证明书（熏蒸除虫证明

书）。

（7） sanitary certificate 卫生证书。

（8） health certificate 卫生（健康）证书。

（9） analysis certificate 分析（化验）证书。

（10） tank inspection certificate 油仓检验证明书。

（11） record of ullage and oil temperature 空距及油温记录单。

（12） certificate of aflatoxin negative 黄曲霉素检验证书。

（13） non-aflatoxin certificate 无黄曲霉素证明书。

（14） survey report on weight issued by…由××签发之重量检验证明书。

（15） inspection certificate 检验证书。

（16） inspection and testing certificate issued by… 由××签发之检验证明书。

（十二）其他单据 Other Documents

（1） full set of forwarding agents' cargo receipt 全套运输行所出具之货物承运收据。

（2） air way bill for goods condigned to…quoting our credit number 以××为收货人，注明本证号码的空运货单。

（3） parcel post receipt 邮包收据。

（4） parcel post receipt showing parcels addressed to…a/c accountee 邮包收据注明收件人通过××转交开证人。

（5） parcel post receipt evidencing goods condigned to…and quoting our credit number 以××为收货人并注明本证号码的邮包收据。

（6） certificate customs invoice on form 59A combined certificate of value and origin for developing countries 适用于发展中国家的包括价值和产地证明书的格式 59A 海关发票证明书。

（7） pure foods certificate 纯食品证书。

（8） combined certificate of value and Chinese origin 价值和中国产地联合证明书。

（十三）装运条款 The Stipulation for Shipping Terms

1. loading port and destinaltion 装运港与目的港

（1） despatch/shipment from Chinese port to…从中国港口发送/装运往××。

（2） evidencing shipment from China to…CFR by steamer in transit Saudi Arabia not later than 15th July, 2021 of the goods specified below 列明下面的货物按成本加运费价格用轮船，不得迟于 2021 年 7 月 15 日从中国通过沙特阿拉伯装运到××。

2. date of shipment 装船期

（1） bills of lading must be dated not later than August 15, 2021 提单日期不得迟于 2021 年 8 月 15 日。

（2） shipment must be effected not later than July 30, 2021 货物不得迟于 2021 年 7 月 30 日装运。

（3） shipment latest date：…最迟装运日期：××年××月××日。

（4） evidencing shipment/despatch on or before…列明货物在××年××月××日或在该日之前装运/发送。

（5）from China port to … not later than 31st August, 2021 不迟于2021年8月31日从中国港口至××。

3. partial shipments and transhipment 分运与转运

（1）partial shipments are (not) permitted（不）允许分运。

（2）partial shipments (are) allowed (prohibited) 准许（不准）分运。

（3）without transhipment 不允许转运。

（4）transhipment at Hong Kong allowed 允许在香港转船。

（5）partial shipments are permissible, transhipment is allowed except at… 允许分运，除在××外允许转运。

（6）partial/prorate shipments are perimtted 允许分运/按比例装运。

（7）transhipment are permitted at any port against, through B/lading 凭联运提单允许在任何港口转运。

（十四）有效日期与地点 Date & Place of Expiry

（1）valid in…for negotiation until… 在××议付至××止。

（2）draft (s) must be presented to the negotiating (or drawee) bank not later than… 汇票不得迟于××交议付行（受票行）。

（3）expiry date for presention of documents… 交单到期日为××年××月××日。

（4）draft (s) must be negotiated not later than… 汇票要不迟于××年××月××日议付。

（5）this L/C is valid for negotiation in China until 15th, July 2021 本证于2021年7月15日前在中国议付有效。

（6）bills of exchange must be negotiated within 15 days from the date of bills of lading but not later than August 8, 2021 汇票须在提单日起15天内议付，但不得迟于2021年8月8日。

（7）this credit remains valid in China until 23rd May, 1977 (inclusive) 本证到1977年5月23日为止，包括当日在内在中国有效。

（8）expiry date August 15, 2021 in country of beneficiary for negotiation 于2021年8月15日在受益人国家议付到期。

（9）draft (s) drawn under this credit must be presented for negoatation in China on or before 30th August, 2021 根据本证项下开具的汇票须在2021年8月30日或该日前在中国交单议付。

（10）expiry (expiring) date…到期日（效期）……

（11）negotiation on or before… 在××日或该日以前议付。

（12）this credit shall remain in force until 15th August 2021 in China 本证到2021年8月15日为止在中国有效。

（13）the credit is available for negotiation or payment abroad until…本证在国外议付或付款的日期到××年××月××日为止。

（14）documents to be presented to negotiation bank within 15 days after shipment 单据需在装船后15天内交给议付行。

（15）documents must be presented for negotiation within…days after the on board date of bill of lading/after the date of issuance of forwarding agents' cargo receipts 单据需在已装船提单/

运输行签发之货物承运收据日期后××天内提示议付。

（十五）开证行付款保证 the Guarantee of the Opening Bank

（1） we hereby engage with you that all drafts drawn under and in compliance with the terms of this credit will be duly honored 我行保证及时对所有根据本信用证开具，并与其条款相符的汇票兑付。

（2） we undertake that drafts drawn and presented in conformity with the terms of this credit will be duly honoured 我行保证对提交符合本证条款的汇票付款。

（3） we hereby engage with the drawers, endorsers and bona-fide holders of draft （s） drawn under and in compliance with the terms of the credit that such draft （s） shall be duly honoured on due presentation and delivery of documents as specified (if drawn and negotiated with in the validity date of this credit) 凡根据本证开具与本证条款相符的汇票，并能按时提示和交出本证规定的单据，我行保证对出票人、背书人和善意持有人承担付款责任（须在本证有效期内开具汇票并议付）。

（4） provided such drafts are drawn and presented in accordance with the terms of this credit, we hereby engage with the drawers, endorsors and bona-fide holders that the said drafts shall be duly honoured on presentation 凡根据本证的条款开具并提示汇票，我们担保对其出票人、背书人和善意持有人在交单时承付。

（5） we hereby undertake to honour all drafts drawn in accordance with the terms of this credit 所有按照本条款开具的汇票，我行保证兑付。

（十六）特别条款 Special Conditions

（1） for special instructions please see overleaf 特别事项请看背面。

（2） at the time of negotiations you will be paid the draft amount less 5% due to…议付时汇票金额应少付 5% 给××（注：这种条款是开证行对议付行的指示）。

（3） which amount the negotiation bank must authorise us to pay… 该项金额须由议付行授权我行付给××（注：指佣金的金额）。

（4） if the terms or conditions of this credit are not acceptable to you please contact the openers for necessary amendments 如你方不接受本证条款，请与开证人联系以作必要修改。

（5） negotiations unrestricted/restricted to advising bank 不限制议付行/限于通知行。

（6） （the price） including packing charges（价格）包括包装费用。

（7） all documents must be separated 各种单据须分开（即联合单证不接受）。

（8） beneficiary's drafts are to be made out for 95% of invoice value, being 5% commission payable to credit opener 受益人的汇票按发票金额 95% 开具，5% 佣金付给开证人。

（9） drafts to be drawn for full CIF value less 5% commission, invoice to show full CIF value 汇票按 CIF 总金额减少 5% 开具，发票须表明 CIF 的全部金额。

（10） 5% commission to be remitted to credit openers by way of bank drafts in USD drawn on…this commission not to be showed on the invoice5% 佣金用美元开成以××为付款人的银行汇票付给开证人，该佣金勿在发票上表明。

（11） freight and charges to be showed on bill of lading etc. 提单（单据）等须标明运费及附加费。

（12） cable copy of shipping advice despatched to the accountee immediately after shipment 装船后，即将装船通知电报副本寄交开证人。

（13） one copy of commercial invoice and packing list should be sent to the credit openers 15 days before shipment 商业发票和装箱单各一份须在装船前 15 天寄给开证人。

（14） the beneficiary is to cable Mr. …stating L/C No. , quantity shipped name & ETD of vessel within 5 days after shipment, a copy of this cable must accompany the documents for negotiation 受益人应在装船后 5 天内将信用证号码、装船数量、船名和预计开航日期电告××先生，该电报的副本须随同单据一起议付。

（15） all documents except bills of exchange and B/Lading to be made out in name of A. B. C. Co. , Ltd. and which name is to be shown in B/Lading as joint notifying party with the applicant 除汇票和提单外，所有单据均须作成以 A. B. C. 有限公司为抬头，并以该公司和申请人作为提单的通知人。

（16） amount of credit and quantity of merchandise more or less acceptable 证内金额与货物数量允许增减。

（17） credit amount and shipment quantity more or less allowed 证内金额与装运数量允许增减。

（18） shipment samples to be sent direct by airmail to buyer before shipment 装运前须将装船货样直接航寄买方。

（19） cable accountee name of steamer/carriage number, quantity of goods and shipment date （or E. T. A. ） 将船名/车号、货物数量及装船期（或预抵期）电告开证人。

（20） all banking charges outside Hong Kong are for account of accountee 香港以外的全部银行费用由开证人负担。

（21） drawee Bank's charges and acceptance commission are for buyer's account 付款行的费用和承兑费用由买方负担。

（22） port congestion surcharge, if any, is payable by openers in excess of this documentary credit amount against evidence 如果有港口拥挤费，超过本证金额部分凭证明由开证人支付。

（23） amount of this credit may be exceeded by cost of insurance 本证金额可以超过保险费部分。

（24） this letter of credit is transferable in China only, in the event of a transfer, a letter from the first beneficiary must accompany the documents for negotiation 本信用证仅在中国可转让，如实行转让，由第一受益人发出的书面（证明）须连同单据一起议付。

（25） admixture 5% max, including organic matter such as weed and inorganic 杂质最高 5%，包括有机物（如杂草）和无机物。

（十七）索偿文句 in Reimbursement

1. instruction to the negotiation bank 对议付行指示

（1） the amount and date of negotiation of each draft must be endorsed on reverse hereof by the negotiation bank 每份汇票的议付金额和日期必须由议付行在本证背面签注。

（2） without your confirmation（本证）无需你行保兑。

（3） documents must be sent by consecutive airmails 单据须分别由连续航次邮寄，即不要将两套或数套单据同一航次寄出。

(4) all original documents are to be forwarded to us by airmail and duplicate documents by seamail 全部单据的正本须用航邮，副本用平邮寄交我行。

(5) please despatch the first set of documents including three copies of commercial invoices direct to us by registered airmail and the second set by following airmail 请将包括3份商业发票在内的第一套单据用挂号航邮经寄我行，第二套单据在下一次航邮寄出。

(6) original documents must be sent by registered airmail, and duplicate by subsequent airmail 单据的正本须用挂号航邮寄送，副本在下一班航邮寄送。

(7) documents must be sent by successive (or succeeding) airmails 单据要由连续航邮寄送。

(8) all documents made out in English must be sent to our bank in one lot 用英文缮制的所有单据须一次寄交我行。

2. method of reimbursement 索偿办法

(1) after negotiation, you may reimburse yourselves by debiting our RMB account with you, please forward all relative documents in one lot to us by airmail 议付后请借记我行在你行开立的人民币账户，并将全部有关单据用航邮一次寄给我行。

(2) all bank charges outside U. K. are for our principals account, but must claimed at the time of presentation of documents 在英国境外发生的所有银行费用，应由开证人负担，但须在提交单据时索取。

(3) negotiating bank may claim reimbursement by T. T. on the…bank 议付行可向××银行电索。

【样单1-2】

信用证		
SEQUENCE OF TOTAL	*27:	1/1
FORM DOC CREDIT	*40 A:	IRREVOCABLE
DOC CREDIT NUM	*20:	BKKB1103043
DATE OF ISSUE	31 C:	001103
DATE/PLACE EXP	*31 D:	DATE 010114 PLACE BENEFICIARIES' COUNTRY
APPLICANT	*50:	MOUN CO., LTD NO. 443, 249 ROAD BANGKOK THAILAND
BENEFICIARY	*59:	// SHANGHAI FOREIGN TRADE CORP. SHANGHAI, CHINA
AMOUNT	*32 B:	CODE USD AMOUNT 18.000
AVAILABLE	*41 D:	ANY BANK IN CHINA BY NEGOTIATION
DRAFTS AT	42 C:	SIGHT IN DUPLICATE INDICATING THIS L/C NUMBER
DRAWEE	42 A:	// ISSUING BANK
PARTIAL SHIPMTS	43 P:	NOT ALLOWED
TRANSSHIPMENT	43 T:	ALLOWED

PORT OF LOADING	44 E:	CHINA MAIN FORT, CHINA
PORT OF DISCHARGE	44 F:	BANGKOK, THAILAND
LATEST SHIPMENT	44 C:	001220
GOODS DESCRIPT.	45 A:	2,000 KGS ISONIAZID BP98 AT USD9.00 PER KG C AND F BANGKOK
DOCS REQUIRED	46 A:	+ COMMERCIAL INVOICE IN ONE ORIGINAL PLUS 5 COPIES INDICATING FOB VALUE, FREIGHT CHARGES AND THIS L/C NUMBER, ALL OF WHICH MUST BE MANUALLY SIGNED. + FULL SET OF 3/3 CLEAN ON BOARD OCEAN BILLS OF LADING AND TWO NON - NEGOTIABLE, COPIES MADE OUT TO ORDER OF BANGKOK BANK PUBLIC COMPANY LIMITED, BANGKOK MARKED FREIGHT PREPAID AND NOTIFY APPLICANT AND INDICATING THIS L/C NUMBER. + PACKING LIST IN ONE ORIGINAL PLUS 5 COPIES, ALL OF WHICH MUST BE MANUALLY SIGNED.
ADDITIONAL COND	47 A:	ADDITIONAL CONDITION: A DISCREPANCY FEE OF USD50.00 WILL BE IMPOSED ON EACH SET OF DOCUMENTS PRESENTED FOR NEGOTIATION UNDER THIS L/C WITH DISCREPANCY. THE FEE WILL BE DEDUCTED FROM THE BILL AMOUNT.
CHARGES	71 B:	ALL BANK CHARGES OUTSIDE THAILAND INCLUDING REIMBURSING BANK COMMISSION AND DISCREPANCY FEE (IF ANY) ARE FOR BENEFICIARIES' ACCOUNT.
CONFIRMATION	*49:	WITHOUT
REIMBURS. BANK	53 D:	// BANGKOK BANK PUBLIC COMPANY LIMITED, NEW YORK BRANCH ON T/T BASIS
INS PAYING BANK	78:	DOCUMENTS TO BE DESPATCHED IN ONE LOT BY COURIER. ALL CORRESPONDENCE TO BE SENT TO/BANGKOK BANK PUBLIC COMPANY LIMITED HEAD OFFICE, 333 SILOM ROAD, BANGKOK 10500, THAILAND.
SEND REC INFO	72:	REIMBURSEMENT IS SUBJECT TO ICC URR 525

工作任务

假设你是刘华，请仔细阅读以上信用证，并找出下列内容。

（1）跟单信用证类型。
（2）跟单信用证号码。
（3）开证日期。
（4）到期日、到期地点。
（5）开证申请人银行。
（6）受益人。
（7）货币币种与金额。
（8）汇票汇款期限。
（9）汇票付款人。
（10）分批装运与转运。
（11）装运港与目的港。
（12）最迟装运日期。
（13）货物/劳务描述。
（14）单据要求。
（15）费用负担。
（16）交单期限。
（17）附加款件。
（18）保兑指示。
（19）给付款行/承兑行/议付行的指示。
（20）货物数量。

能力训练

1. 请翻译以下信用证

【样单 1-3】

SEQUENCE OF TOTAL	*27：	1 / 1
FORM DOC. CREDIT	*40 A：	IRREVOCABLE
DOC. CREDIT NUMBER	*20：	63211020049
DATE OF ISSUE	31 C：	110129
EXPIRY	*31 D：	DATE110410 PLACE IN BENEFICIARY'S COUNTRY
APPLICANT	*50：	FASHION FORCE CO. , LTD P. O. BOX 8935 NEW TERMINAL, ALTA, VISTA OTTAWA, CANADA
BENEFICIARY	*59：	NANJING GARMENT CO. , LTD. HUARONG MANSION RM2901 NO. 85 GUANJIAQIAO, NANJING 210005, CHINA
AMOUNT	*32 B：	CURRENCY USD AMOUNT 3, 264
AVAILABLE WITH/BY	*41 D：	ANY BANK BY NEGOTIATION
DRAFTS AT	42 C：	SIGHT

DRAWEE	42 A:	BNP ACAMMXXX * BNP PARIBAS (CANADA) * MONTREAL
PARTIAL SHIPMTS	43 P:	NOT ALLOWED
TRANSSHIPMENT	43 T:	NOT ALLOWED
PORT OF LOADING	44 E:	CHINA
PORT OF DISCHARGE	44 F:	MONTREAL
LATEST DATE OF SHIP.	44 C:	110325
DESCRIPT OF GOODS	45 A:	SALES CONDITIONS: CIF MONTREAL/CANADA SALES CONTRACT NO. F01LCB05127 LADIES COTTON BLAZER (100% COTTON, 40SX20/140X60) STYLE NO. PO NO. QTY/PCS USD/PC 46-301A 10337 2, 560 12. 80
DOS REQUIRED	46 A:	+COMMERCIAL INVOICES IN 3 COPIES SIGNED BY BENEFICIARY'S REPRESENTATIVE. +CANADA CUSTOMS INVOICES IN 4 COPIES. +FULL SET OF ORIGINAL MARINE BILLS OF LADING CLEAN ON BOARD PLUS 2 NON NEGOTIABLE COPIES MADE OUT OR ENDORSED TO ORDER OF BNP PARIBAS (CANADA) MARKED FREIGHT PREPAID AND NOTIFY APPLICANT'S FULL NAME AND ADDRESS. +DETAILED PACKING LISTS IN 3 COPIES. +COPY OF CERTIFICATE OF ORIGIN FORM A. +COPY OF EXPORT LICENCE. +BENEFICIARY'S LETTER STATING THAT ORIGINAL CERTIFICATE OF ORIGIN FORM A, ORIGINAL EXPORT LICENCE, COPY OF COMMERCIAL INVOICE, DETAILED PACKING LISTS AND A COPY OF BILL OF LADING WERE SENT DIRECT TO APPLICANT BY COURIER WITHIN 5 DAYS AFTER SHIPMENT. THE RELATIVE COURIER RECEIPT IS ALSO REQUIRED FOR PRESENTATION. +COPY OF APPLICANT'S FAX APPROVING PRODUCTION SAMPLES
BEFORE SHIPMENT.		
		+LETTER FROM SHIPPER ON THEIR LETTERHEAD INDICATING THEIR NAME OF COMPANY AND ADDRESS, BILL OF LADING NUMBER, CONTAINER NUMBER AND THAT THIS SHIPMENT, INCLUDING ITS CONTAINER, DOES NOT CONTAIN ANY NON-MANUFACTURED WOODEN MATERIAL, DUNNAGE, BRACING MATERIAL, PALLETS, CRATING OR OTHER NON-MANUFACTURED WOODEN PACKING MATERIAL. +INSPECTION CERTIFICATE ORIGINAL SINGED AND ISSUED BY FASHION FORCE CO., LTD STATING THE SAMPLES OF FOUR STYLE GARMENTS HAS BEEN APPROVED, WHICH SEND

THROUGH DHL BEFORE 15DAYS OF SHIPMENT.
+INSURANCE POLICY OR CERTIFICATE IN 1 ORIGINAL AND 1 COPY ISSUED OR ENDORSED TO THE ORDER OF BNP PARIBAS (CANADA) FOR THE CIF INVOICE PLUS 10 PERCENT COVERING ALL RISKS, INSTITUTE STRIKES, INSTITUTE WAR CLAUSES AND CIVIL COMMOTIONS CLAUSES.

ADDITIONAL COND. 47 A:

+IF DOCUMENTS PRESENTED ARE FOUND BY US NOT TO BE UN FULL COMPLIANCE WITH CREDIT TERMS, WE WILL ASSESS A CHARGE OF USD 55.00 PER SET OF DOCUMENTS.
+ALL CHARGES IF ANY RELATED TO SETTLEMENTS ARE FOR ACCOUNT OF BENEFICIARY.
+3 PCT MORE OR LESS IN AMOUNT AND QUANTITY IS ALLOWED.
+ ALL CERTIFICATES/LETTERS/STATEMENTS MUST BE SIGNED AND DATED
+THE CANADIAN GOVERNMENT NOW INSIST THAT EVERY SHIPMENT ENTERING CANADA MUST HAVE THE ABOVE DOCUMENTATION WITH THE SHIPMENT.
+BILL OF LADING AND COMMERCIAL INVOICE MUST CERTIFY THE FOLLOWING: THIS SHIPMENT, INCLUDING ITS CONTAINER DOES NOT CONTAIN ANY NON-MANUFACTURED WOODEN MATERIAL, DUNNAGE, BRACING MATERIAL PALLETS, CRATING OR OTHER NON MANUFACTURED WOODEN PACKING MATERIAL.
+BENEFICIARY'S BANK ACCOUNT NO. 07773108201140121

CHARGES 71 B: OUTSIDE COUNTRY BANK CHARGES
TO BE BORNE BY THE BENEFICIARY
OPENING BANK CHARGES
TO BE BORNE BY THE APPLICANT

CONFIRMATION *49: WITHOUT

INSTRUCTIONS 78:

+WE SHALL COVER THE NEGOTIATING BANK AS PER THEIR INSTRUCTIONS
+FORWARD DOCUMENTS IN ONE LOT BY SPECIAL COURIER PREPAID TO BNP PARIBAS (CANADA) 1981 MCGILL COLLEGE AVE. MONTREAL QC H3A 2W8 CANADA.

SEND. TO REC. INFO. 72: THIS CREDIT IS SUBJECT TO UCP FOR
DOCUMENTARY CREDIT 1993 REVISION
ICC PUBLICATION 500 AND IS THE
OPERATIVE INSTRUMENT

TRAILER ORDER IS <MAC: > <PAC: > <ENC: > <CHK: > <TNG: > <PDE: >
MAC: F344CA36
CHK: AA6204FFDFC2

2. 翻译以下合同

【样单 1-4】

销售合同 **SALES CONTRACT**				
卖方 SELLER：	NANJING TANG TEXTILE GARMENT CO. , LTD. HUARONG MANSION RM2901 NO. 85 GUANJIAQIAO, NANJING 210005, CHINA	编号 NO. 日期 DATE 地点 SIGNED IN	F01LCB05127 JAN. 03, 2011 NANJING	
买方 BUYER：	FASHION FORCE CO. , LTD P. O. BOX 8935 NEW TERMINAL, ALTA, VISTA OTTAWA, CANADA			
买卖双方同意以下条款达成交易： This contract is made by and agreed between the BUYER and the SELLER, in accordance with the terms and conditions stipulated below.				
1. 品名及规格 Commodity & Specification		2. 数量 Quantity	3. 单价及价格条款 Unit Price & Trade Terms	4. 金额 Amount
				CIF MONTREAL
LADIES COTTON BLAZER (100% COTTON, 40SX20/140X60)		2, 550PCS	USD12. 80	USD32, 640. 00
Total:		2, 550PCS		USD32, 640. 00
5. 总值 Total Value	SAY USD THIRTY TWO THOUSAND SIX HUNDRED AND FORTY ONLY			
6. 包装 Packing	IN CARTONS OF 30PCS EACH TOTAL: 85 CARTONS.			
7. 唛头 Shipping Marks	FASHION FORCE F01LCB05127 CTN NO. MONTREAL MADE IN CHINA			
8. 装运期及运输方式 Time of Shipment & Means of Transportation	TO BE EFFECTED BEFORE MAR 25, 2011 WITH PARTIAL SHIPMENT NOT ALLOWED AND TRANSHIPMENT ALLOWED.			
9. 装运港及目的地 Port of Loading & Destination	FROM: CHINA TO: MONTREAL			
10. 保险 Insurance	THE SELLER SHALL COVER INSURANCE AGAINST ALL RISKS, INSTITUTE STRIKES, INSTITUTE WAR FOR 110% OF THE TOTAL INVOICE VALUE AS PER THE RELEVANT OCEAN MARINE CARGO OF P. I. C. C. DATED 1/1/1981.			
11. 付款方式 Terms of Payment	BY IRREVOCABLE SIGHT LETTER OF CREDIT.			
12. 备注 Remarks				
The Buyer		The Seller		
FASHION FORCE CO. , LTD		NANJING TANG TEXTILE GARMENT CO. , LTD.		

(signature)　　　　　　　　(signature)

模块评估

1. 模块课程评价表

模块内容________　　班级_______　学号_______　姓名_______　　_______年__月___日

1. 你认为本模块最有价值的内容是：
2. 本堂课上教师使用的教学方法是否对学习有帮助，你对此有何建议。
3. 你是否有计划地组织学习？是否在朝学习目标努力？
4. 下列问题我需要得到进一步的了解和帮助：
教师签名 学生签名

2. 基本能力测评表

核心能力	评价指标	测评结果	备注
自我管理能力	1. 培养自己的责任心 2. 掌握时间管理能力 3. 将所学知识运用到工作中		
交流能力	1. 知道如何尊重他人的观点、价值和信仰等 2. 能与其他人有效沟通 3. 在团队合作中表现积极 4. 能正确获取并反馈信息		
解决问题的能力	1. 学会搜集、使用信息资源 2. 能发现并解决常规及特殊问题		
创新能力	1. 面对问题，能用所学知识和技能提出有价值的观点 2. 使用不同的思维方式		
其他			
教师评语 教师签字			
成绩		学生签字	

模块二 单项制作出口单据

项目一：催证、审证与改证

项目目标

能够正确催证，审证并撰写信用证修改函。

学习情境二

公司业务员于芳接到一笔订单，与加拿大 AFG 公司签订了一笔出口合同。由于对方没有在规定时间内开具信用证，刘华在于芳的指导下向对方催证。2021 年 4 月对方开来信用证，于芳带着刘华根据合同和 UCP 对信用证进行审核，确认信用证有无要修改的地方。审核后发现几处与合同不符，需要修改，刘华向对方发出了修改函。

价值引领

在信用证结算方式下，及时向开证行申请开立信用证是买方的责任之一，若买方未在合同约定时间内申请开证，卖方需进行催证，以保障合同的顺利履行。受益人收到信用证后，要认真审核，确保信用证条款和合同条款一致，信用证内容符合收证时国家相关政策、法令和国际惯例的要求，备货和船期等实际情况能够满足信用证的单据要求。否则，受益人需要与开证申请人沟通，要求其通过开证行修改信用证，以便受益人安全收汇，保证自己的正当权益。

任务一：催证

相关知识

催证是卖方通知或催促国外买方按照合同规定迅速通过开证银行开出信用证，以便卖方能按时交货。

在实际业务中，由于种种原因买方未按合同规定及时开证，这就需要卖方及时催促买方尽快开证。在开证银行开出信用证后，买方才能要求卖方履行交货义务，所以，买方按时开立信用证是卖方履行合同的前提条件。如果买方未按合同规定申请开立信用证，卖方一般会发函指出其违约行为，催促其立即开证或展延开证期限，要求再勿逾期；或提出其他相应措施，如适当调整数量、价格、装运期等。但对一再拖延催而不回复者，卖方经过慎重考虑，可及时作出处理，或宣告撤约，或提出索赔。对逾期来证，卖方多数是能通融接受的，但根据货源供应等情况，也可以有条件地接受或不予接受，根据实际情况与买方进行协商。

工作任务

根据业务员于芳与国外客户签订的合同（见样单2-1），双方约定信用证不迟于3月30前到达，但现在期限已到，卖方仍未收到信用证。请你给AFG公司的业务员Andy Burns去函催证，并提醒对方我方通知行为“中国银行上海分行”，而非只是“中国银行”，以免寄错，致函时间为2021年4月5日。

【样单2-1】

LINJIANG TRADING CO., LTD.	29TH FLOOR KINGSTAR MANSION, 623JINLIN RD., SHANGHAI, CHINA TEL: (021) 82588666 FAX: (021) 82588999 ZIP CODE: 200002

APR. 5,2021

Dear Mr. Andy Burns,

We are in receipt of your returning signed Sales Confirmation No. NEO2011026.

However, we regret to inform you that we did not receive your L/C concerning the above contract till today. It is clearly stipulated in the said contract that the relevant L/C should reach us date APR 5. Please be assured to open your L/C strictly in accordance with our offered bank information, especially it should be "Bank of China, Shanghai branch" not "Bank of China" only. Please pay attention to it because last time another customer's L/C reached to Bank of China in shanghai.

Owing to the punctual shipment, the early arrival of your L/C will be highly appreciated.

Yours faithfully,
Linjiang Trading Co., Ltd.
Hua Liu

任务二：审证

相关知识

什么是审核

审证即审核信用证，是对国外进口方通过银行开来的信用证内容进行全面审核，以确定接受或修改。

从理论上讲，国外来证应与买卖合同相符。但在很多实际业务中，买方开来的信用证并非与合同完全相符，将会给卖方履行合同、安全收汇造成隐患。对此，出口商必须提高警惕，注意审核国外来证。

审核的依据是合同和《UCP600》，基本原则是要求信用证条款与合同的规定相一致，除非事先征得出口企业的同意，在信用证中不得增减或改变合同条款的内容。

审证内容

审核信用证是银行（通知行）与出口企业的共同责任，双方各有侧重。业务中，银行重点审核开证行的政治背景、资信能力、付款责任、索汇路线及信用证真伪等。出口企业则审查信用证的内容与买卖合同是否一致。具体包括以下几个方面：

1. 银行审证

（1）从政策上审核。主要看来证各项内容是否符合我方的方针政策以及是否存在歧视性内容，有则须根据实际情况向开证行交涉修改。

（2）对开证行的审核。主要对开证行所在国家的政治经济状况、开证行的资信、经营作风等进行审查。对于资信欠佳的银行应酌情采取适当的保全措施。

（3）对信用证性质与开证行付款责任的审核。出口业务中，我方不接受带“可撤销”字样的信用证；对于不可撤销的信用证，如附有限制性条款或保留字句，使“不可撤销”名不副实，应要求对方修改。

2. 出口企业审证

出口企业只需作复核性审核，其审证重点主要包括下述几项：

（1）对信用证金额与货币的审核。审核信用证金额是否与合同金额一致，大小写金额是否一致。如合同订有溢短装条款，信用证金额是否包括溢短装部分金额；信用证使用的货币是否与合同规定的计价和支付货币一致。

（2）对有关货物条款的审核。主要是对商品的品质、规格、数量、包装等依次进行审核，如发现信用证内容与合同规定不一致，原则上要修改信用证。

（3）对信用证的装运期、有效期和到期地点的审核。信用证的装运期必须与合同的规定相同；信用证的有效期一般规定在装运期限后 7 ~ 15 天，以便卖方制单。关于信用证的到期地点，通常规定在中国境内，对于在国外到期的信用证，出口商一般不接受，应要求修改。

（4）对开证申请人、受益人的审核。开证申请人的名称和地址应仔细审核，以防错发错运。受益人的名称和地址也须正确无误，以免影响收汇。

（5）对单据的审核。主要对来证中要求提供的单据种类、份数及填制方法等进行审核，如发现有不正常规定或出口商难以履行的条款，应要求对方修改。

（6）对其他运输、保险、商检等条款的审核。仔细审核信用证对分批装运、转船、保险险别、投保加成以及商检条款的规定是否与合同一致，如有不符，应要求对方修改。

（7）对特殊条款的审核。审证时，如发现超越合同规定的附加或特殊条款，一般不轻易接受，如对我方无太大影响，也可酌情考虑。

审证方式

1. 全面审核信用证

全面审核信用证具体内容如下：

（1）根据合同条款全面审核信用证条款。

按照合同上的签约人、商品描述、价格条款、支付条款、装运条款、保险条款、合同金额、商检、仲裁等全部内容，全面仔细审核信用证的受益人名称、品名、价格、货币、金额、包装、运输方式、装运路线、装期、有效期、交单期、信用证到期地点、保险险别、投保加成等详细具体规定的信用证条款，把合同条款与信用证条款一一对应起来进行审核，逐条检查信用证条款是否符合合同条款的规定，发现信用证规定有不符合合同规定的地方，一定要与进口方联系。如果信用证条款与合同条款不一致，但不会给出口方带来不利，可要求进口方书面确认修改合同条款即可；如果信用证条款与合同条款不一致，会对出口方产生不利影响，出口方应该要求进口方按照合同条款对信用证条款进行修改。

（2）根据信用证知识来审核合同，检查合同条款是否有缺陷，为顺利执行合同条款把好最后的关。

如果发现合同条款有缺陷，此时，可利用最后的修补机会，对不利于顺利履约、不利于出口商顺利取得相应单据结汇的信用证条款，即使该信用证条款与合同条款一致，也应与进口方协商，要求修改合同、修改信用证，在货物装运前解决问题，以保证安全结汇。

2. 着重审核信用证

信用证是一项独立的约定，一般说来，受益人按照信用证规定要求执行，就应取得相应的单据，议付结汇。但是，有的信用证在开出之时就设置了条款陷阱，即“软条款”。信用证软条款是比较常见的信用证风险，它限制了出口方对信用证操作的主动权，出口方在履约操作过程中，很难获得或者根本不能获得符合信用证规定的单据，影响信用证收汇安全。

软条款的表现形式多种多样，如执行信用证的主动权被进口方掌握，装船需要进口方的指示；结汇单据依赖进口方提供；收取货款需要进口方同意；信用证条款与要求不配套，单据条款与操作条款不衔接，相关规定自相矛盾；如果接受信用证软条款，出口企业必然承担相应的收汇风险。当然，并非所有的信用证软条款都必须修改，出口企业可根据市场、客户资信、产品、运输及软条款的具体要求等，区别对待不同条件下的软条款。对确实需要修改的信用证软条款，应与客户协商，要求修改信用证，在收到相关信用证修改前，出口方应谨慎行事。

工作任务

收到信用证之后（见样单 2-2），刘华在于芳指导下，根据 NEO2021026 出口合同对信用证进行审核，指出信用证存在的问题，并提出具体的信用证修改要求。

【样单 2-2】

MAR. 22，2021 09：18：11		LOGICAL TERMINALE102
MT S700	ISSUE OF A DOCUMENTARY CREDIT	PAGE00001
		FUNCMSG700
		UMR06881051

MSGACK DWS765I AUTH OK, KEY B198081689580FC5, BKCHCNBJ RJHISARI RECORD		
BASIC HEADER		F 01 BKCHCNBJA940 0588 550628
APPLICATION HEADER		0 700 1057 010320 RJHISARIAXXX 7277 977367 020213 1557 N * ALRAJHI BANKING AND INVESTMENT * CORPORATION * RIYADH * (HEAD OFFICE)
USER HEADER		SERVICE CODE 103: (银行盖信用证通知专用章) BANK. PRIORITY 113: MSG USER REF. 108: INFO. FROM CI 115:
SEQUENCE OF TOTAL	*27:	1 / 1
FORM OF DOC. CREDIT	*40 A:	IRREVOCABLE
DOC. CREDIT NUMBER	*20:	0011LC123756
DATE OF ISSUE	31 C:	210408
DATE/PLACE EXP.	*31 D:	DATE210505 PLACE CHINA
APPLICANT	*50:	AFG GENERAL TRADING CO. P. O. BOX 99552, RIYADH 22766, KSA TEL: 00966-1-4659220 FAX: 00966-1-4659213
BENEFICIARY	*59:	LINJIANG TRADING CO., LTD. HUARONG MANSION RM2901 NO. 85 GUANJIAQIAO, NANJING 210005, CHINA TEL: 0086-25-4715004 FAX: 0086-25-4711363
AMOUNT	*32 B:	CURRENCY USD AMOUNT 13, 260
AVAILABLE WITH/BY	*41 D:	ANY BANK IN CHINA, BY NEGOTIATION
DRAFTS AT	42 C:	SIGHT
DRAWEE	42 A:	RJHISARI * ALRAJHI BANKING AND INVESTMENT * CORPORATION * RIYADH * (HEAD OFFICE)
PARTIAL SHIPMTS	43 P:	NOT ALLOWED
TRANSSHIPMENT	43 T:	NOT ALLOWED
PORT OF LOADING	44 E:	CHINA MAIN FORT, CHINA
PORT OF DISCHARGE	44 F:	DAMMAM PORT, SAUDI ARABIA
LATEST SHIPMENT	44 C:	210430
GOODS DESCRIPT.	45 A:	ABOUT 1, 700 CARTONS CANNED MUSHROOM PIECES & STEMS 24 TINS X 425 GRAMS NET WEIGHT (D. W. 227 GRAMS) AT USD7. 80 PER CARTON. ROSE BRAND.
DOCS REQUIRED	46 A:	DOCUMENTS REQUIRED: + SIGNED COMMERCIAL INVOICE IN TRIPLICATE ORIGINAL AND MUST SHOW BREAK DOWN OF THE AMOUNT AS FOLLOWS: FOB

		VALUE, FREIGHT CHARGES AND TOTAL AMOUNT C AND F.
		+ FULL SET CLEAN ON BOARD BILL OF LADING MADE OUT TO THE ORDER OF ALRAJHI BANKING AND INVESTMENT CORP, MARKED FREIGHT PREPAID AND NOTIFY APPLICANT, INDICATING THE FULL NAME, ADDRESS AND TEL NO. OF THE CARRYING VESSEL'S AGENT AT THE PORT OF DISCHARGE.
		+ PACKING LIST IN ONE ORIGINAL PLUS 5 COPIES, ALL OF WHICH MUST BE MANUALLY SIGNED.
		+ INSPECTION (HEALTH) CERTIFICATE FROM C. I. Q. (ENTRY-EXIT INSPECTION AND QUARANTINE OF THE PEOPLE'S REPUBLIC OF CHINA) STATING GOODS ARE FIT FOR HUMAN BEING.
		+ CERTIFICATE OF ORIGIN DULY CERTIFIED BY C. C. P. I. T. STATING THE NAME OF THE MANUFACTURERS OF PRODUCERS AND THAT GOODS EXPORTED ARE WHOLLY OF CHINESE ORIGIN.
		+ THE PRODUCTION DATE OF THE GOODS NOT TO BE EARLIER THAN HALF MONTH AT TIME OF SHIPMENT. BENEFICIARY MUST CERTIFY THE SAME.
		+ SHIPMENT TO BE EFFECTED BY CONTAINER AND BY REGULARE LINE. SHIPMENT COMPANY'S CERTIFICATE TO THIS EFFECT SHOULD ACCOMPANY THE DOCUMENTS.
		+ INSURANCE POLICY OR CERTIFICATE IN 1 ORIGINAL AND 1 COPY ISSUED OR ENDORSED TO THE ORDER OF ALRAJHI BANKING AND INVESTMENT CORPORATION FOR THE INVOICE PLUS 10 PERCENT COVERING ALL RISKS, INSTITUTE CARGO CLAUSES, INSTITUTE STRIKES.
ADDITIONAL COND.	47 A:	A DISCREPANCY FEE OF USD50.00 WILL BE IMPOSED ON EACH SET OF DOCUMENTS PRESENTED FOR NEGOTIATION UNDER THIS L/C WITH DISCREPANCY. THE FEE WILL BE DEDUCTED FROM THE BILL AMOUNT. PAYMENT UNDER THE GOODS WERE APPROVED BY SAUDI GOVERNMENT LAB.
CHARGES	71 B:	ALL CHARGES AND COMMISSIONS OUTSIDE KSA ON BENEFICIARIES' ACCOUNT INCLUDING REIMBURSING, BANK COMMISSION, DISCREPANCY FEE (IF ANY) AND COURIER CHARGES.
CONFIRMAT INSTR	*49:	WITHOUT
REIMBURS. BANK	53 D:	// ALRAJHI BANKING AND INVESTMENT CORP RIYADH (HEAD OFFICE)
INS PAYING BANK	78:	 DOCUMENTS TO BE DESPATCHED IN ONE LOT BY COURIER. ALL CORRESPONDENCE TO BE SENT TO ALRAJHI BANKING AND INVESTMENT COPRORATION RIYADH (HEAD OFFICE)

SEND REC INFO	72:	REIMBURSEMENT IS SUBJECT TO ICC URR 525
TRAILER		ORDER IS <MAC: > <PAC: > <ENC: > <CHK: > <TNG: > <PDE: > MAC: E55927A4 CHK: 7B505952829A

对照【样单1-1】审核上述信用证，得出如下审核结果：

信用证审核结果

信用证号	IRREVOCABLE
合 同 号	NEO2021026
审证结果	1. 信用证上并没有将合同上要求的“提单日期之后，15 天之内交单”显示在信用证上。效期太短，不符合同规定的“有效至装运日后 15 天内在中国议付”。装运日是 4 月 30 日，而信用证有效期到 5 月 5 日，5 天内根本来不及议付。建议将信用证有效期改到 5 月 15 日。 2. 合同规定由买方提供保险“TO BE COVERED BY THE BUYER”，而信用证中有关议付单据部分，却要求我方提供保险单据的条款“+ INSURANCE POLICY OR CERTIFICATE IN 1 ORIGINAL AND...”，应当要求删除该项条款。 3. 附加条款中的“PAYMENT UNDER THE GOODS WERE APPROVED BY SAUDI GOVERNMENT LAB（货物经沙特官方实验室检验合格后方可付款）”使出口商完全处于被动的境地，属软条款，不能接受，应当要求删除该项条款。

任务三：改证

相关知识

信用证修改函

1. 基本框架

①感谢对方开来的信用证。

②列明不符点，并说明应如何修改。

③希望早日收到信用证修改书。

2. 关键点

①审证质量。

审核信用证的质量这一步非常关键，如果没有发现存在的问题，将会造成严重的损失。

②准确表达。

需对方修改的地方要用准确规范的英文进行表达，避免因表达问题造成进一步的失误。

3. 基本内容

第一个主题：感谢来证

Thank you for your L/C No. ... issued by ... dated ...

We are pleased to receive L/C No. ... established by ... dated ... against S/C No. ...

第二个主题：列明不符点

However, we are sorry to find it contains the following discrepancies.

But the following points are in discrepancy with the stipulations of our S/C No. …

Please add the word… before…

Please delete the clause…and insert the wording.

Please amend the…to…

The amount should be…not/instead of…

Please extend the shipment date and the validity of the L/C to…and…respectively.

第三个主题：催促改证

Thank you for your kind cooperation.

Please see to it that the L/C amendment reach us before … (date), falling which we shall not be able to effect punctual shipment.

工作任务

根据任务二中的审核结果，给加拿大 AFG 公司写修改函。

【样单 2-3】

LINJINGTRADING CO., LTD.	29TH FLOOR KINGSTAR MANSION, 623JINLIN RD., SHANGHAI, CHINA TEL: (021) 82588666　　FAX: (021) 82588999 ZIP CODE: 200002

APR. 9,2021

Dear Mr. Andy Burns,

We are very glad to receive your L/C NO. 0011LC123756, but we are quite sorry to find that it contains some discrepancies with the S/C. Please instruct your bank to amend the L/C as quickly as possible.

The L/C is to be amended as follows:

1. Please amend the "DATE20210505 PLACE CHINA" to "DATE 20210515 PLACE CHINA".
2. Please delete the clause "INSURANCE POLICY OR CERTIFICATE IN 1 ORIGINAL AND 1 COPY ISSUED OR ENDORSED TO THE ORDER OF ALRAJHI BANKING AND INVESTMENT CORP FOR THE INVOICE PLUS 10 PERCENT COVERING ALL RISKS, INSTITUTE CARGO CLAUSES, INSTITUTE STRIKES".
3. Please delete the clause "PAYMENT UNDER THE GOODS WERE APPROVED BY SAUDI GOVERNMENT LAB.".

Please try your best to amend the above soon and email advising your confirmation. We are looking forward to hearing from you at an early date.

Yours faithfully,
Linjiang Trading Co., Ltd.
Hua Liu

能力训练

请根据模块一中的合同【样单 1-4】审核信用证【样单 1-3】，找出需要修改的地方，并给买方写一份修改函。

项目二：制作商业发票和装箱单

项目目标

根据具体情况，能够按要求独立完成商业发票和装箱单的制作。

学习情境三

根据我方提出的修改意见，买方及时通知开证行进行信用证修改，2021 年 4 月 12 日，中国银行上海分行通知我方信用证修改书已经收到。我方积极组织生产、包装产品。刘华根据修改后审核无误的信用证（见样单 2-2）及货物基本情况制作商业发票和装箱单。

价值引领

商业发票是最重要的基本单据，是制作其他单据的依据。装箱单是对商业发票的一种补充。单证人员要认真、准确、规范制单，以便安全收汇。

任务一：制作商业发票

相关知识

制作商业发票操作指导图

<table>
<tr><td>ISSUER
按合同和信用证的规定填写卖方名称和地址全称，一般名称和地址要分行排列。</td><td colspan="2">商业发票
COMMERCIAL INVOICE</td></tr>
<tr><td>TO
买方栏目又称发票的收货人或抬头人。当采用信用证方式付款时，除非信用证另有规定，商业发票必须以信用证申请人为抬头。跟单托收业务，发票上的收货人应根据合同所列买方或指定名称缮制，并列明详细地址。</td><td>NO.
发票号码由出口商自行编制。</td><td>DATE
发票的出票日期，信用证方式付款时一般在信用证开证日期之后，装运日期之前，或至少在交单或有效期之前。</td></tr>
<tr><td rowspan="2">TRANSPORT DETAILS
启运地和目的地，按信用证填写。</td><td>S/C NO.
合同号码，应与信用证上所列的一致，须在发票上列明，若一笔交易有几个合同号码，都应打在发票上。</td><td>L/C NO.
信用证号码，按信用证填写。</td></tr>
<tr><td colspan="2">TERMS OF PAYMENT
填写付款方式。</td></tr>
</table>

<table>
<tr><td>Marks and Numbers</td><td>Number and Kind of Package
Description of Goods</td><td>Quantity</td><td>Unit Price</td><td>Amount</td></tr>
<tr><td rowspan="2">唛头
凡是信用证上规定唛头的，必须逐字逐行按规定缮制，并与其他单据的唛头相一致。信用证中没有规定唛头的，则按合同条款中指明的唛头或买方已提供的唛头缮制；如果都没有规定的，则由卖方自行设计，并注意单单相符。</td><td colspan="4">贸易术语</td></tr>
<tr><td>商品名称及规格必须与合同和信用证一致。

其他需要证明的文句。</td><td>数量或重量既要与实际装运货物相符，又要符合信用证规定。以件数计算价格的商品，发票要列明件数；以重量计算价格的，必须列出重量。如果货品规格较多，每种商品应注明小计数量，最后表示出总数量。</td><td>单价</td><td>单价和总值是发票的重点，特别要注意发票金额不能超过信用证上所列金额，发票的货币要与信用证相一致。</td></tr>
<tr><td colspan="2">SAY TOTAL　　总金额的大写</td><td colspan="3">TOTAL　　总计　　总计

SIGNATURE
出具人和签章。一般发票必须经出口商正式签字盖章才有效，并注意使用的图章和签字与其他单据的签章相一致。如果对方国家要求手签名，就只能采用手签名，要注意根据各国的习惯来确认签字盖章形式。</td></tr>
</table>

工作任务

根据样单1-1，样单2-2及本模块任务一的知识介绍，参考下列补充资料，制作商业发票。

补充资料：

（1）有关商品重量及体积计算：

①商品净重描述：24 TINS X 425 GRAMS NET WEIGHT。

②包装纸箱尺寸：长45cm、宽20cm、高14.9cm。

③此项商品按净重×1.1估算毛重。

④所有计算结果保留两位小数。

（2）运费：总价798.00美元。

（3）商业发票编号：2011SDT001。

（4）公司联系人：李佳。

【样单2-4】

临江国际贸易有限公司

LINJIANG TRADING CO., LTD.

Room 2901, HuaRong Mansion, Guanjiaqiao 85#, Nanjing 210005, P. R. CHINA

TEL: 025-4715004 025-4715619 FAX: 4691619

COMMERCIAL INVOICE

To	AFG GENERAL TRADING CO. P. O. BOX 99552, RIYADH 22766, KSA TEL: 00966-1-4659220 FAX: 00966-1-4659213	Invoice No.	2021SDT001
		Invoice Date	2021-04-18
		S/C No.	NEO2021026
		S/C Date	2021-02-28
From	SHANGHAI PORT, CHINA	To	DAMMAM PORT, SAUDI ARABIA
Letter of credit No.	0011LC123756	Date	2021-03-20

Marks and Numbers	Number and Kind of Package Description of Goods	Quantity	Unit price	Amount
				CFR DAMMAM PORT, SAUDI ARABIA
ROSE BRAND 178/2001 RIYADH	ABOUT 1 700 CARTONS CANNED MUSHROOMS PIECES & STEMS 24 TINS X 425 GRAMS NET WEIGHT (D. W. 227 GRAMS) AT USD7.80 PER CARTON. ROSE BRAND.	1,700CARTONS	USD7.80	USD13,260.00
	TOTAL	1,700CARTONS		USD13,260.00
SAY TOTAL	USD THIRTEEN THOUSAND TWO HUNDRED AND SIXTY ONLY.			

LINJIANG TRADING CO., LTD.

李佳

任务二：制作装箱单

相关知识

制作装箱单操作指导图

出口公司名称地址
装箱单名称（Packing list） 应按照信用证规定使用。通常用 "Packing List" " Packing Specification" "Detailed Packing List "。如果来证要求用中性包装单（Neutral Packing List），则包装单名称打 "Packing List "，如果包装单内不打卖方名称，则不能签章。

To	买方名称和地址	Invoice No.	商业发票号码
		Invoice Date	商业发票日期
		S/C No.	合同号码
		S/C Date	合同日期

From	装运港	To	目的港
Letter of Credit No.	信用证号码	Date of Shipment	信用证日期

Marks and Numbers	Number and Kind of Package Description of Goods	Quantity	Package	G. W	N. W	Meas.
唛头 与合同一致，有的注明实际唛头，有时也可只注明 "as per invoice No. ×××"。唛头的具体写法请参见发票制单。	货物描述，与发票一致。	数量，与合同一致	填写包装的数量和材料	分别注明单位包装的数据和总包装的数据，最后在合计栏处计总。	分别注明单位包装的数据和总包装的数据，最后在合计栏处计总。	分别注明不同商品的总体积，最后在合计栏处计总。
	Total	总计	总计	总计	总计	总计

SAY TOTAL：总包装件数的大写

SIGNATURE

出单人的签字或盖章。装箱单只能由信用证的受益人出具，除非信用证另有规定，装箱单无须签字。

工作任务

根据样单1-1，样单2-2，结合以上知识，参考制作商业发票中的补充资料，独立制作装箱单。

【样单2-5】

临江国际贸易有限公司

LINJIANGTRADING CO.，LTD.

Room 2901，HuaRong Mansion，Guanjiaqiao 85#，Nanjing 210005，P. R. CHINA

TEL：025-4715004 025-4715619 FAX：4691619

PACKING LIST

To	AFG GENERAL TRADING CO. P. O. BOX 99552，RIYADH 22766，KSA TEL：00966-1-4659220 FAX：00966-1-4659213	Invoice No.	2021SDT001
		Invoice Date	2021-04-18
		S/C No.	NEO2021026
		S/C Date	2011-02-28
From	SHANGHAI PORT，CHINA	To	DAMMAM PORT，SAUDI ARABIA
Letter of Credit No.	0011LC123756	Date of Shipment	2021-04-25

Marks and Numbers	Number and Kind of Package Description of Goods	Quantity	Package	G. W	N. W	Meas.
ROSE BRAND 178/2001 RIYADH	ABOUT 1，700 CARTONS CANNED MUSHROOMS PIECES & STEMS 24 TINS × 425 GRAMS NET WEIGHT（D. W. 227 GRAMS） AT USD7. 80 PER CARTON. ROSE BRAND.	1，700 CARTONS	1，700 CARTONS	19，074 KGS	17，340 KGS	22. 80 CBM
	TOTAL	1，700 CARTONS	1，700 CARTONS	19，074KGS	17，340KGS	22. 80CBM
SAY TOTAL	USD ONE THOUSAND SEVEN HUNDRED CARTONS ONLY.					

能力训练

根据模块一中的信用证【样单1-3】和合同【样单1-4】以及审核结果，参考以下补充资料，制作商业发票和装箱单。

补充资料：

（1）每30件装一箱。

（2）总毛总：19KGS。

（3）总净重：17KGS。

（4）总尺码：21.583CBM。

（5）商业发票号码：NT01FF004。

【样单 2-6】

COMMERCIAL INVOICE				
To			Invoice No.	
			Invoice Date	
			S/C No.	
			S/C Date	
From		To		
Letter of Credit No.		Date		
Marks and Numbers	Number and Kind of Package Description of Goods	Quantity	Unit price	Amount
Total				
SAY TOTAL				

【样单 2-7】

PACKING LIST						
To				Invoice No.		
				Invoice Date		
From		To				
Marks and Numbers	Number and Kind of Package Description of Goods	Quantity	Package	G. W	N. W	Meas.
Total						
SAY TOTAL						

项目三：制作运输单据

项目目标

能够根据具体情况，按要求独立完成订舱委托书、海运提单、装船通知的制作。

学习情境四

在落实信用证和备货时，临江国际贸易公司开始根据信用证的有关规定备货出运。4月12日，临江公司委托货运代理人（上海凯通国际货运代理有限公司）向船公司订舱。刘华在业务员的指导下根据信用证及合同的有关规定填写“货物出运委托书”，并提交货代委托订舱。临江国际贸易公司配合货运公司安排装运、装船事宜，之后刘华开始与货运公司核对提单内容，协助货运公司按要求制作海运提单。装船后，刘华及时向买方发出装船通知。

价值引领

订舱委托书是制作海运提单的主要背景材料，海运提单是重要的运输单据，装船通知也可能是提交银行结汇的单据之一。正确制作上述单据，便于合同的正常履行，保障卖方安全收汇。

任务一：制作订舱委托书

相关知识

制作订舱委托书操作指导图

出口货物订舱委托书			日期	
1）发货人	4）信用证号码	参考信用证		
托运人的名称和地址 信用证：受益人 汇款和托收：卖方	5）开证银行	参考信用证		
	6）合同号码	参考合同	7）成交金额	参考信用证
	8）装运口岸	参考信用证	9）目的港	参考信用证
2）收货人	10）转船运输	参考信用证，填写 YES 或 NO	11）分批装运	参考信用证，填写 YES 或 NO

续表

<table>
<tr><td rowspan="3">信用证：参考信用证提单收货人的规定即：MADE OUT 后面的内容
汇款和托收：买方</td><td>12）信用证有效期</td><td>参考信用证</td><td>13）装船期限</td><td>按照合同或信用证规定填写装运期限，但同时要结合实际备货情况在“注意事项”栏目写明预订船期。</td></tr>
<tr><td>14）运费</td><td>在 CFR、CPT、CIF、CIP 贸易术语下，运费预付 Freight prepaid；在 FOB 和 FCA 贸易术语下，运费到付 Freight collect/Freight payable at destination 。</td><td>15）成交条件</td><td>填贸易术语</td></tr>
<tr><td>16）公司联系人</td><td>按公司实际情况填写</td><td>17 电话/传真</td><td>按公司实际情况填写</td></tr>
<tr><td>3）通知人</td><td>18）公司开户行</td><td>按公司实际情况填写</td><td>19）银行账号</td><td>按公司实际情况填写</td></tr>
<tr><td rowspan="2">信用证：按照信用证要求填写通知人的名称、地址、联系电话和传真。
汇款和托收：一般填写进口商的名称、地址、联系电话和传真。
若收货人是记名抬头，则本栏目往往填写 Same as the consignee。</td><td colspan="4">20）特别要求</td></tr>
<tr><td colspan="4">该栏目往往填写提单的特殊条款，如对集装箱的冷冻、熏蒸等特殊要求。
以上 12-15 项内容，在有些订舱委托书中是分栏填写，也有合并填写在“注意事项”或“声明事项”栏目。</td></tr>
</table>

<table>
<tr><td>21）标记唛码</td><td>22）货号规格</td><td>23）包装件数</td><td>24）毛重</td><td>25）净重</td><td>26）数量</td><td>27）单价</td><td>28）总价</td></tr>
<tr><td rowspan="3">参考商业发票</td><td>货物描述，一般只写统称</td><td>参考装箱单</td><td>参考装箱单</td><td>参考装箱单</td><td>参考装箱单</td><td>参考装箱单</td><td>参考装箱单</td></tr>
<tr><td colspan="2">29）总件数</td><td>30）总毛重</td><td>31）总净重</td><td colspan="2">32）总尺码</td><td>33）总金额</td></tr>
<tr><td colspan="2">参考装箱单</td><td>参考装箱单</td><td>参考装箱单</td><td colspan="2">参考装箱单</td><td>参考装箱单</td></tr>
<tr><td colspan="8">34）备注</td></tr>
<tr><td colspan="8">其他事项</td></tr>
</table>

工作任务

根据合同【样单 1-1】和信用证【样单 2-2】，以及商业发票【样单 2-4】和装箱单【样单 2-5】，参考下列补充资料，制作订舱委托书。

补充资料：

（1）公司开户行：中国银行。

（2）银行账号：48625935148。

【样单 2-8】

出口货物订舱委托书		日期	Apr. 12,2021	
1）发货人	4）信用证号码	0011LC123756		
SHANGHAI TRADING CO., LTD. HUARONG MANSION RM2901 NO. 85 GUANJIAQIAO, NANJING 210005, CHINA TEL: 0086 - 25 - 4715004 FAX: 0086-25-4711363	5）开证银行	ALRAJHI BANKING AND INVESTMENT CORP.		
	6）合同号码	NEO2021026	7）成交金额	USD13, 260. 00
	8）装运口岸	SHANGHAI	9）目的港	DAMMAM PORT
2）收货人	10）转船运输	N	11）分批装运	N
ALRAJHI BANKING AND INVESTMENT CORP.	12）信用证有效期	2021-05-15	13）装船期限	2021-04-30
	14）运费	PREPAID	15）成交条件	CFR
	16）公司联系人	李佳	17）电话/传真	025-4715004
3）通知人	18）公司开户行	中国银行	19）银行账号	48625935148
AFG GENERAL TRADING CO. P. O. BOX 99552, RIYADH 22766, KSA TEL: 00966 - 1 - 4659220 FAX: 00966-1-4659213	20）特别要求			

21）标记唛码	22）货号规格	23）包装件数	24）毛重	25）净重	26）数量	27）单价	28）总价
ROSE 178/2001 RIYADH	ABOUT 1, 700 CARTONS CANNED MUSHROOMS PIECES & STEMS 24 TINS×425 GRAMS NET WEIGHT (D. W. 227 GRAMS) AT USD7. 80 PER CARTON. ROSE BRAND.	1, 700 CARTONS	19, 074 KGS	17, 340 KGS	1, 700 CARTONS	USD7. 80	USD 13, 260. 00

29）总件数	30）总毛重	31）总净重	32）总尺码	33）总金额
1, 700 CARTONS	19, 074 KGS	17, 340 KGS	22. 80CBM	USD13, 260. 00

34）备注

任务二：制作海运提单

相关知识

制作海运提单操作指导图

<table>
<tr><td colspan="2">Shipper</td><td></td><td>B/L No.</td><td></td></tr>
<tr><td colspan="2">一般填写出口公司的名称（即信用证中的受益人）</td><td colspan="3" rowspan="11">SINOTRANS
中国外运广东公司
SINOTRANS GUANGDONG COMPANY

OCEAN BILL OF LADING
Shipped on board in apparent good order and condition (unless otherwise indicated) the goods or packages specified herein and to be discharged at the mentioned port of discharge or as near thereto as the vessel may safely get and be always afloat.
The weight, measure, marks and numbers, quality, contents and value, being particulars furnished by the Shipper, are not checked by the Carrier on loading.
The Shipper, Consignee and the Holder of this Bill of Lading hereby expressly accept and agree to all printed, written or stamped provisions, exceptions and conditions of this Bill of Lading, including those on the back hereof.
In witness whereof the number of original Bills of Lading stated below have been signed, one of which being accomplished the other (s) to be void.</td></tr>
<tr><td colspan="2">Consignee or order</td></tr>
<tr><td colspan="2">严格按照信用证要求填写
(1) 记名提单
例如：ABC CO.
(2) 指示提单
例如：TO ORDER
TO ORDER OF SHIPPER
TO ORDER OF ABC BANK
(3) 不记名提单
例如：TO BEARER</td></tr>
<tr><td colspan="2">Notify Address</td></tr>
<tr><td colspan="2">一般是货物的进口人或其代理，信用证情况下应严格按来证规定填写</td></tr>
<tr><td>Pre-carriage by</td><td>Port of Loading</td></tr>
<tr><td>前程运输，在联运方式下要填</td><td>填写装运港名称</td></tr>
<tr><td>Vessel</td><td>Port of Transshipment</td></tr>
<tr><td>一般填写第一程船船名航次</td><td>转运港</td></tr>
<tr><td>Port of Discharge</td><td>Final Destination</td></tr>
<tr><td>填写卸货港名称</td><td>最终目的地，在联运方式下填</td><td colspan="3"></td></tr>
<tr><td>Container. seal No. or marks and Nos.</td><td>Number and Kind of Package</td><td>Description of Goods</td><td>Gross Weight (kgs.)</td><td>Measurement (m^3)</td></tr>
<tr><td>填写唛头，如果货物以集装箱运输，则还要填写集装箱号和封箱号</td><td>填写最大包装件数
如果是散装货，则填写 IN BULK</td><td>填写货物描述，可以使用统称
成交价格为 CIF 或 CFR，这一栏里填写 FREIGHT PREPAID 成交价格为 FOB，这一栏里填写 FREIGHT COLLECT 信用证要求在提单里显示的附加信息可以填写在本栏</td><td>填写总毛重</td><td>填写总体积，一般保留小数点后 3 位</td></tr>
<tr><td colspan="2">Freight and Charges</td><td colspan="3" rowspan="2">REGARDING TRANSHIPMENT
INFORMATION PLEASE CONTACT</td></tr>
<tr><td colspan="2">成交价格为 CIF 或 CFR，这一栏里填写 FREIGHT PREPAID
成交价格为 FOB，这一栏里填写 FREIGHT COLLECT</td></tr>
</table>

续表

Ex. rate	Prepaid at	Freight Payable at	Place and Date of Issue
			出单地点和日期
	Total Prepaid	Number of Original B/L	Signed for or on Behalf of the Master
		正本提单的份数，按信用证的要求填写，如果信用证无明确要求或要求“FULL SET”，一般用大写注明“TWO”或者“THREE”	签署 （1）承运人签字，必须表明承运人的身份 例如：提单的上部：COSCO 提单签字处：COSCO （签字） AS CARRIER （2）代理人签字，除表明代理人身份外，还必须表明所代表的委托人的名称和身份 例如：提单的上部：COSCO 提单签字处：ABC SHIPPING CO. （签字） AS AGENT FOR THE CARRIER，COSCO
			As Agent

工作任务

根据合同【样单 1-1】和信用证【样单 2-2】，以及商业发票【样单 2-4】和装箱单【样单 2-5】，参考订舱委托书【样单 2-8】和下列补充资料，制作海运提单。

补充资料：

（1）船名航次：HANTIN / 059W。

（2）出运日期：2021 年 4 月 25 日。

（3）签署人：杨威。

【样单 2-9】

<table>
<tr><td colspan="2">Shipper</td><td>B/L No.</td></tr>
<tr><td colspan="2">SHANGHAI TRADING CO.，LTD.
HUARONG MANSION RM2901 NO. 85 GUANJIAQIAO，
NANJING 210005，CHINA
TEL：0086-25-4715004　FAX：0086-25-4711363</td><td rowspan="11">SINOTRANS
中国外运广东公司
SINOTRANS GUANGDONG COMPANY

OCEAN BILL OF LADING
Shipped on board in apparent good order and condition (unless otherwise indicated) the goods or packages specified herein and to be discharged at the mentioned port of discharge or as near thereto as the vessel may safely get and be always afloat.
The weight，measure，marks and numbers，quality，contents and value，being particulars furnished by the Shipper，are not checked by the Carrier on loading.
The Shipper，Consignee and the Holder of this Bill of Lading hereby expressly accept and agree to all printed，written or stamped provisions，exceptions and conditions of this Bill of Lading，including those on the back hereof.
In witness whereof the number of original Bills of Lading stated below have been signed，one of which being accomplished the other (s) to be void.</td></tr>
<tr><td colspan="2">Consignee</td></tr>
<tr><td colspan="2">TO THE ORDER OF ALRAJHI BANKING AND INVESTMENT CORP.</td></tr>
<tr><td colspan="2">Notify Address</td></tr>
<tr><td colspan="2">AFG GENERAL TRADING CO.
P. O. BOX 99552，RIYADH 22766，KSA
TEL：00966-1-4659220　FAX：00966-1-4659213</td></tr>
<tr><td>Pre-carriage by</td><td>Port of Loading</td></tr>
<tr><td></td><td>SHANGHAI PORT</td></tr>
<tr><td>Vessel</td><td>Port of Transshipment</td></tr>
<tr><td>HANTIN / 059W</td><td></td></tr>
<tr><td>Port of Discharge</td><td>Final Destination</td></tr>
<tr><td>DAMMAM PORT</td><td></td></tr>
</table>

续表

Container. seal No. or marks and Nos.	Number and Kind of Package	Description of Goods	Gross Weight (kgs)	Measurement (m^3)
ROSE BRAND 178/2001 RIYADH	1, 700CTNS FREIGHT PREPAID	CANNED MUSHROOMS PIECES & STEMS 24 TINS×425 GRAMS NET WEIGHT (D. W. 227 GRAMS) ROSE BRAND.	19, 074	22. 80

Freight and charges	REGARDING TRANSHIPMENT INFORMATION PLEASE CONTACT
FREIGHT PREPAID	

Ex. rate	Prepaid at	Freight payable at	Place and Date of Issue
			SHANGHAI , APR. 25, 2021
	Total Prepaid	Number of Original B/L	Signed for or on Behalf of the Master
		THREE	Yang Wei
			As Agent

任务三：制作装船通知

相关知识

制作装船通知操作指导

出口公司名称

SHIPPING ADVICE

单据名称 Shipping/Shipment Advice，Advice of Shipment 等，也有人将其称为 Shipping Statement/Declaration，如信用证有具体要求，从其规定。

FAX 传真

TEL 电话

INVOICE NO. 发票号码

L/C NO. 信用证号码

S/C NO. 合同号码

MESSRS：

通知对象

应按信用证规定，具体讲可以是开证申请人、申请人的指定人或保险公司等。

DEAR SIRS，

WE HEREBY INFORM YOU THAT THE GOODS UNDER THE ABOVE MENTIONED CREDIT HAVE BEEN SHIPPED. THE DETAILS OF THE SHIPMENT ARE STATED BELOW.

SHIPPING MARKS：

唛头

COMMODITY： 商品名称

TOTAL G. W.： 总毛重

OCEAN VESSEL： 船名航次

DATE OF DEPARTURE： 装船日期

B/L NO.： 提单号码

PORT OF LOADING： 装运港

DESTINATION： 目的地

签署

一般可以不签署，如信用证要求“certified copy of shipping advice”，通常加盖受益人条形章。

工作任务

根据以下提单【样单2-10】和补充资料，制作装船通知。

补充资料：

（1）传真：56489542。

（2）电话：56489545。

（3）发票号码：JS03256。

（4）信用证号码：H2108。

（5）销售合同号码：ST355。

【样单2-10】

<table>
<tr><td colspan="2">Shipper</td><td colspan="3">B/L No. HJSHB142323</td></tr>
<tr><td colspan="2">NANJING FORGIGN TRADE IMP. AND EXP. CORP.</td><td colspan="3" rowspan="11">SINOTRANS
中国外运广东公司
SINOTRANS GUANGDONG COMPANY

OCEAN BILL OF LADING
Shipped on board in apparent good order and condition (unless otherwise indicated) the goods or packages specified herein and to be discharged at the mentioned port of discharge or as near thereto as the vessel may safely get and be always afloat.
The weight, measure, marks and numbers, quality, contents and value, being particulars furnished by the Shipper, are not checked by the Carrier on loading.
The Shipper, Consignee and the Holder of this Bill of Lading hereby expressly accept and agree to all printed, written or stamped provisions, exceptions and conditions of this Bill of Lading, including those on the back hereof.
In witness whereof the number of original Bills of Lading stated below have been signed, one of which being accomplished the other (s) to be void.</td></tr>
<tr><td colspan="2">Consignee or Order</td></tr>
<tr><td colspan="2">TO ORDER</td></tr>
<tr><td colspan="2">Notify Address</td></tr>
<tr><td colspan="2">EAST AGENT COMPANY
126 ROOM STREET, ANTERWEIP, BELGIUM</td></tr>
<tr><td>Pre-carriage by</td><td>Port of Loading</td></tr>
<tr><td></td><td>NANJING</td></tr>
<tr><td>Vessel</td><td>Port of Transshipment</td></tr>
<tr><td>DAFENG E002</td><td></td></tr>
<tr><td>Port of Discharge</td><td>Final Destination</td></tr>
<tr><td>LONDON</td><td></td></tr>
<tr><td>Container. seal No. or Marks and Nos.</td><td>Number and Kind of Package</td><td>Description of Goods</td><td>Gross Weight (kgs.)</td><td>Measurement (m^3)</td></tr>
<tr><td>CBD
LONDON
NOS1-200</td><td>SHIPPED IN ONE 20'CY TO CY CONTAINER

FREIGHT: USD2, 635. 00</td><td>LADIES LYCRA LONG PANT</td><td>2, 000</td><td>6</td></tr>
</table>

续表

<table>
<tr><td colspan="3">Freight and Charges</td><td rowspan="2">REGARDING TRANSHIPMENT
INFORMATION PLEASE CONTACT</td></tr>
<tr><td colspan="3"></td></tr>
<tr><td colspan="3">FREIGHT PREPAID</td><td></td></tr>
<tr><td>Ex. rate</td><td>Prepaid at</td><td>Freight Payable at</td><td>Place and Date of Issue</td></tr>
<tr><td rowspan="4"></td><td></td><td></td><td>NANJING OCT 20,2004</td></tr>
<tr><td>Total Prepaid</td><td>Number of Original B/L</td><td>Signed for or on Behalf of the Master</td></tr>
<tr><td rowspan="2"></td><td rowspan="2">THREE</td><td>FOR PACIFIC INTERNATIONAL LINES (PTE) LTD
AS CARRIER</td></tr>
<tr><td>As Agent</td></tr>
</table>

制作装船通知如下：

【样单 2-11】

NANJING FOREIGN TRADE IMP. AND EXP. CORP.
SHIPPING ADVICE

FAX　56489542　　　　INVOICE NO.　JS03256

TEL　56489545　　　　L/C NO.　H2108

S/C NO.　ST355

MESSRS:

EAST AGENT COMPANY

126 ROOM HUAPU STREET, ANTERWEIP, BELGIUM

DEAR SIRS:

WE HEREBY INFORM YOU THAT THE GOODS UNDER THE ABOVE MENTIONED CREDIT HAVE BEEN SHIPPED. THE DETAILS OF THE SHIPMENT ARE STATED BELOW.

SHIPPING MARKS:		
	COMMODITY :	LADIES LYCRA LONG PANT
	TOTAL G. W. :	2,000KGS
CBD	OCEAN VESSEL:	DAFENG　E002
LONDON	DATE OF DEPARTURE:	OCT. 20,2021
NOS1-200	B/L NO. :	HJSHB142323
	PORT OF LOADING:	NANJING
	DESTINATION:	LONDON

拓展任务 制作航空运单

相关知识

航空运单填写规范详解

航空运单与海运提单类似，也有正面、背面条款之分，不同的航空公司也有其独特的航空运单格式。航运公司的海运提单可能有差异，但各航空公司所使用的航空运单大多借鉴 IATA 所推荐的标准格式，本文主要介绍这种标准格式，也称中性运单。下面就有关需要填写的栏目说明如下：

（1）始发站机场：需填写 IATA 统一制定的始发站机场或城市的三字代码，这一栏应与 11 栏相一致。

①IATA 统一编制的航空公司代码，如我国的国际航空公司代码为 999。

②运单号。

（2）发货人姓名、住址（Shipper's Name and Address）：填写发货人姓名、地址、所在国家及联络方法。

（3）发货人账号：只在必要时填写。

（4）收货人姓名、住址（Consignee's Name and Address）：填写收货人姓名、地址、所在国家及联络方法。与海运提单不同，因为空运单不可转让，不能标注“凭指示”之类的字样。

（5）收货人账号：同第 3 栏一样，只在必要时填写。

（6）承运人代理的名称和所在城市（Issuing Carrier's Agent Name and City）。

（7）代理人的 IATA 代号。

（8）代理人账号。

（9）始发站机场及所要求的航线（Airport of Departure and Requested Routing）：始发站应与第 1 栏填写的内容一致。

（10）支付信息（Accounting Information）：此栏只在采用特殊付款方式时才填写。

（11）①（C、E）. 去往（To）：分别填入第一（二、三）中转站机场的 IATA 代码。②（D、F）. 承运人（By）：分别填入第一（二、三）段运输的承运人。

（12）货币（Currency）：填入 ISO 货币代码。

（13）收费代号：填写支付方式。

（14）运费及声明价值费（WT/VAL, Weight Charge/Valuation Charge）：

此处可能有两种情况：预付（PPD, Prepaid）或到付（COLL, collected）。如预付，在 14A 中填入“*”，否则填在 14B 中。需要注意的是，航空货物运输中运费与声明价值费支付的方式必须一致，不能分别支付。

（15）其他费用（Other）：也有预付和到付两种支付方式。

（16）运输声明价值（Declared Value for Carriage）：在此栏填入发货人要求的用于运输的声明价值。如果发货人不要求声明价值，则填入“NVD（No Value Declared）”。

（17）海关声明价值（Declared Value for Customs）：发货人在此填入对海关的声明价值，或者填入“NCV（No Customs Valuation）”，表明没有声明价值。

（18）目的地机场（Airport of Destination）：填写最终目的地机场全称。

（19）航班及日期（Flight/Date）：填入货物所搭乘航班及日期。

（20）保险金额（Amount of Insurance）：只有在航空公司提供代保险业务而客户也有此需要时才填写。

（21）操作信息（Handling Information）：一般填入承运人对货物处理的有关注意事项，如“托运人提供活动物证明（Shipper's Certification for Live Animals）”等。

（22）货物运价、运费细节。

①货物件数和运价组成点（No. of Pieces RCP，Rate Combination Point）：填入货物包装件数。如 10 包即填“10”。当需要组成比例运价或分段相加运价时，在此栏填入运价组成点机场的 IATA 代码。

②毛重（Gross Weight）：填入货物总毛重。

③重量单位：可选择公斤（kg）或磅（lb）。

④运价等级（Rate Class）：一般而言，航空运价有 6 种代码，分别是 M（Minimum，起码运费）、C（Specific Commodity Rates，特种运价）、S（Surcharge，高于普通货物运价的等级货物运价）、R（Reduced，低于普通货物运价的等级货物运价）、N（Normal，45 公斤以下货物适用的普通货物运价）、Q（Quantity，45 公斤以上货物适用的普通货物运价）。

⑤商品代码（Commodity Item No.）：在使用特种运价时需要在此栏填写商品代码。

⑥计费重量（Chargeable Weight）：此栏填入航空公司据以计算运费的计费重量，该重量可与货物毛重相同，也可以不同。

⑦运价（Rate/Charge）：填入该货物适用的费率。

⑧运费总额（Total）：此栏数值应为起码运费值，或为运价与计费重量两栏数值的乘积。

⑨货物的品名、数量，含尺码或体积（Nature and Quantity of Goods incl. Dimensions or Volume）：货物的尺码应以厘米或英寸为单位，尺寸分别以货物最长、最宽、最高边为基础。体积则是上述三边的乘积，单位为立方厘米或立方英寸。

⑩该运单项下货物总件数。

⑪该运单项下货物总毛重。

⑫该运单项下货物总运费。

（23）其他费用（Other Charges）：除运费和声明价值附加费以外的其他费用。根据 IATA 规则各项费用分别用三个英文字母表示。其中前两个字母是某项费用的代码，如运单费就表示为 AW（Air Waybill Fee）。第三个字母是 C 或 A，表示费用应支付给承运人（Carrier）或货运代理人（Agent）。

（24）①分别记录运费、声明价值费和税款金额，有预付与到付两种方式。

②分别记录需要付与货运代理人（Due Agent）和承运人（Due Carrier）的其他费用合计金额。

（25）需预付或到付的各种费用。

（26）预付、到付的总金额。

（27）发货人的签字。

（28）签单时间（日期）、地点、承运人或其代理人的签字。

（29）货币换算及目的地机场收费记录。

以上所有内容不一定要全部填入空运单，IATA 也不限制在运单中写入其他所需的内容，这种标准化的单证对航空货运经营人提高工作效率、促进航空货运业向电子商务方向迈进有积极的意义。

工作任务

根据以下信用证和补充资料，制作航空运单。

补充资料：

2021 年 4 月 7 日，世格贸易公司（DESUN TRADING CO.，LTD.）的货物从南京起运，航班为 FX0910，请根据信用证制作航空运单。

（1）商品毛重：19,074.44KGS。

（2）体积：36.85CBM。

（3）Rate Class 运价分类代号：N。

（4）Rate/Charge 费率：20.61。

（5）Other Charge 其他费用：AWC（运单费）50.00。

（6）信用证：

SEQUENCE OF TOTAL	*27：	1 / 1
FORM OF DOC. CREDIT	*40 A：	IRREVOCABLE
DOC. CREDIT NUMBER	*20：	63211020049
DATE OF ISSUE	31 C：	210129
Date/Place EXPIRY	*31 D：	DATE Apr. 10，2021 PLACE IN BENEFICIARY'S COUNTRY
APPLICANT	*50：	FASHION FORCE CO.，LTD P. O. BOX 8935 NEW TERMINAL，ALTA，VISTA OTTAWA，CANADA
BENEFICIARY	*59：	NANJING TANG TEXTILE GARMENT CO.，LTD. HUARONG MANSION RM2901 NO. 85 GUANJIAQIAO，NANJING 210005，CHINA
AMOUNT	*32 B：	CURRENCY USD AMOUNT 32,640
AVAILABLE WITH/BY	*41 D：	ANY BANK BY NEGOTIATION
DRAFTS AT	42 C：	SIGHT
DRAWEE	42 A：	BNPACAMMXXX *BNP PARIBAS（CANADA） *MONTREAL
PARTIAL SHIPMTS	43 P：	NOT ALLOWED
TRANSSHIPMENT	43 T：	ALLOWED
PORT OF LOADING	44 E：	CHINA
PORT OF DISCHARGING	44 F：	MONTREAL
LATEST DATE OF SHIP.	44 C：	210325
DESCRIPT OF GOODS	45 A：	
		SALES CONDITIONS：CIF MONTREAL/CANADA SALES CONTRACT NO. F01LCB05127 LADIES COTTON BLAZER（100% COTTON，40SX20/140X60）

	STYLE NO. PO NO. QTY/PCS USD/PC 46-301A 10 337 2 550 12. 80
DOCUMENTS REQUIRED 46 A:	
	+ COMMERCIAL INVOICES IN 3 COPIES SIGNED BY BENEFICIARY'S REPRESENTATIVE. + CANADA CUSTOMS INVOICES IN 4 COPIES. + FULL SET OF ORIGINAL MARINE BILLS OF LADING CLEAN ON BOARD FLUS 2 NON NEGOTIABLE COPIES MADE OUT OR ENDORSED TO ORDER OF BNP PARIBAS (CANADA) MARKED FREIGHT PREPAID AND NOTIFY APPLICANT'S FULL NAME AND ADDRESS. + DETAILED PACKING LISTS IN 3 COPIES. + COPY OF CERTIFICATE OF ORIGIN FORM A. + COPY OF EXPORT LICENCE. + BENEFICIARY'S LETTER STATING THAT ORIGINAL CERTIFICATE OF ORIGIN FORM A, ORIGINAL EXPORT LICENCE, COPY OF COMMERCIAL INVOICE, DETAILED PACKING LISTS AND A COPY OF BILL OF LADING WERE SENT DIRECT TO APPLICANT BY COURIER WITHIN 5 DAYS AFTER SHIPMENT. THE RELATIVE COURIER RECEIPT IS ALSO REQUIRED FOR PRESENTATION. + COPY OF APPLICANT'S FAX APPROVING PRODUCTION SAMPLES BEFORE SHIPMENT. + LETTER FROM SHIPPER ON THEIR LETTERHEAD INDICATING THEIR NAME OF COMPANY AND ADDRESS, BILL OF LADING NUMBER, CONTAINER NUMBER AND THAT THIS SHIPMENT, INCLUDING ITS CONTAINER, DOES NOT CONTAIN ANY NON-MANUFACTURED WOODEN MATERIAL, DUNNAGE, BRACING MATERIAL, PALLETS, CRATING OR OTHER NON-MANUFACTURE WOODEN PACKING MATERIAL. + INSPECTION CERTIFICATE ORIGINAL SIGNED AND ISSUED BY FASHION FORCE CO. , LTD STATING THE SAMPLES OF FOUR STYLE GARMENTS HAS BEEN APPROVED, WHICH SEND THROUGH DHL BEFORE 15DAYS OF SHIPMENT. + INSURANCE POLICY OR CERTIFICATE IN 1 ORIGINAL AND

		1 COPY ISSUED OR ENDORSED TO THE ORDER OF BNP PARIBAS (CANADA) FOR THE CIF INVOICE PLUS 10 PERCENT COVERING ALL RISKS, INSTITUTE STRIKES, INSTITUTE WAR CLAUSES AND CIVIL COMMOTIONS CLAUSES.
ADDITIONAL COND.	47 A：	
		+ IF DOCUMENTS PRESENTED ARE FOUND BY US NOT TO BE UNFULL COMPLIANCE WITH CREDIT TERMS. WE WILL ASSESS A CHARGE OF USD 55. 00 PER SET OF DOCUMENTS. + ALL CHARGES IF ANY RELATED TO SETTLEMENTS ARE FOR AC-COUNT OF BENEFICIARY. + 3 PCT MORE OR LESS IN AMOUNT AND QUANTITY IS ALLOWED. + ALL CERTIFICATES/LETTERS/STATEMENTS MUST BE SIGNED AND DATED + FOR INFORMATION ONLY, PLEASE NOTE AS OF JUN. 4, 2020 THAT ALL SHIPMENTS FROM CHINA THAT ARE PACKED WITH UN-TREATED WOOD WILL BE BANNED FROM CANADA DUE TO THE THREAT POSED BY THE ASIAN LONGNORNED BEETLE. + THE CANADIAN GOVERNMENT NOW INSIST THAT EVERY SHIP-MENT ENTERING CANADA MUST HAVE THE ABOVE DOCUMENTATION WITH THE SHIPMENT. + BILL OF LADING AND COMMERCIAL INVOICE MUST CERTIFY THE FOLLOWING： THIS SHIPMENT, INCLUDING ITS CONTAINER DOES NOT CONTAIN ANY NON - MANUFACTURED WOODEN MATERIAL, DUNNAGE, BRACING MATERIAL PALLETS, CRATING OR OTHER NON-MANUFACTURED WOODEN PACKING MATERIAL. + BENEFICIARY'S BANK ACCOUNT NO. 07773108201140121
CHARGES	71 B：	OUTSIDE COUNTRY BANK CHARGES TO BE BORNE BY THE BENEFICIARY OPENING BANK CHARGES TO BE BORNE BY THE APPLICANT
CONFIRMATION	*49：	WITHOUT
INSTRUCTIONS	78：	

		+ WE SHALL COVER THE NEGOTIATING BANK AS PER THEIR INSTRUCTIONS + FORWARD DOCUMENTS IN ONE LOT BY SPECIAL COURIER PREPAID TO BNP PARIBAS (CANADA) 1981 MCGILL COLLEGE AVE. MONTREAL QC H3A 2W8 CANADA.
SEND. TO REC. INFO.	72:	THIS CREDIT IS SUBJECT TO UCP FOR DOCUMENTARY CREDIT2007 REVISION ICC PUBLICATION600AND IS THE OPERATIVE INSTRUMENT

制作的航空运单如下：

【样单 2-12】

<table>
<tr><td>999</td><td></td><td colspan="2"></td><td>999-</td></tr>
<tr><td colspan="2">Shipper's Name and Address</td><td colspan="2">Shipper's Account Number</td><td rowspan="2"></td></tr>
<tr><td colspan="4">DESUN TRADING CO. , LTD.
HUARONG MANSION RM2901 NO. 85 GUANJIAQIAO,
NANJING 210005, CHINA
TEL: 0086-25-4715004 FAX: 0086-25-4711363</td></tr>
<tr><td colspan="4"></td><td>Copies 1, 2 and 3 of this Air Waybill are originals and have the same validity.</td></tr>
<tr><td colspan="2">Consignee's Name and Address</td><td colspan="2">Consignee's Account Number</td><td rowspan="2">It is agreed that the goods described herein are accepted for carriage in apparent good order and condition (except as noted) and subject to the conditions of contract on the reverse hereof. All goods may be carried by and other means including road or any other carrier unless specific contrary instructions are given hereon by the shipper. the shipper's attention is drawn to the notice concerning carrier's limitation of liability. Shipper may increase such limitation of liability by declaring a higher value for carriage and paying a supplemental charge if required.</td></tr>
<tr><td colspan="4">NEO GENERAL TRADING CO. , LTD
P. O. BOX 99552, RIYADH 22766, KSA
TEL: 00966-1-4659220 FAX: 00966-1-4659213</td></tr>
</table>

续表

Issuing Carrier's Agent Name and City		Accounting Information FREIGHT PREPAID
Agent's IATA Code	Account No.	
Airport of Departure (Addr. of first carrier) and Requested Routing NANJING		

To	By First Carrier	to	by	to	by	Currency	CHGS Code	WT/VAL PPD	WT/VAL COLL	Other PPD	Other COLL	Declared Value for Carriage	Declared Value for Customs
						USD		X		X			

Airport of Destination	Flight/Date for Carrier Use Only Flight/Date		Amount of Insurance	INSURANCE: If Carrier offers insurance, and such insurance is requested in accordance with the conditions thereof, indicate amount to be insured in figures in box marked "Amount of Insurance."
DAMMAM PORT	FX0910	APR 7, 2021		

Handing Information

(For USA only) These commodities licensed by U. S. for ultimate destination…Diversion contrary to U. S. law is prohibited

No. of Pieces, RCP	Gross Weight	kg/Lb	Rate Class N	Commodity Item No.	Chargeable Weight	Rate Charge	Total	Nature and Quantity of Goods (incl. Dimensions or Volume)
1, 700 CTNS	19, 074. 44	kg			19, 074. 44	20. 61	393, 124. 21	CANNED MUSHROOM PIECES & STEMS 24 TINS X 425 GRAMS

Prepaid	Weight Charge	Collect	Other Charges
393, 124. 21			
Valuation Charge			AWC: 50. 00
Tax			
Total other Charges Due Agent			Shipper certifies that the particulars on the face hereof are correct and that insofar as any part of the consignment contains dangerous goods, such part is properly described by name and is in proper condition for carriage by air according to the applicable dangerous goods regulations.
Total other Charges Due Carrier 50. 00			…………………………………… Signature of Shipper or its Agent
Total Prepaid 393, 174. 21	Total Collect		7/APRIL/2021 NANJING DESUN TRADING CO. , LTD.
Currency Conversion Rates	CC Charges in Dest. Currency		…………………………………… Executed on (date) at (place) Signature of Issuing Carrier or its Agent
For Carrier's Use only at Destination	Charges at Destination		Total Collect Charges 999-

ORIGINAL 3 (FOR SHIPPER)

能力训练

根据模块一中的信用证【样单 1-3】和合同【样单 1-4】，模块二中已做好的发票【2-6】和装箱单【2-7】，参考下列补充资料，制作提单和装船通知：

补充资料：

（1）船名航次：HUA CHANG　　　V. 09981。

（2）货物装一个集装箱，集装箱号和封志号：MSKU2612114 / 1681316 20'。

（3）装运日期：MAR. 20，2021。

（4）提单号码：COS6314203208。

【样单 2-13】

Shipper			B/L No.	
		SINOTRANS 中国外运广东公司 SINOTRANS GUANGDONG COMPANY OCEAN BILL OF LADING Shipped on board in apparent good order and condition (unless otherwise indicated) the goods or packages specified herein and to be discharged at the mentioned port of discharge or as near thereto as the vessel may safely get and be always afloat. The weight, measure, marks and numbers, quality, contents and value, being particulars furnished by the Shipper, are not checked by the Carrier on loading. The Shipper, Consignee and the Holder of this Bill of Lading hereby expressly accept and agree to all printed, written or stamped provisions, exceptions and conditions of this Bill of Lading, including those on the back hereof. In witness whereof the number of original Bills of Lading stated below have been signed, one of which being accomplished the other (s) to be void.		
Consignee or Order				
Notify Address				
Pre-carriage by	Port of Loading			
Vessel	Port of Transshipment			
Port of Discharge	Final Destination			
Container. Seal No. or Marks and Nos.	Number and Kind of Package	Description of Goods	Gross Weight (kgs)	Measurement (m^3)
Freight and Charges		REGARDING TRANSSHIPMENT INFORMATION PLEASE CONTACT		
Ex. rate	Prepaid at	Freight Payable at	Place and Date of Issue	
	Total Prepaid	Number of Original B/L	Signed for or on Behalf of the Master	
			As Agent	

【样单 2-14】

SHIPPING ADVICE

FAX	INVOICE NO.
TEL	L/C NO.
	S/C NO.

MESSRS:

DEAR SIRS:

WE HEREBY INFORM YOU THAT THE GOODS UNDER THE ABOVE MENTIONED CREDIT HAVE BEEN SHIPPED. THE DETAILS OF THE SHIPMENT ARE STATED BELOW.

SHIPPING MARKS:

COMMODITY :
TOTAL G. W. :
OCEAN VESSEL:
DATE OF DEPARTURE:
B/L NO. :
PORT OF LOADING:
DESTINATION:

项目四：制作保险单据

项目目标

能按要求独立制作投保单和保险单。

学习情境五

在完成订舱手续之后，在货物装船前，单证员根据合同和信用证条款的规定，向当地保险公司办理出口货物运输保险。单证员按照信用证规定填制投保单、确定保险金额，并附上商业发票和装箱单向中国人民保险公司办理保险手续。中国人民保险公司按照约定的保险费率收讫保险费后，依据投保单出具保险单给出口公司。

价值引领

国际货物运输保险是国际贸易的一个重要环节，正确缮制投保单和保险单，按要求及时投保，可以转嫁国际货物运输途中的风险损失，有利于进出口企业加强经济核算，保持正常经营。

任务一：制作投保单

相关知识

制作投保单操作指导

出口货物运输保险投保单

<table>
<tr><td>发票号码</td><td colspan="2">根据具体情况填写</td><td>投保条款和险别</td></tr>
<tr><td rowspan="2">被保险人</td><td colspan="2">客户抬头
一般填信用证的受益人，即出口公司的名称。
若信用证另有要求，按信用证填写</td><td rowspan="15">(　　) PICC CLAUSE
(　　) ICC CLAUSE
(　　) ALL RISKS
(　　) W. P. A. /W. A.
(　　) F. P. A.
(　　) WAR RISKS
(　　) S. R. C. C
(　　) STRIKE
(　　) ICC CLAUSE A
(　　) ICC CLAUSE B
(　　) ICC CLAUSE C
(　　) AIR TPT ALL RISKS
(　　) AIR TPT RISKS
(　　) O/L TPT ALL RISKS
(　　) O/L TPT RISKS
(　　) TRANSSHIPMENT RISKS
(　　) W TO W
(　　) T. P. N. D.
(　　) F. R. E. C.
(　　) R. F. W. D.
(　　) RISKS OF BREAKAGE
I. O. P.
以上按L/C选择</td></tr>
<tr><td colspan="2">过户
买方
根据信用证计算得出，不保留小数位，出现小数，向上进位。</td></tr>
<tr><td rowspan="3">保险金额</td><td>USD</td><td>(　　　)</td></tr>
<tr><td>HKD</td><td>(　　　)</td></tr>
<tr><td>(　)</td><td>(　　　)</td></tr>
<tr><td>启运港</td><td colspan="2">根据具体情况填写</td></tr>
<tr><td>目的港</td><td colspan="2">根据具体情况填写</td></tr>
<tr><td>转内陆</td><td colspan="2"></td></tr>
<tr><td>开航日期</td><td colspan="2">根据具体情况填写</td></tr>
<tr><td>船名航次</td><td colspan="2">根据具体情况填写</td></tr>
<tr><td>赔款地点</td><td colspan="2">按 L/C，无明确规定，一般将目的港/地作为赔付地点</td></tr>
<tr><td>赔付币别</td><td colspan="2">按 L/C，无明确规定，按发票币制</td></tr>
<tr><td>正本份数</td><td colspan="2">按 L/C</td></tr>
<tr><td>其他特别条款</td><td colspan="3">按 L/C</td></tr>
<tr><td colspan="4">以下由保险公司填写</td></tr>
<tr><td>保单号码</td><td></td><td>费率</td><td></td></tr>
<tr><td>签单日期</td><td></td><td>保费</td><td></td></tr>
</table>

投保日期：　　如实填写　　　　　　　　投保人签章：

补充资料：

我国广东省机械进出口公司（GUANGDONG MACHINE IMPORT AND EXPORT COMPANY）向荷兰罗纳度贸易公司（HOLLAND RONALDO TRADE COMPANY）出口不锈钢铲头（STAINLESS SCOOP）12 000 件，每件 9.60 美元，CIF Rotterdam（鹿特丹）、纸箱包装，每箱 12 件。合同规定按发票金额的 110% 投保一切险和战争险，运输标志为：

F. V.

ART NO=9099

ROTTERDAM

NOS：1-1000

该货物于 2021 年 3 月 20 日在广州装“Pessession V16”轮运往鹿特丹

商业发票号：NM134

合同号：05MP561009

信用证号：T-027651

【样单 2-15】

出口货物运输保险投保单

<table>
<tr><td>发票号码</td><td colspan="2">NM134</td><td>投保条款和险别</td></tr>
<tr><td rowspan="2">被保险人</td><td colspan="2">客户抬头
GUANGDONG MACHINE IMPORT AND EXPORT COMPANY</td><td rowspan="13">(√) PICC CLAUSE
(　) ICC CLAUSE
(√) ALL RISKS
(　) W. P. A. /W. A.
(　) F. P. A.
(√) WAR RISKS
(　) S. R. C. C.
(√) STRIKE
(　) ICC CLAUSE A
(　) ICC CLAUSE B
(　) ICC CLAUSE C
(　) AIR TPT ALL RISKS
(　) AIR TPT RISKS
(　) O/L TPT ALL RISKS
(　) O/L TPT RISKS
(　) TRANSSHIPMENT RISKS
(　) W TO W
(　) T. P. N. D.
(　) F. R. E. C.
(　) R. F. W. D.
(　) RISKS OF BREAKAGE
(　) I. O. P.</td></tr>
<tr><td colspan="2">过户
HOLLAND RONALDO TRADECOMPANY</td></tr>
<tr><td rowspan="3">保险金额</td><td colspan="2">USD (126 720)</td></tr>
<tr><td colspan="2">HKD (　　)</td></tr>
<tr><td colspan="2">(　) (　　)</td></tr>
<tr><td>启运港</td><td colspan="2">GUANGZHOU</td></tr>
<tr><td>目的港</td><td colspan="2">ROTTERDAM</td></tr>
<tr><td>转内陆</td><td colspan="2"></td></tr>
<tr><td>开航日期</td><td colspan="2">2021. 3. 20</td></tr>
<tr><td>船名航次</td><td colspan="2">PESSESSION V16</td></tr>
<tr><td>赔款地点</td><td colspan="2">ROTTERDAM</td></tr>
<tr><td>赔付币别</td><td colspan="2">USD</td></tr>
<tr><td>正本份数</td><td colspan="2">1 份正本，1 份副本</td></tr>
<tr><td>其他特别条款</td><td colspan="3"></td></tr>
<tr><td colspan="4">以下由保险公司填写</td></tr>
<tr><td>保单号码</td><td></td><td>费率</td><td></td></tr>
<tr><td>签单日期</td><td></td><td>保费</td><td></td></tr>
</table>

投保日期：　2021 年 3 月 16 日　　　　投保人签章：

任务二：制作保险单

相关知识

制作保险单操作指导图

<table>
<tr><td colspan="8">中国人民保险公司广州市分公司
The People's Insurance Company of China Guangzhou Branch</td></tr>
<tr><td colspan="2"></td><td colspan="2">总公司设于北京
Head Office Beijing</td><td colspan="2">一九四九年创立
Established in 1949</td><td colspan="2"></td></tr>
<tr><td colspan="8">货物运输保险单
CARGO TRANSPORTATION INSURANCE POLICY</td></tr>
<tr><td colspan="2">发票号码（INVOICE NO.）</td><td>如实填写</td><td colspan="2" rowspan="2"></td><td rowspan="2">保险单号次
Policy No.</td><td colspan="2" rowspan="2">如实填写</td></tr>
<tr><td colspan="2">合同号（CONTRACT NO.）</td><td>如实填写</td></tr>
<tr><td colspan="2">信用证号（L/C NO.）</td><td colspan="6">如实填写</td></tr>
<tr><td colspan="2">被保险人
Insured</td><td colspan="6">一般填信用证的受益人，即出口公司的名称。</td></tr>
<tr><td colspan="8">中国人民保险有限公司（以下简称本公司）根据被保险人的要求，由被保险人向本公司缴付约定的保险费，按照本保险单承担险别和背面所载条款与下列特别条款承保下列货物运输保险，特立本保险单。
This policy of Insurance witnesses that the People's Insurance Company of China（hereinafter called "The Company"），at the request of the Insured and in consideration of the agreed premium paid to the company by the insured, undertakes to insure the undermentioned goods in transportation subject to conditions of the Policy as the Clauses printed overleaf and other special clauses attached hereon.</td></tr>
<tr><td colspan="2">标记
Marks & Nos</td><td colspan="2">包装及数量
Packing & Quantity</td><td colspan="2">保险货物项目
Descriptions of Goods</td><td colspan="2">保险金额
Amount Insured</td></tr>
<tr><td colspan="2">唛头</td><td colspan="2">如实填写</td><td colspan="2">如实填写</td><td colspan="2">参考投保单的填写</td></tr>
<tr><td colspan="2">总保险金额：
Total Amount Insured</td><td colspan="6">保险金额的大写</td></tr>
<tr><td>保费
Premium</td><td>如实填写</td><td colspan="2">启运日期
Date of commencement：</td><td>如实填写，参考提单</td><td colspan="2">装载运输工具
Per conveyance</td><td>如实填写</td></tr>
<tr><td>自
From</td><td colspan="2">装运港</td><td>经
Via</td><td colspan="2">转运港</td><td>至
To</td><td>目的港</td></tr>
<tr><td>承保险别
Conditions</td><td colspan="7">按信用证约定填</td></tr>
</table>

续表

所保货物，如发生本保险单项下可能引起索赔的损失或损坏，应立即通知本公司下述代理人查勘。如有索赔，应向本公司提交保险单正本（本保险单共有____份正本）及有关文件。如一份正本已用于索赔，其余正本则自动失效。 In the event of loss or damage which may result in acclaim under this Policy, immediate notice must be given to the Company's Agent as mentioned here under. Claims, if any, one of the Original Policy which has been issued in ____ original (s) together with the relevant documents shall be surrendered to the Company. If one of the Original Policy has been accomplished, the others to be void.
中国人民保险公司广州市分公司 The People's Insurance Company of China Guangzhou Branch

赔款偿付地点 Claim payable at	参考投保单	签名
出单日期 Issuing Date	不得晚于提单日期	Authorized Signature
地址 Address	保险人地址	电话（TEL）：如实填写 传真（FAX）：如实填写

工作任务

根据本项目任务一的相关资料，制作保险单。

【样单 2-16】

中国人民保险公司广州市分公司 The People's Insurance Company of China Guangzhou Branch			
	总公司设于北京 Head Office Beijing	一九四九年创立 Established in 1949	
货物运输保险单 CARGO TRANSPORTATION INSURANCE POLICY			
发票号码（INVOICE NO.）	NM134	保险单号次 Policy No.	PLC876
合同号（CONTRACT NO.）	05MP561009		
信用证号（L/C NO.）	T-027651		
被保险人 Insured	GUANGDONG MACHINE IMPORT AND EXPORT COMPANY		
中国人民保险有限公司（以下简称本公司）根据被保险人的要求，由被保险人向本公司缴付约定的保险费，按照本保险单承担险别和背面所载条款与下列特别条款承保下列货物运输保险，特立本保险单。			

续表

<table>
<tr><td colspan="12">This policy of Insurance witnesses that the People's Insurance Company of China (hereinafter called "The Company"), at the request of the Insured and in consideration of the agreed premium paid to the company by the insured, undertakes to insure the undermentioned goods in transportation subject to conditions of the Policy as per the Clauses printed overleaf and other special clauses attached hereon.</td></tr>
<tr><td colspan="3">标记
Marks & Nos</td><td colspan="3">包装及数量
Packing & Quantity</td><td colspan="3">保险货物项目
Descriptions of Goods</td><td colspan="3">保险金额
Amount Insured</td></tr>
<tr><td colspan="3">F. V.
ART NO = 9099
ROTTERDAM
NOS：1-1000</td><td colspan="3">12, 000PCS， 1, 000CTNS</td><td colspan="3">STAINLESS SCOOP</td><td colspan="3">USD126, 720</td></tr>
<tr><td colspan="3">总保险金额：
Total Amount Insured</td><td colspan="9">U. S. DOLLARS ONE HUNDRED AND TWENTY SIX THOUSAND SEVEN HUNDRED AND TWENTY ONLY</td></tr>
<tr><td>保费
Premium</td><td colspan="2">AS ARRANGED</td><td colspan="3">启运日期
Date of commencement</td><td colspan="2">2021-03-20</td><td colspan="2">装载运输工具
Per conveyance</td><td colspan="2">Pessession
V16</td></tr>
<tr><td>自
Form</td><td colspan="3">GUANGZHOU</td><td>经
Via</td><td colspan="4"></td><td>至
To</td><td colspan="2">ROTTERDAM</td></tr>
<tr><td colspan="2">承保险别
Conditions</td><td colspan="10">COVERING OCEAN MARINE TRANSPORTATION ALL RISKS AND WAR RISK AS PER AND SUBJECT TO THE OCEAN MARINE CARGO CLAUSES OF PICC DATED 1/1/1981 INCL. WAREHOUSE TO WAREHOUSE.</td></tr>
<tr><td colspan="12">所保货物，如发生本保险单项下可能引起索赔的损失或损坏，应立即通知本公司下述代理人查勘。如有索赔，应向本公司提交保险单正本（本保险单共有　　份正本）及有关文件。如一份正本已用于索赔，其余正本则自动失效。
In the event of loss or damage which may result in acclaim under this Policy, immediate notice must be given to the Company's Agent as mentioned here under. Claims, if any, one of the Original Policy which has been issued in ________ original(s) together with the relevant documents shall be surrendered to the Company. If one of the Original Policy has been accomplished, the others to be void.</td></tr>
<tr><td colspan="12">中国人民保险公司广州市分公司
The People's Insurance Company of China Guangzhou Branch</td></tr>
<tr><td colspan="3">赔款偿付地点
Claim payable at</td><td colspan="5">ROTTERDAM</td><td colspan="4">王天华</td></tr>
<tr><td colspan="3">出单日期
Issuing Date</td><td colspan="5">MAR. 17， 2021</td><td colspan="4">Authorized Signature</td></tr>
<tr><td colspan="3">地址
Address</td><td colspan="5">中国广州黄河路 112 号
邮编（POST CODE）：518000</td><td colspan="4">电话（TEL）：(020) 86521049
传真（FAX）：(020) 84404593</td></tr>
</table>

能力训练

根据模块一中的信用证【样单 1-3】和合同【样单 1-4】以及模块二中已做好的发票【2-6】和装箱单【2-7】，以及提单【样单 2-13】制作投保单和保险单。

【样单 2-17】

出口货物运输保险投保单

发票号码		投保条款和险别
被保险人	客户抬头	( ) PICC CLAUSE ( ) ICC CLAUSE ( ) ALL RISKS ( ) W. P. A. /W. A. ( ) F. P. A. ( ) WAR RISKS ( ) S. R. C. C. ( ) STRIKE ( ) ICC CLAUSE A ( ) ICC CLAUSE B ( ) ICC CLAUSE C ( ) AIR TPT ALL RISKS ( ) AIR TPT RISKS ( ) O/L TPT ALL RISKS ( ) O/L TPT RISKS ( ) TRANSSHIPMENT RISKS ( ) W TO W ( ) T. P. N. D. ( ) F. R. E. C. ( ) R. F. W. D. ( ) RISKS OF BREAKAGE ( ) I. O. P.
	过户	
保险金额	USD ( )	
	HKD ( )	
	( ) ( )	
启运港		
目的港		
转内陆		
开航日期		
船名航次		
赔款地点		
赔付币别		
正本份数		
其他特别条款		

以下由保险公司填写			
保单号码		费率	
签单日期		保费	

投保日期：　　　　　　　　投保人签章：

【样单 2-18】

中保财产保险有限公司

The People's Insurance (Property) Company of China, Ltd.

发票号码 Invoice No.		保险单号次 Policy No.	

海洋货物运输保险单
MARINE CARGO TRANSPORTATION INSURANCE POLICY

被保险人： Insured：	

中保财产保险有限公司（以下简称本公司）根据被保险人的要求，及其所缴付约定的保险费，按照本保险单承担险别和背面所载条款与下列特别条款承保下列货物运输保险，特签发本保险单。

This policy of Insurance witnesses that the People's Insurance (Property) Company of China, Ltd. (hereinafter called "The Company"), at the request of the Insured and in consideration of the agreed premium paid by the insured, undertakes to insure the undermentioned goods in transportation subject to conditions of the Policy as per the Clauses printed overleaf and other special clauses attached hereon.

保险货物项目 Descriptions of Goods	包装 单位 数量 Packing Unit Quantity	保险金额 Amount Insured

承保险别 Conditions	货物标记 Marks of Goods

总保险金额 Total Amount Insured	

保费 Premium		装载运输工具 Per conveyance S. S		开航日期 Slg. on or abt	

起运港 From		目的港 To	

续表

<table>
<tr><td colspan="5">所保货物，如发生本保险单项下可能引起索赔的损失或损坏，应立即通知本公司下述代理人查勘。如有索赔，应向本公司提交保险单正本（本保险单共有____份正本）及有关文件。如一份正本已用于索赔，其余正本则自动失效。
In the event of loss or damage which may result in acclaim under this Policy, immediate notice must be given to the Company's Agent as mentioned here under. Claims, if any, one of the Original Policy which has been issued in ________ original (s) together with the relevant documents shall be surrendered to the Company. If one of the Original Policy has been accomplished, the others to be void.</td></tr>
<tr><td colspan="2">赔款偿付地点
Claim payable at</td><td colspan="2"></td><td></td></tr>
<tr><td>日期
Date</td><td></td><td>在
At</td><td colspan="2"></td></tr>
<tr><td>地址
Address</td><td colspan="4"></td></tr>
</table>

项目五：制作出境货物报检相关单据

项目目标

能按要求独立完成出境货物报检的相关单据，包括报检委托书、报检单、检验证书。

学习情境六

货物在出境之前需要检验，刘华协助报检员刘磊准备商业发票、装箱单、报检委托书，委托徐州盛通食品厂报检，申请签发出境货物换证凭单与健康证书。

价值引领

进出口商品检验是国际货物买卖中不可缺少的一个环节，商检证书也可能是结汇单据之一。实事求是地缮制、申请和办理商检证书，关乎合同的履行和顺利结汇，也体现外贸单证员的诚信和职业道德修养。

任务一：制作代理报检委托书

相关知识

制作代理报检委托书操作指导图

代理报检委托书

编号：

　填写出入境口岸出入境检验检疫局的名称　出入境检验检疫局：

本委托人（备案号/组织机构代码　按实际情况填写　）保证遵守国家有关检验检疫法律、法规的规定，保证所提供的委托报检事项真实、单货相符。否则，愿承担相关法律责任。具体委托情况如下：

填写该票货物的出口日期。

本委托人将于______年______月间进口/出口如下货物：

品名	填写该票货物的名称，并与发票上的货名一致。	HS 编码	按海关规定的商品分类编码规则填写该出口货物的商品编号。
数（重）量	填写该票货物的数量或重量，并与其他单据同项内容一致。	包装情况	填包装数量和材料。
信用证/合同号	填写该票货物的编号/填写该票货物的信用证编号。	许可文件号	根据有关法律法规的规定，将该出口货物报检必须提供的文件名称填入此栏。
进口货物收货单位及地址		进口货物提/运单号	
其他特殊要求	委托人在报检中必须达到的要求，在此注明。		

特委托　受托单位：填写受理该报检业务单位的名称　（代理报检注册登记号　按实际情况填写　），代表本委托人办理上述货物的下列出入境检验检疫事宜：

□1. 办理报检手续；
□2. 代缴纳检验检疫费；
□3. 联系和配合检验检疫机构实施检验检疫；
□4. 领取检验检疫证单；
□5. 其他与报检有关的相关事宜：______________

选择代理报检业务单位事宜，在相关事宜前的“□”内打“√”。

委托人签名盖章，并注明日期。

联 系 人：______________

联系电话：______________

本委托书有效期至______年____月____日

委托人（加盖公章）

年　　月　　日

受托人确认声明

本企业完全接受本委托书。保证履行以下职责：

1. 对委托人提供的货物情况和单证的真实性、完整性进行核实；
2. 根据检验检疫有关法律法规规定办理上述货物的检验检疫事宜；
3. 及时将办结检验检疫手续的有关委托内容的单证、文件移交委托人或其指定的人员；
4. 如实告知委托人检验检疫部门对货物的后续检验检疫及监管要求。

如在委托事项中发生违法或违规行为，愿承担相关法律和行政责任。

联 系 人：________________

联系电话：________________

受托人（加盖公章）

年　月　日

受托人签名盖章，并注明日期。

工作任务

根据合同【样单1-1】和信用证【样单2-2】，以及商业发票【样单2-4】和装箱单【样单2-5】，参考订舱委托书【样单2-8】和海运提单【样单2-9】及以下的补充资料，制作代理报检委托书。

补充资料：

（1）2021年4月16日，临江国际贸易公司委托盛州盛通食品厂报检（3201120673），申请签发出境货物换证凭单与健康证书。临江国际贸易公司资料如下：

法人代表：张亮

业务联系人：胡爱玲

联系电话：025-4715004

企业性质：私营有限责任公司

组织机构代码：3201003830

（2）商品资料如下：

中文名称：碎片蘑菇罐头

英文名称：CANNED MUSHROOMS PIECES & STEMS

商品描述：24 TINS×425 GRAMS NET WEIGHT（D. W. 227 GRAMS）

包装纸箱：长45cm、宽20cm、高14.9cm，装一个20’集装箱

海关编码：2003.1011

（3）有关重量及体积计算：

①此项商品按净重×1.1来估算毛重。

②所有计算结果保留两位小数。

（4）装运日期：2021年4月25日。

（5）发票编号：2021SDT001。

【样单 2-19】

代理报检委托书

编号：

上海 出入境检验检疫局：

本委托人（备案号/组织机构代码 3201003830 ）保证遵守国家有关检验检疫法律、法规的规定，保证所提供的委托报检事项真实、单货相符。否则，愿承担相关法律责任。具体委托情况如下：

品名	碎片蘑菇罐头 CANNED MUSHROOMS PIECES & STEMS	HS 编码	2003. 1011
数（重）量	1, 700 CARTONS	包装情况	1, 700 CARTONS
信用证/合同号	NEO2011026 / 0011LC123756	许可文件号	
进口货物收货单位及地址		进口货物提/运单号	
其他特殊要求			

特委托 盛州盛通食品厂 （代理报检注册登记号 3201120673 ），代表本委托人办理上述货物的下列出入境检验检疫事宜：

☑1. 办理报检手续；

☑2. 代缴纳检验检疫费；

☑3. 联系和配合检验检疫机构实施检验检疫；

☑4. 领取检验检疫证单。

☐5. 其他与报检相关的事宜：________________

联 系 人：________________

联系电话：________________

本委托书有效期至______年____月____日

委托人（加盖公章）

2021 年 4 月 16 日

受托人确认声明

本企业完全接受本委托书，保证履行以下职责：

1. 对委托人提供的货物情况和单证的真实性、完整性进行核实；
2. 根据检验检疫有关法律法规办理上述货物的检验检疫事宜；
3. 及时将办理检验检疫手续的有关委托内容的单证、文件移交委托人或其指定人员；
4. 如实告知委托人检验检疫部门对货物的后续检验检疫及监管要求。

如在委托事项中发生违法或违规行为，愿承担相关法律和行政责任。

联 系 人：________________

联系电话：________________

受托人（加盖公章）

年 月 日

任务二：制作报检单

相关知识

制作报检单操作指导图

中华人民共和国出入境检验检疫

出境货物报检单

填写报检单位在检验检疫机构备案或注册登记的代码。

填写报检人员的联系电话。

由检验检疫机构报检受理人员填写。

报检单位 (加盖公章)：填写报检单位的全称，并盖报检单位印章。 *编 号

报检单位登记号： 联系人： 电话： 报检日期： 年 月 日

填写报检人员姓名。

检验检疫机构实际受理报检的日期，由检验检疫机构受理报检人员填写。

填写本货物实际申请检验检疫数/重量，重量还应注明毛重或净重。

发货人	（中文） 卖方					
	（外文） 卖方英文名称					
收货人	（中文） 买方					
	（外文） 买方英文名称					
货物名称（中/外文）	H.S. 编码	产地	数/重量	货物总值	包装种类及数量	
填写出口贸易合同上的货物名称及规格。	填写货物的商品编码（8位数或10位数编码），以当年海关公布的商品税则编码分类为准。	填写本货物的生产或加工地的省、市和县名称。		填写本批货物的总值及币种，应与出口贸易合同和发票上的货物总值一致。	填写本批货物实际运输包装的种类及数量，应注明包装的材质。	
运输工具名称号码	如实填写，不确定时填写运输方式，如“海运”。	贸易方式	如实填写，如一般贸易、来料加工、进料加工、易货贸易。	货物存放地点	填写本批货物存放的具体地点、厂库。	
合同号	如实填写	信用证号	如实填写	用途	种用或繁殖、食用、奶用、观赏或演艺、伴侣动物、实验、药用、饲用、其他从以上选择	
发货日期	出口装运日期	输往国家（地区）	买方所在国家和地区，或合同注明的最终输往国家和地区。	许可证/审批号	如为实施许可/审批制度管理的货物，必须填写其编号，不得留空。	
启运地	如实填写	到达口岸	如实填写	生产单位注册号	填写本批货物生产、加工的单位在检验检疫机构注册登记编号。	
集装箱规格、数量及号码	货物若以集装箱运输，应填写集装箱的规格、数量及号码。					
合同、信用证订立的检验检疫条款或特殊要求	标 记 及 号 码	随附单据（划“✓”或补填）				
填写在出口贸易合同中特别订立的有关质量、卫生等条款，或报检单位对本批货物检验检疫的特别要求。	填写本批货物的标记号码，若没有标记号码，则填“N/M”。不得留空。	□合同 □信用证 □发票 □换证凭单 □装箱单 □厂检单	□包装性能结果单 □许可/审批文件 □ 根据向检验检疫机构提供的实际单据，在同名的“□”上打“√”，或在“□”后补填其名称。			

续表

需要证单名称（划“✓”或补填）		*检验检疫费	
□品质证书 __正__副 □重量证书 __正__副 □数量证书 __正__副 □兽医卫生证书 __正__副 □健康证书 __正__副 □卫生证书 __正__副 □动物卫生证书 __正__副	□植物检疫证书 __正__副 □熏蒸/消毒证书 __正__副 □出境货物换证凭单 __正__副 □ 根据所需由检验检疫机构出具的证单，在对应的“□”上打“√”或补填，并注明所需证单的正副本数量。	总金额（人民币元）	由检验检疫机构计费人员填写。
		计费人	
		收费人	

报检人郑重声明：	领 取 证 单	
1. 本人被授权报检。 2. 上列填写内容正确属实，货物无伪造或冒用他人的厂名、标志、认证标志，并承担货物质量责任。 签名：________		
	日期	报检人在领取证单时填写领证日期并签名。
	签名	

注：有“*”号栏由出入境检验检疫机关填写

◆国家出入境检验检疫局制

[1-2 (2000.1.1)]

注：报检数据由报检单位按照检验检疫报检数据规范的要求，通过电子报检系统录入。录入人员应审核报检数据的齐全性、正确性与有效性，遵循如实申报的原则。（“出/入境货物报检单”所列各栏必须填写完整、准确、清晰，无申报内容的栏目应以斜杠“/”表示，不得留空。）

工作任务

根据合同【样单 1-1】和信用证【样单 2-2】，商业发票【样单 2-4】和装箱单【样单 2-5】，参考代理报检委托书【样单 2-19】，以及下列补充资料制作报检单。

补充资料：随附单据，包括合同、信用证、发票、装箱单

【样单 2-20】

中华人民共和国出入境检验检疫
出境货物报检单

报检单位（加盖公章）：临江国际贸易公司 *编 号 ________

报检单位登记号：3201003830 联系人：刘磊 电话：025-4715004 报检日期：2021 年 4 月 16 日

发货人	（中文）临江国际贸易公司				
	（外文）LINJIANG TRADING CO.，LTD.				
收货人	（中文）/				
	（外文）AFG GENERAL TRADING CO.				
货物名称（中/外文）	H. S. 编码	产地	数/重量	货物总值	包装种类及数量

续表

碎片蘑菇罐头 CANNED MUSHROOMS PIECES & STEMS	2003. 1011	徐州	1 700 箱	USD13 260. 00	1 700 箱

运输工具名称号码	海运	贸易方式	一般贸易	货物存放地点		工厂仓库
合同号	NEO2011026	信用证号	0011LC123756		用途	食用
发货日期	2021-04-25	输往国家（地区）	沙特阿拉伯	许可证/审批号		
启运地	上海	到达口岸	达曼	生产单位注册号		
集装箱规格、数量及号码	20′×1					

合同、信用证订立的检验检疫条款或特殊要求	标 记 及 号 码	随附单据（划“√”或补填）	
	ROSE BRAND 178/2001 RIYADH	☑合同 ☑信用证 ☑发票 ☐换证凭单 ☑装箱单 ☐厂检单	☐包装性能结果单 ☐许可/审批文件 ☐ ☐ ☐ ☐

需要证单名称（划“√”或补填）		*检验检疫费	
☐品质证书 _正_副 ☐重量证书 _正_副 ☐数量证书 _正_副 ☐兽医卫生证书 _正_副 ☑健康证书 _正_副 ☐卫生证书 _正_副 ☐动物卫生证书 _正_副	☐植物检疫证书 _正_副 ☐熏蒸/消毒证书 _正_副 ☑出境货物换证凭单 _正_副 ☐ ☐ ☐ ☐	总金额（人民币元）	
		计费人	
		收费人	

报检人郑重声明：	领 取 证 单	
1. 本人被授权报检。 2. 上列填写内容正确属实，货物无伪造或冒用他人的厂名、标志、认证标志，并承担货物质量责任。 签名：______	日期	
	签名	

注：有“*”号栏由出入境检验检疫机关填写

◆国家出入境检验检疫局制

［1-2（2000. 1. 1）］

任务三：制作检验证书

相关知识

一、外贸企业或生产企业出具的检验证书相关知识

【样单 2-21】

1. THE NAME AND ADDRESS OF BENEFICIARY /FACTORY

2. INSPECTION CERTIFICATE

3. INVOICE NO.：

4. DATE：

5. COMMODITY：

6. SHIPPING MARKS：

7. QUANTITY：

8. WEIGHT：

9. RESULTS OF INSPECTION：

10. SIGNATURE

二、出入境检验检疫局出具的检验证书相关知识

（一）证书种类

1. 品质检验证书

品质检验证书是出口商品交货结汇和进口商品结算索赔的有效凭证。法定检验商品的证书，是进出口商品报关、输出输入的合法凭证；商检机构签发的放行单和在报关单上加盖的放行章与商检证书有同等的通关效力。签发的检验情况通知单同为商检证书性质。

2. 重量或数量检验证书

重量或数量检验证书是出口商品交货结汇、签发提单和进口商品结算索赔的有效凭证；出口商品的重量证书，也是国外报关征税和计算运费、装卸费用的证件。

3. 兽医检验证书

兽医检验证书是证明出口动物产品或食品经过检疫合格的证件，适用于冻畜肉、冻禽、禽畜罐头、冻兔、皮张、毛类、绒类、猪鬃、肠衣等出口商品，是对外交货、银行结汇和进口国通关输入的重要证件。

4. 卫生/健康证书

卫生/健康证书是证明可供人类食用的出口动物产品、食品等经过卫生检验或检疫合格的证件，适用于肠衣、罐头、冻鱼、冻虾、蛋品、乳制品、蜂蜜等，是对外交货、银行结汇和通关验放的有效证件。

5. 消毒检验证书

消毒检验证书是证明出口动物产品经过消毒处理，保证安全卫生的证件，适用于猪鬃、马尾、皮张、山羊毛、羽毛、人发等商品，是对外交货、银行结汇和国外通关验放的有效凭证。

6. 熏蒸证书

熏蒸证书是用于证明出口粮谷、油籽、豆类、皮张等商品，以及包装用木材与植物性填充物等，已经过熏蒸灭虫的证明。

7. 残损检验证书

残损检验证书是证明进口商品残损情况的证件，适用于进口商品发生残、短、渍、毁等情况；可作为收货人向发货人、承运人或保险人等有关责任方索赔的有效证件。

8. 积载鉴定证书

积载鉴定证书是证明船方和集装箱装货部门正确配载积载货物，履行运输契约义务的证件，可供货物交接或发生货损时处理争议之用。

9. 财产价值鉴定证书

财产价值鉴定证书是作为对外贸易关系人和司法、仲裁、验资等有关部门索赔、理赔、评估或裁判的重要依据。

10. 船舱检验证书

船舱检验证书证明承运出口商品的船舱清洁、密固、冷藏效能及其他技术条件是否符合保护承载商品的质量和数量完整与安全的要求，可作为承运人履行租船契约适载义务，对外贸易关系方进行货物交接和处理货损事故的依据。

11. 生丝品级及公量检验证书

生丝品级及公量检验证书是出口生丝的专用证书，其作用相当于品质检验证书和重量/数量检验证书。

12. 产地证明书

产地证明书是出口商品在进口国通关输入和享受减免关税优惠待遇和证明商品产地的凭证。

13. 其他相关证书

舱口检视证书、监视装/卸载证书、舱口封识证书、油温空距证书、集装箱监装/拆证书，作为证明承运人履行契约义务、明确责任界限、便于处理货损货差责任事故的证明。

14. 价值证明书

价值证明书作为进口国管理外汇和征收关税的凭证，在发票上签盖商检机构的价值证明章与价值证明书具有同等效力。

15. 货载衡量检验证书

货载衡量检验证书是证明进出口商品的重量、体积吨位的证件，可作为计算运费和制订配载计划的依据。

（二）证书中英文名称

（1）certificate of weight 重量证明书

（2）certificate of inspection certifying quality & quantity in triplicate issued by C. I. B. C. 由中国商品检验局出具的品质和数量检验证明书一式三份

（3）phytosanitary certificate 植物检疫证明书

（4）plant quarantine certificate 植物检疫证明书

（5）fumigation certificate 熏蒸证明书

（6）certificate stating that the goods are free from live weevil 无活虫证明书（熏蒸除虫证明书）

（7）sanitary certificate 卫生证书

（8）health certificate 卫生（健康）证书

（9）analysis certificate 分析（化验）证书

（10）tank inspection certificate 油仓检验证明书

（11）record of ullage and oil temperature 空距及油温记录单

（12）certificate of aflatoxin negative 黄曲霉素检验证书

（13）non-aflatoxin certificate 无黄曲霉素证明书

（14）survey report on weight issued by C. I. B. C. 中国商品检验局签发之重量检验证明书

（15）inspection certificate 检验证书

（16）inspection and testing certificate issued by C. I. B. C. 中国商品检验局签发之检验证明书

（三）检验证书操作指导图

中华人民共和国出入境检验检疫

ENTRY-EXIT INSPECTION AND QUARANTINE

OF THE PEOPLE'S REPUBLIC OF CHINA

品质检验证书　编号

> 名称应与信用证或合同规定完全相符。

> 如证书不止一页，每页上的编号应该一致，另外要注意页数的连续

INSPECTION CERTIFICATE OF QUALITY

发货人

Consignor

> 应与信用证的受益人或合同的卖方相一致。如第三方作为发货人，应与提单上的发货人一致。

收货人

Consignee

> 通常是信用证的开证人或合同的买方。如果是中间交易，可打实际买方。如果信用证规定要求本栏留空，可打上"＊＊＊"符号。

品名

Description of Goods

> 商品名称应与发票完全一致。如发票货名过多，可打总称。

标记及号码

> 唛头，如实填写

报检数量/重量

Quantity /Weight Declared　如实填写

包装种类及数量

Number and Type of Packages　如实填写

产地

Place of Origin　如实填写

到达口岸

Port of Destination　如实填写

运输工具

Means of Conveyance s. s. 如实填写

检验日期

Date of Inspection 如实填写

检验结果：

Results of Inspection:

这是商检证的核心部分，不同的检验证，或同种检验证而不同的检验目的，应出具不同的证明内容。以上内容，凡信用证有规定，均应与规定相符，如无规定，应与合同相符，如合同也无规定，应按惯例或根据检验目的决定填写的证明内容。

> 应有检验机构盖章和检验人员签字。

> 应在提单日之前。

签证地点 Place of Issue　　签证日期 Date of Issue

授权签字人 Authorized Officer　　签名 Signature

工作任务

根据合同【样单1-1】和信用证【样单2-2】，商业发票【样单2-4】和装箱单【样单2-5】，参考报检单【样单2-20】，根据信用证的要求制作健康证书。

【样单2-22】

中华人民共和国出入境检验检疫
ENTRY-EXIT INSPECTION AND QUARANTINE OF THE PEOPLE'S REPUBLIC OF CHINA

健康证书　编号 210100312347665

HEALTH　CERTIFICATE

发货人 Consignor	LINJIANG TRADING CO. , LTD.	
收货人 Consignee	AFG GENERAL TRADING CO. , LTD.	
品名 Description of Goods	CANNED MUSHROOMS PIECES & STEMS	标记及号码 ROSE BRAND 178/2001 RIYADH
报检数量/重量 Quantity /Weight Declared	1, 700 CARTONS	
包装种类及数量 Number and Type of Packages	1, 700 CARTONS	
产地 Place of Origin	徐州	
到达口岸 Port of Destination	DAMMAM	
运输工具 Means of Conveyance s. s. HANTIN / 059W	检验日期 Date of Inspection　2021-4-17	

检验结果

Results of Inspection

THIS IS TO CERTIFY THAT GOODS ARE FIT FOR HUMAN BEING.

签证地点 Place of Issue　SHANGHAI　　　签证日期 Date of Issue　2021-4-17

授权签字人 Authorized Officer　　　签名 Signature

能力训练

根据模块一中的信用证【样单 1-3】和合同【样单 1-4】以及模块二中已做好的发票【2-6】和装箱单【2-7】，结合下列补充资料，制作报检单和品质检验证书。

（1）报检单位登记号：3020027661。

（2）报检员：李丽　联系电话：82717883。

（3）随附单据：合同、信用证、商业发票、装箱单。

【样单 2-23】

中华人民共和国出入境检验检疫

出境货物报检单

报检单位（加盖公章）：　　　　　　　　　　　　　*编　　号 ________

报检单位登记号：　　　联系人：　　　电话：　　　报检日期：____年____月____日

<table>
<tr><td rowspan="2">发货人</td><td colspan="5">（中文）</td></tr>
<tr><td colspan="5">（外文）</td></tr>
<tr><td rowspan="2">收货人</td><td colspan="5">（中文）</td></tr>
<tr><td colspan="5">（外文）</td></tr>
<tr><td>货物名称（中/外文）</td><td>H. S. 编码</td><td>产地</td><td>数/重量</td><td>货物总值</td><td>包装种类及数量</td></tr>
<tr><td colspan="6"></td></tr>
<tr><td>运输工具名称号码</td><td></td><td>贸易方式</td><td></td><td>货物存放地点</td><td></td></tr>
<tr><td>合同号</td><td></td><td>信用证号</td><td></td><td>用途</td><td></td></tr>
<tr><td>发货日期</td><td></td><td>输往国家（地区）</td><td></td><td>许可证/审批号</td><td></td></tr>
<tr><td>启运地</td><td></td><td>到达口岸</td><td></td><td>生产单位注册号</td><td></td></tr>
<tr><td>集装箱规格、数量及号码</td><td colspan="5"></td></tr>
<tr><td colspan="2">合同、信用证订立的检验检疫条款或特殊要求</td><td colspan="2">标 记 及 号 码</td><td colspan="2">随附单据（划“√”或补填）</td></tr>
<tr><td colspan="2"></td><td colspan="2"></td><td>□合同
□信用证
□发票
□换证凭单
□装箱单
□厂检单</td><td>□包装性能结果单
□许可/审批文件
□
□
□
□</td></tr>
<tr><td colspan="4">需要证单名称（划“√”或补填）</td><td colspan="2">*检验检疫费</td></tr>
</table>

续表

<table>
<tr>
<td rowspan="3">□品质证书　＿正＿副
□重量证书　＿正＿副
□数量证书　＿正＿副
□兽医卫生证书　＿正＿副
□健康证书　＿正＿副
□卫生证书　＿正＿副
□动物卫生证书　＿正＿副</td>
<td rowspan="3">□植物检疫证书　＿正＿副
□熏蒸/消毒证书　＿正＿副
□出境货物换证凭单　＿正＿副
□
□
□
□</td>
<td>总金额
（人民币元）</td>
<td></td>
</tr>
<tr>
<td>计费人</td>
<td></td>
</tr>
<tr>
<td>收费人</td>
<td></td>
</tr>
<tr>
<td colspan="2" rowspan="3">报检人郑重声明：
1. 本人被授权报检。
2. 上列填写内容正确属实，货物无伪造或冒用他人的厂名、标志、认证标志，并承担货物质量责任。
签名：＿＿＿＿</td>
<td colspan="2">领 取 证 单</td>
</tr>
<tr>
<td>日期</td>
<td></td>
</tr>
<tr>
<td>签名</td>
<td></td>
</tr>
</table>

注：有“＊”号栏由出入境检验检疫机关填写　　◆国家出入境检验检疫局制

［1-2（2000. 1. 1）］

【样单 2-24】

品质检验证书

1. THE NAME AND ADDRESS OF BENEFICIARY /FACTORY

2. INSPECTION CERTIFICATE

3. INVOICE NO.：

4. DATE：

5. COMMODITY：

6. SHIPPING MARKS：

7. QUANTITY：

8. WEIGHT：

9. RESULTS OF INSPECTION：

10. SIGNATURE

项目六：制作出口货物报关相关单据

项目目标

能根据要求独立完成出口报关单、报关委托书的填写。

学习情境七

订舱成功之后，由于要从上海出运，临江国际贸易公司委托上海凯通国际货运代理有限公司代理报关。目前，临江国际贸易公司已取得商检换证凭单。如果你是刘华，请准备报关单、报关委托书、商业发票、装箱单、合同，委托上海凯通国际货运代理有限公司报关。

价值引领

报关单在对外经济贸易活动中具有十分重要的法律地位，正确、如实填写报关委托书和报关单，有利于商品及时通关，也有利于办理出口退税。单证人员要熟悉《中华人民共和国海关进出口货物报关单填制规范》，遵纪守法，诚信通关。

任务：制作报关单

相关知识

制作报关单操作指示

中华人民共和国海关出口货物报关单

预录入编号：不填　　　　海关编号：不填

出口口岸 实际出境口岸海关名+4位海关代码	备案号 手册（BCDE）纸质手册、电子手账册/征免税证明 Z 特定减免税、国家减免税/原产地代码及编号 Y	出口日期 装载该货物的运输工具申报进出境日期：例 20110809 是船不是货物的日期，一般可不填	申报日期 海关接受货物报关的日期：例 20110811
经营单位 对外签订并执行合同的境内单位中文名+10位单位代码	运输方式 1. 水路运输 2. 航空运输	运输工具名称 1. 船名/航次 2. 航班号	提运单号 1. 提单号（B/L NO.） 2. 如果是航空运输，则填总运单号-分运单号
发货单位 出口货物在境内的最初生产销售单位中文名+10位单位代码	贸易方式 由备案号决定	征免性质 由备案号、贸易方式决定	结汇方式 不能为空
许可证号 限制出口、两用物项出口、废物出口等需要填写。	运抵国 直接运到或中转未发生交易到达的国家，如发生中转及交易，则填中转地	指运港 已知的出口货物的最终卸货港	境内货源地 发货单位所在地，填发货单位10位代码的前5位

续表

<table>
<tr><td>批准文号
填写出口收汇核销单编号</td><td>成交方式
1. CIF
2. CFR
3. FOB</td><td>运费
1. 不填
2. 不填
3. 要填</td><td>保费
1. 不填
2. 要填
3. 要填</td><td>杂费
折扣、佣金或手续费，如要扣除，应在金额前面加负号。
502/-1000/3　如发票单独列出才需要填写</td></tr>
<tr><td>合同协议号
CONTRACT NO.</td><td>件数
除集装箱外的货物最大外包装数量</td><td>包装种类
除集装箱外的货物最大外包装材料</td><td>毛重（公斤）
GROSS WEIGHT　或 G/W</td><td>净重（公斤），同装箱单保持一致
NET WEIGHT
或 N/W</td></tr>
<tr><td colspan="2">集装箱号
不能空非集装箱 填 0
CONTAINER　NO. /SIZE/TARE WEIGHT
只填一个，有多的填在备注栏</td><td colspan="2">随附单据
出入境通关单（A/B）、自动进口许可证（7/O/V）、原产地证书（Y）、关税配额许可证（e）
只填一个，有多的填在备注栏</td><td>生产厂家
一般不填</td></tr>
<tr><td colspan="5">标记唛码及备注
MARKS
备注：1. 多的集装箱号
2. 随附单据</td></tr>
<tr><td colspan="5">项号　商品编号　商品名称、规格型号　数量及单位　最终目的国（地区）　单价　总价　币制　征免</td></tr>
<tr><td colspan="5">依次填商品项目，例如：1
出口货物的商品编码
第一行：中文商品名称；第二行：规格型号。必要时加注原文
第一行：法定第一计量单位；第二行：法定第二计量单位，依次填写；第三：其他成交单位。
产地（地区）代码，无法确认的填报“国别不详”代码701。
单位价格
商品总价
成交币种
征免由备案号、贸易方式决定，一般填写照章征免。</td></tr>
<tr><td colspan="5">后面的内容一般不填</td></tr>
<tr><td colspan="5">税费征收情况</td></tr>
<tr><td colspan="2">录入员　录入单位</td><td colspan="2">兹声明以上申报无讹并承担法律责任</td><td>海关审单批注及放行日期（签章）
审单　审价</td></tr>
<tr><td colspan="4" rowspan="2">报关员
申报单位（签章）　单位地址
邮编　电话　填制日期</td><td>征税　统计</td></tr>
<tr><td>查验　放行</td></tr>
</table>

工作任务

根据合同【样单1-1】和信用证【样单2-2】，商业发票【样单2-4】和装箱单【样单2-5】，参考报检单【样单2-20】，根据下列资料制作报关单。

补充资料：

（1）出境货物换证凭单。

中华人民共和国出入境检验检疫
出境货物换证凭单

类别：口岸申报换证　　　　编号：3200000202000368

<table>
<tr><td>发货人</td><td colspan="2">临江国际贸易有限公司</td><td rowspan="7">标记及号码
ROSE BRAND
178/2001
RIYADH</td></tr>
<tr><td>收货人</td><td colspan="2">* * *</td></tr>
<tr><td>品名</td><td colspan="2">碎片蘑菇罐头 24×425G</td></tr>
<tr><td>H. S. 编码</td><td colspan="2">2003. 1011</td></tr>
<tr><td>报检数/重量</td><td colspan="2">1 700 箱/17 340 千克</td></tr>
<tr><td>包装种类及数量</td><td colspan="2">纸箱 1 700 箱</td></tr>
<tr><td>申报总值</td><td colspan="2">13 260 美元</td></tr>
<tr><td>产地</td><td>江苏省徐州市</td><td>生产单位（注册号）</td><td>6500/554433</td></tr>
<tr><td>生产日期</td><td>2021/04</td><td>生产批号</td><td>* * *</td></tr>
<tr><td rowspan="2">包装性能检验结果单号</td><td rowspan="2">320100381005836</td><td>合同/信用证号</td><td>AFG2011026 / 0011LC123756</td></tr>
<tr><td>运输工具名称及号码</td><td>HANTIN / 059W</td></tr>
<tr><td>输往国家或地区</td><td>沙特阿拉伯</td><td>集装箱规格及数量</td><td>* * * * * *</td></tr>
<tr><td>发货日期</td><td>* * *</td><td>检验依据</td><td>合同、SN0400-1995</td></tr>
<tr><td>检验检疫结果</td><td colspan="3">本批商品经按 QB1006-90 抽取代表性样品，检验结果如下：
一、物理检验
1. 外观无膨胀，无损坏，密封良好。
2. 罐外无锈，罐内壁无腐蚀，罐内无杂质。
3. 内容物形状、块粒、色泽、香味正常。
4. 净重 425 克，固形物大于等于 70%。
5. NACL：1. 75%。
二、化学检验（重金属含量：每公斤制品中含量）
锡不超过 200 毫克　铜不超过 5 毫克　铅不超过 1 毫克　砷不超过 0. 5 毫克
三、细菌检验
商业无菌。
结论：本批商品符合上述检验依据，适合人类食用。
* * * * * * * *（出入境检验检疫局检验检疫专用章）
签字：张天戟　　日期：2021 年 4 月 17 日</td></tr>
<tr><td>本单有效期</td><td colspan="3">截至 2022 年 8 月 17 日</td></tr>
<tr><td>备注</td><td colspan="3">查验合格</td></tr>
</table>

续表

分批出境核销栏	日期	出境数/重量	结存数/重量	核销人	日期	出境数/重量	结存数/重量	核销人

说明：1. 货物出境时，经口岸检验检疫机关查验货证相符，且符合检验检疫要求的予以签发通关单或换发检验检疫证书；2. 本单不作为国内贸易的品质或其他证明；3. 涂改无效。

①办理换证　　[5-3（2021.1.1）＊1]

（2）报关单预录入编号：619110008。

（3）出口口岸：上海海关，口岸代码：2200。

（4）出运日期：2021-04-25。

（5）申报日期：2021-04-18。

（6）运输方式：江海运输。

（7）贸易方式：一般贸易，代码（0110）。

（8）征免性质：一般征税，代码（101）。

（9）目的国：沙特阿拉伯，代码（131）；目的港：达曼，代码（1463）。

（10）产地：徐州，代码（32039）。

（11）集装箱号：FCIU8283952。

（12）币制：美元，代码（502）。

（13）征免方式：照章征税。

（14）有关商品重量及体积计算：

①商品净重描述：24 TINS×425 GRAMS NET WEIGHT。

②包装纸箱尺寸：长 45cm、宽 20cm、高 14.9cm。

③此项商品按净重×1.1 估算毛重。

④所有计算结果保留两位小数。

（15）运费：总价 798.00 美元。

（16）商业发票编号：2011SDT001。

【样单 2-25】

中华人民共和国海关出口货物报关单

预录入编号：619110008　　　　海关编号：

<table>
<tr><td>出口口岸　上海海关　2200</td><td colspan="2">备案号</td><td>出口日期
2021-04-25</td><td>申报日期
2021-04-23</td></tr>
<tr><td>经营单位　临江国际贸易有限公司
3201003830</td><td>运输方式
江海运输</td><td>运输工具名称
HANTIN / 059W</td><td colspan="2">提运单号</td></tr>
<tr><td>发货单位　临江国际贸易有限公司
3201003830</td><td colspan="2">贸易方式
一般贸易（0110）</td><td>征免性质
一般征税（101）</td><td>结汇方式
信用证</td></tr>
</table>

续表

<table>
<tr><td>许可证号</td><td colspan="2">运抵国（地区）
沙特阿拉伯（131）</td><td>指运港
达曼（1463）</td><td>境内货源地
徐州（32039）</td></tr>
<tr><td>批准文号</td><td>成交方式
CFR</td><td>运费　　美元
总价　　798.000</td><td>保费</td><td>杂费</td></tr>
<tr><td>合同协议号　NEO2001026</td><td>件数
1 700</td><td>包装种类
纸箱</td><td>毛重（公斤）
19 074</td><td>净重（公斤）
17 340</td></tr>
<tr><td>集装箱号　FCIU8283952</td><td colspan="3">随附单据</td><td>生产厂家</td></tr>
<tr><td colspan="5">标记唛码及备注
ROSE BRAND
178/2001
RIYADH</td></tr>
</table>

项号	商品编号	商品名称、规格型号	数量及单位	最终目的国（地区）	单价	总价	币制	征免
1	20031011	碎片蘑菇罐头 24×425G	1 700 箱	沙特阿拉伯 （131）	7.80	13 260.00	USD 美元	照章 征税

<table>
<tr><td colspan="3">税费征收情况</td></tr>
<tr><td>录入员　录入单位</td><td>兹声明以上申报无讹并承担法律责任</td><td>海关审单批注及放行日期（签章）
审单　　审价</td></tr>
<tr><td colspan="2" rowspan="2">报关员

申报单位（签章）

单位地址

邮编　　电话　　填制日期</td><td>征税　　统计</td></tr>
<tr><td>查验　　放行</td></tr>
</table>

拓展任务 制作报关委托书

相关知识

制作代理报关委托书说明

代理报关委托书是托运人委托承运人或其代理人办理报关等通关事宜，明确双方责任和义务的书面证明，具体样式见【样单 2-26】，填写要求如下：

委托报关协议通用条款

(1)《代理报关委托书》是进出口货物收发货人根据《海关法》和相关法律法规要求提交报关企业的具有法律效力的授权证明。《代理报关委托书》由进出口货物收发货人填写，并加盖单位行政公章和法定代表人或被授权人签字。

(2) 根据《中华人民共和国海关进出口货物申报管理规定》要求，《代理报关委托书/委托报关协议》作为代理报关时报关单的必备随附单证使用，其编号为 11 位阿拉伯数字，是代理报关业务的流水号。

(3) 双方经办人员应在开始委托报关操作前认真填写格式化《代理报关委托书/委托报关协议》，并按格式提示签字、加盖章后生效。

(4)《委托报关协议》是进出口货物收发货人（或单位）与报关企业按照《海关法》的要求签署的明确具体委托报关事项和双方责任的具有法律效力的文件，分正文表格和通用条款两大部分。

(5) 规范统一的《代理报关委托书/委托报关协议》纸质格式，将两个独立的文件印制在一张 A4 无碳复写纸上，一式三联，由中国报关协会监制。

(6) 其中《委托报关协议》正文表格分必填项、补填项，没有标记的各项为必填项，应在签署前填写；标明“＊”的各项为补填项，应在本文本作为报关单随附单证递交海关前填写。

(7) 委托方是关税的纳税义务人，应承担 HS 编码的填写责任。但因被委托方业务熟悉，故也可在“其他要求”一栏中委托被委托方帮助填写。

(8) 如遇两种以上的货物在同一票报关单申报时，“主要货物名称”一栏填写涉税额最多的一种货物品名。

(9) 填写“收到单证情况”一栏时，标记“√”表示收到，否则表示没有收到。

(10) 委托方“其他要求”一栏，是对被委托方服务内容的具体要求和《代理报关委托书》中的 C、D、E、F 项委托事项的进一步描述。被委托方“服务承诺”一栏，是被委托方对能否满足委托方“其他要求”的承诺。

(11) 填写《代理报关委托书/委托报关协议》应使用签字笔，字迹工整。涂改处盖章后才能生效。

【样单 2-26】

代理报关委托书

编号：

我单位现　　（A 逐票、B 长期）委托贵公司代理　　等通关事宜。（A. 报关查验　B. 垫缴税款　C. 办理海关证明联　D. 审批手册　E. 核销手册　F. 申办减免税手续　G. 其他）详见《委托报关协议》。

我单位保证遵守《海关法》和国家有关法规，保证所提供的情况真实、完整、单货相符。否则，愿承担相关法律责任。

本委托书有效期自签字之日起至　　年　　月　　日止。

委托方（盖章）：

法定代表人或其授权签署《代理报关委托书》的人（签字）

年　　月　　日

委托报关协议

为明确委托报关具体事项和各自责任，双方经平等协商签订协议如下：

委托方		被委托方		
主要货物名称		*报关单编码	No.	
HS 编码		收到单证日期	年　月　日	
进出口日期	年　月　日	收到单证情况	合同	发票
提单号			装箱清单	提（运）单
贸易方式			加工贸易手册	许可证件
原产地/货源地			其他	
传真电话		报关收费	人民币　　元	
其他要求		承诺说明：		
背面所列通用条款是本协议不可分割的一部分，对本协议的签署构成了对背面通用条款的同意。		背面所列通用条款是本协议不可分割的一部分，对本协议的签署构成了对背面通用条款的同意。		
委托方业务盖章： 经办人签章： 联系人电话： 年　月　日		被委托方业务盖章： 经办人签章： 联系人电话： 年　月　日		

能力训练

根据模块一中的信用证【样单 1-3】和合同【样单 1-4】，参考模块二中已做好的发票【2-6】和装箱单【2-7】，以及下列补充资料，制作出口报关单。

（1）报关单预录入编号：619110013。

（2）出口口岸：上海海关，口岸代码：2200。

（3）运输方式：江海运输。

（4）贸易方式：一般贸易，代码（0110）。

（5）征免性质：一般征税，代码（101）。

（6）目的国：加拿大，代码（501）；目的港：蒙特利尔港，代码（3042）。

（7）币制：美元，代码（502）。

（8）征免方式：照章征税。

（9）运费：总价 627.000 美元。

【样单 2-27】

中华人民共和国海关出口货物报关单

预录入编号：　　　　　　　　　　　　海关编号：

出口口岸	备案号	出口日期	申报日期		
经营单位	运输方式	运输工具名称	提/运单号		
发货单位	贸易方式	征免性质	结汇方式		
许可证号	运抵国（地区）	指运港	境内货源地		
批准文号	成交方式	运费	保费	杂费	
合同协议号	件数	包装种类	毛重（公斤）	净重（公斤）	
集装箱号	随附单据	生产厂家			
标记唛码及备注					

项号	商品编号	商品名称、规格型号	数量及单位	最终目的国（地区）	单价	总价	币制	征免

续表

<table>
<tr><td colspan="3"></td></tr>
<tr><td colspan="3"></td></tr>
<tr><td colspan="3"></td></tr>
<tr><td colspan="3">税费征收情况</td></tr>
<tr><td>录入员　录入单位</td><td>兹声明以上申报无讹并承担法律责任</td><td>海关审单批注及放行日期（签章）
审单　审价</td></tr>
<tr><td colspan="2" rowspan="2">报关员
申报单位（签章）
单位地址
邮编　电话　填制日期</td><td>征税　统计</td></tr>
<tr><td>查验　放行</td></tr>
</table>

项目七：制作原产地证书

项目目标

能根据要求独立完成一般原产地证和普惠制原产地证的填写。

学习情境八

根据国家有关规定，临江国际贸易公司最迟于装运前3天向签证机构申请办理原产地证书，并按签证机构要求提供已缮制的《中华人民共和国出口货物原产地证明申请书》和《中华人民共和国原产地证明书》各一套，出口货物商业发票和签证机构所需要的其他证明文件。如果你是刘华，请准备相关单据向中国国际贸易促进委员会（China Council for The Promotion of International Trade，CCPIT，简称贸促会）申请签发一般原产地证书。

价值引领

原产地证明书是证明货物原产地和制造地的文件，是进口国海关采取不同国别政策和关税待遇的依据，也是常用的结汇单据之一。正确填写原产地证明书，有利于顺利结汇，维护企业和国家的正当权益。

任务一：制作一般原产地证

相关知识

制作一般原产地证操作指示

ORIGINAL

<table>
<tr>
<td>1. Exporter
出口方，填写出口方的名称、详细地址及国家（地区）。若经其他国家或地区需填写转口商名称时，可在出口商后面加填英文 O/B，然后再填写转口商名称、地址和国家（转口商应为境外公司）。</td>
<td rowspan="2">Certificate No.

CERTIFICATE OF ORIGIN
OF
THE PEOPLE'S REPUBLIC OF
CHINA</td>
</tr>
<tr>
<td>2. Consignee
收货方，最终收货方的名称、详细地址及国家（地区），通常是外贸合同中的买方或信用证上规定的提单通知人。但往往由于贸易的需要，信用证规定所有单证收货人一栏留空，在这种情况下，此栏应加注“TO WHOM IT MAY CONCERN”或“TO ORDER”，不得留空。</td>
</tr>
<tr>
<td>3. Means of Transport and Route
运输方式和路线，运输方式，如海运、空运、陆运；运输路线，海运、陆运应填写装货港、到货港。如经转运，还应注明转运地。注意装运港必须在中国境内。多式联运要分阶段说明。由于珠海暂无国际航线，因此如由珠海陆运至香港地区，再空运至德国，应注明“FROM ZHUHAI TO HONGKONG BY TRUCK，THEN TO GERMANY BY AIR”。如不确定何时出运，建议不用显示出运日期。</td>
<td rowspan="2">5. For Certifying Authority Use Only
签证机构用栏
为签证机构在签发后发证书、补发证书或加注其他声明时使用。证书申领单位应将此栏留空。</td>
</tr>
<tr>
<td>4. Country / Region of Destination
目的地国家（地区），货物最终运抵目的地的国家或地区，即货物最终进口国（地区），一般应与最终收货人所在国家（地区）一致，或最终目的港国别一致，不能填写中间商国家名称。</td>
</tr>
</table>

续表

6. Marks and Numbers 唛头，不可简单地填写"按照发票（AS PER INVOICE NO.）"或者"按照提单（AS PER B/L NO.）"。如无唛头，应填写 NO MARK（N/M）。此栏不得留空。此栏不可打印中国以外的其他国家制造的字样，如 MADE IN U. S. A. 字样。	7. Number and Kind of Packages; Description of Goods 商品名称、包装数量及种类，商品名称要求填写具体名称。包装数量及种类要求填明多少箱、包、袋等，注意在阿拉伯数字后加括号加注英文数量。如货物系散装，填写商品名称后加注"散装"英文"IN BULK"。此栏填打完毕后，在末行加上表示结束的符号（＊＊＊），以防再添加内容。此栏中一般能够接受的声明内容如下： 制造商名称、地址（若制造商名称与出口商不一致，需提供保函，声明该 CO 项下货物由所打印厂家生产，并盖制造商公章或出口商公章）；信用证号码、合同号码；根据领事馆要求、需要加打的声明；开户银行名称或许可证号码（IMPORT LICENSE）等。	8. H. S. Code 商品编码，要求填写四位数的 HS 编码，与报关单一致。若同一证书包含几种商品，则应将相应的税目号全部填写。此栏不得留空。	9. Quantity 量值，填写出口货物的量值即数量或重量，应以商品的计量单位填定，以重量计算的要填注毛重或净重。	10. Number and Date of Invoices 发票号码及日期，必须按照所申请出口货物的商业发票填写。此栏不得留空。日期的表达要求：月份一定要用英文，年份一定要完整。 原产地证中的三个日期：发票日期、申办日期、签发日期，其中发票日期最早，签发日期最迟，但三个日期可为同一日。若打印出运日期，则要遵循出运日期不可早于发票日期的原则，出运日期和发票日期可为同一日。 一份发票只能申领一份产地证。当同一发票项下的货物分批出运时，可将发票拆成多份，并在每份发票号后加 A、B、C 或"-1""-2""-3"等以示区别，并分别凭发票申领产地证。

11. Declaration by the Exporter The undersigned hereby declares that the above details and statements are correct, that all the goods were produced in China and that they comply with the Rules of Origin of the People's Republic of China. 出口方声明 该栏由申请单位已在签证机构注册的原产地证手签人员签字，并加盖申请单位在签证机构备案的中英文印章，手签人的签字与印章不得重合。必须在该栏填写申领地点和日期，申领日期一律用英文表述。 签发日期迟于出运日期的原产地证为后发证，企业在申办时除提供申请书和发票外，须另外提供报关单或提单，并提交迟办原因解释，签证机构在第 5 栏加注"ISSUED RETROSPECTIVELY"的英文印章。办后发证或补发遗失、损毁证书时，第十一栏和第十二栏日期应为重发证书的实际申请日期和签发日期。 ------------------------------------ Place and date, signature and stamp of authorized signatory	12. Certification It is hereby certified that the declaration by the exporter is correct. 签证机构证明 此栏由签证机构授权的签证人员签字，并加盖签证机构印章，注明签署地点和日期。签字和盖章不能重合。 ------------------------------------ Place and date, signature and stamp of certifying authority

工作任务

根据合同【样单 1-1】和信用证【样单 2-2】，商业发票【样单 2-4】和装箱单【样单 2-5】，根据下列补充资料制作一般原产地证。

补充资料：

上海贸易公司于 2021 年 4 月 26 日在上海申请签发一般原产地证。

相关工厂资料：

XUZHOU SHENGTONG FOODSTUFFS CO. , LTD.

NO. 15 HEPING ROAD, XUZHOU 221009, CHINA

TEL: 86-0516-3402323　　FAX: 86-0516-3402330

商品海关编码：20031011

【样单 2-28】

ORIGINAL

<table>
<tr><td colspan="2">1. Exporter
LINJIANG TRADING CO. , LTD.
HUARONG MANSION RM2901 NO. 85 GUANJIAQIAO,
NANJING 210005, CHINA
TEL: 0086-25-4715004
FAX: 0086-25-4711363</td><td colspan="3" rowspan="2">Certificate No.

CERTIFICATE OF ORIGIN
OF
THE PEOPLE'S REPUBLIC OF
CHINA</td></tr>
<tr><td colspan="2">2. Consignee
AFG GENERAL TRADING CO. , LTD.
P. O. BOX 99552, RIYADH 22766, KSA
TEL: 00966-1-4659220
FAX: 00966-1-4659213</td></tr>
<tr><td colspan="2">3. Means of Transport and Route
SHIPMENT FROM SHANGHAI PORT, CHINA TO DAMMAM PORT, SAUDI ARABIA BY SEA</td><td colspan="3" rowspan="2">5. For Certifying Authority Use only</td></tr>
<tr><td colspan="2">4. Country / Region of Destination
SAUDI ARABIA</td></tr>
<tr><td>6. Marks and Numbers
ROSE BRAND
178/2001
RIYADH</td><td>7. Number and kind of packages; description of goods
ONE THOUSAND AND SEVEN HUNDRED (1 700) CARTONS OF CANNED MUSHROOMS PIECES & STEMS 24TINS × 425GRAMS NET WEIGHT (D. W. 227 GRAMS) AT USD7. 80 PER CARTON.
ROSE BRAND.</td><td>8. H. S. Code
20031011</td><td>9. Quantity
1, 700 CARTONS</td><td>10. Number and date of invoices
2021SDT001
APR. 25, 2021</td></tr>
</table>

续表

SAY TOTAL：ONE THOUSAND AND SEVEN HUNDRED CARTONS ONLY. THE NAME OF THE MANUFACTURERS： XUZHOU SHENGTONG FOODSTUFFS CO.，LTD. NO. 15 HEPING ROAD，XUZHOU 221009，CHINA TEL：86-0516-3402323 FAX：86-0516-3402330 WE HERBY CERTIFY THAT GOODS EXPORTED ARE WHOLLY OF CHINESE ORIGIN.

11. Declaration by the Exporter The undersigned hereby declares that the above details and statements are correct，that all the goods were produced in China and that they comply with the Rules of Origin of the People's Republic of China. SHANGHAI，CHINA APR. 26，2021 ---------- Place and date，signature and stamp of authorized signatory	12. Certification It is hereby certified that the declaration by the exporter is correct. SHANGHAI，CHINA APR. 26，2021 ---------- Place and date，signature and stamp of certifying authority

任务二：制作普惠制原产地证

相关知识

制作普惠制原产地证操作指示

ORIGINAL

1. Goods Consigned from (Exporter's business name，address，country) 出口商名称、地址、国家，此栏出口商公司名称应与注册时相同。必须打上国名、地址。	Reference No. （证书号） **GENERALIZED SYSTEM OF PREFERENCES** **FORM A** Issued in THE PEOPLE'S REPUBLIC OF CHINA (country) See Notes overleaf
2. Goods Consigned to (Consignee's name，address，country) 收货人的名称、地址、国家 信用证项下一般为开证申请人； 若最终收货人不明确，填发票抬头人的名称与地址； 当给惠国属于某一关税同盟，由同盟名称代替国家或地区名称。	
3. Means of Transport and Route (as far as known) 运输方式和路线 一般应填上装货、到货地点（始启运港、目的港）及运输方式（如海运、陆运、空运）。 例：FROM DONGGUAN TO SHENZHEN BY TRUCK，THENCE TRANSSHIPPED TO HAMBURG BY SEA.	4. For Official Use 供官方使用 此栏由签证当局填写，正常情况下此栏空白。

续表

5. Item Number	6. Marks and Numbers of Packages	7. Number and Kind of Packages; Description of Goods	8. Origin Criterion (see Notes overleaf)	9. Gross Weight or other Quantity	10. Number and Date of Invoices
商品顺序号， 如同批出口货物有不同品种，则按不同品种分列“1”“2”“3”……，以此类推。如为单项商品，此栏填“1”。	唛头及包装号， 此栏与发票栏所列同类内容完全一致；无运输标志时，要填“no mark”或“N M”；有附页时，请在申请书备注栏注明“唛头见附页”。	包件数量及种类，商品的名称包件数量必须用英文和阿拉伯数字同时表示。例如：ONE HUNDRED AND FIFTY (150) CARTONS OF WORKING GLOVES；末行要打上结束语“******”以防伪造或添加。	原产地标准， 完全原产品，不含任何非原产成分，出口到所有给惠国，填写“P”； 含有非原产成分的产品，出口到欧盟、挪威、瑞士和日本，填写“W”，其后加上出口产品的HS品目号，例如“W”42.02。条件：（1）产品列入了上述给惠国的“加工清单”符合其加工条件；（2）产品未列入“加工单”，但产品生产过程中使用的非原产原材料和零部件经过充分加工，产品的HS品目号不同于所用的原材料和零部件的HS品目号； 含有非原产成分的产品，出口到加拿大，填写“F”。条件：非原产成分的价值未超过产品出厂价的40%。 含有非原产成分的产品，出口到俄罗斯、乌克兰、白俄罗斯、哈萨克斯坦、捷克、斯洛伐克六国，填写“Y”，其后加上非原产成分价值占该产品离岸价格的百分比，例如“Y”38%。条件：非原产成分的价值未超过产品离岸价的50%； 输往澳大利亚、新西兰的货物，此栏可以留空。	毛重或其他数量， 此栏应以商品的正常计量单位填，例如“只”“件”“双”“台”“打”等。例如：3 200 DOZ. 或6 270 KGS. 以重量计算的则填毛重，只有净重的，净重亦可，但要标上N. W.（NET WEIGHT）。	发票号码及日期， 此栏不得留空。月份一律用英文（可用缩写）表示，例如：PHK50016 Apr. 6, 2007此栏的日期必须按照正式商业发票填具，发票日期不得迟于出货日期。

11. Certification	12. Declaration by the Exporter
It is hereby certified, on the basis of control carried out, that the declaration by the exporter is correct. 签证当局的证明 此栏填打签证机构的签证地点、日期，例如：SHENZHEN CHINA APR. 6, 2007，检验检疫局签证人经审核后在此栏（正本）签名，盖签证印章。 注：此栏日期不得早于发票日期（第10栏）和申报日期（第12栏），而且应早于货物的出运日期（第3栏）。 签证地点、日期 ------------------------------------ Place and date, signature and stamp of certifying authority	The undersigned hereby declares that the above details and statements are correct, that all the goods were produced in CHINA (country) and that they comply with the origin requirements specified for those goods in the Generalized System of Preferences for goods exported to 最终进口国，进口国必须与第三栏目的港的国别一致。 ------------------------------------ 申报地点、日期（申报日期不得早于发票日期） ------------------------------------ Place and date, signature and stamp of authorized signatory

工作任务

请根据以下资料，制作普惠制产地证。

1. 产地证申请及签发日期：2021 年 1 月 8 日

COMMERCIAL INVOICE

ISSUER
NANJING TANG TEXTILE GARMENT CO., LTD.
HUARONG MANSION RM2901 NO. 85 GUANJIAQIAO,
NANJING 210005, CHINA

INVOICE NO. JS02154
DATE JAN. 3,2021

TO
CHERRY BLOSSOM COMPANY
6-2OHTEMACHI, 1-CHOME, CHIYADA-KU, TOKYO, JAPAN

DESCRIPTION OF GOODS	QUANTITY	UNIT PRICE	CIFTOKYO, JAPAN AMOUNT
100PCT COTTON MEN'S SLACKS	100CTNS/2, 000PCS	USD9. 68	USD19, 360. 00
TOTAL: 100CTNS/2, 000PCS			**USD19, 360. 00**

TOTAL AMOUNT: U. S. DOLLARS NINETEEN THOUSAND THREE HUNDRED AND SIXTY ONLY.

TOTAL QUANTITY: 2, 000PCS IN 100CTNS

TRANSPORT DETAILS: SHIPMENT FROM NANJING, CHINA TO TOKYO, JAPAN BY SEA

TERMS OF PAYMENT: L/C

CREDIT NUMBER: 453439

MARKS AND NUMBERS: CBC SLACKS
TOKYO
CTN 1-100

2. 商业发票

【样单 2-29】

ORIGINAL

1. Goods Consigned from (Exporter's business name, address, country)
NANJING TANG TEXTILE GARMENT CO., LTD.
HUARONG MANSION RM2901 NO. 85 GUANJIAQIAO,
NANJING 210005, CHINA

Reference No.

GENERALIZED SYSTEM OF PREFERENCES CERTIFICATE OF ORIGIN

(Combined declaration and certificate)

FORM A

Issued in THE PEOPLE'S REPUBLIC OF CHINA
(country)

See Notes overleaf

2. Goods Consigned to (Consignee's name, address, country)
CHERRY BLOSSOM COMPANY
6-2OHTEMACHI, 1-CHOME, CHIYADA-KU, TOKYO, JAPAN

3. Means of Transport and Route (as far as known)
SHIPMENT FROM NANJING, CHINA TO TOKYO, JAPAN BY SEA

4. For Official Use

5. Item Number	6. Marks and Numbers of Packages	7. Number and Kind of Packages; Description of Goods	8. Origin Criterion	9. Gross Weight or other Quantity	10. Number and Date of Invoices
1	CBC SLACKS TOKYO CTN: 1-100	ONE HUNDRED (100) CARTONS OF 100PCT COTTON MEN'S SLACKS * * * * * * * * * * *	"P"	2, 000PCS	JS02154 JAN. 3, 2021

11. Certification
It is hereby certified, on the basis of control carried out, that the declaration by the exporter is correct.

NANJING, JIANGSU, JAN. 8, 2021

Place and date, signature and stamp of certifying authority

12. Declaration by the exporter
The undersigned hereby declares that the above details and statements are correct, that all the goods were produced in CHINA
(country)
and that they comply with the origin requirements specified for those goods in the generalized system of Preferences for goods exported to

JAPAN

NANJING, JIANGSU, JAN. 8, 2021

Place and date, signature and stamp of authorized signatory

能力训练

根据模块一中的信用证【样单 1-3】和合同【样单 1-4】，参考模块二中已做好的发票【2-6】和装箱单【2-7】，以及下列补充资料制作出口普惠制原产地证书。

（1）2021 年 3 月 20 日，南京唐朝纺织服装有限公司的货物顺利装船出运。根据信用证要求，3 月 22 日，唐朝公司在南京申请普惠制产地证，并将普惠制产地证及其他随附单据用 DHL 寄给开证人供其作清关用。

（2）普惠制原产地证书由商检局签发。

【样单 2-30】

ORIGINAL

<table>
<tr><td colspan="3">1. Goods Consigned from（Exporter's business name, address, country）</td><td colspan="3" rowspan="2">Reference No.

GENERALIZED SYSTEM OF PREFERENCES
CERTIFICATE OF ORIGIN

（Combined declaration and certificate）

FORM A
Issued in THE PEOPLE'S REPUBLIC OF CHINA
（country）

See Notes overleaf</td></tr>
<tr><td colspan="3">2. Goods Consigned to（Consignee's name, address, country）</td></tr>
<tr><td colspan="3">3. Means of Transport and Route（as far as known）</td><td colspan="3">4. For Official Use</td></tr>
<tr><td>5. Item Number</td><td>6. Marks and Numbers of Packages</td><td>7. Number and Kind of Packages; Description of Goods</td><td>8. Origin Criterion（see Notes overleaf）</td><td>9. Gross Weight or other Quantity</td><td>10. Number and Date of Invoice</td></tr>
<tr><td colspan="3">11. Certification
It is hereby certified, on the basis of control carried out, that the declaration by the exporter is correct.

Place and date, signature and stamp of certifying authority</td><td colspan="3">12. Declaration by the Exporter
The undersigned hereby declares that the above details and statements are correct, that all the goods were produced in CHINA
（country）
and that they comply with the origin requirements specified for those goods in the generalized system of Preferences for goods exported to

----
Place and date, signature and stamp of authorized signatory</td></tr>
</table>

项目八：制作出口收汇核销单和出口许可证

项目目标

根据要求制作出口收汇核销单和出口许可证。

学习情境九

根据本项目提供的信用证和相关补充资料，制作出口收汇核销单和出口许可证。

价值引领

出口收汇核销单是出口单位凭以报关、办理出口收汇和核销、办理出口退税申报的凭证。出口许可证反映国家对出口商品的管理政策。正确而如实地制作出口收汇核销单，准确而及时地填写出口许可证申请表，是履行合同的需要，也是遵守国家相关政策法规的需要。法治社会，诚信经营，遵纪守法。

任务一：制作出口收汇核销单

相关知识

制作出口收汇核销单指示

出口收汇核销单 存根
（沪）编号：核销单编号，已由外汇管理部门预先编印。
出口单位： 签订并执行合同的出口企业名称。
单位编码：出口企业十位数代码。
出口币种总价：按发票金额填。
收汇方式：实际填信用证、托收、T/T 等方式中的一种。
预计收款日期：根据交易中的具体情况填写。
报关日期：填实际报关放行日期。
备注： 可填合同号、出口发票号等须附加说明的内容，原来的出口商品如发生变更，填写原出口商品核销单的编号等情况。
此单报关有效期截至

（出口单位盖章）

出口收汇核销单 监制章				
（沪）编号：核销单编号，已由外汇管理部门预先编印。				
出口单位： 签订并执行合同的出口企业名称。				
单位编码： 出口企业十位数代码。				
银行签注栏	类别	币种金额	日期	盖章
海关签注栏：				
外汇局签注栏 年 月 日（盖章）				

（出口单位盖章）

出口收汇核销单 监制章		
（沪）编号：核销单编号，已由外汇管理部门预先编印。		
出口单位： 签订并执行合同的出口企业名称。		
单位编码： 出口企业十位数代码。		
货物名称	数量	币种总价
按实际品名填写，与发票、报关单一致。	按外包装数或件数填写，与报关单和发票一致。	按发票上金额币制填写，与左边存根一致。
报关单编号：按实际情况填写。		
外汇局签注栏 年 月 日（盖章）		

未经核销此联不得撕开

工作任务

根据下列补充资料，制作出口收汇核销单。

补充资料：

信用证

【样单 2-31】

NATIONAL PARIS BANK
24 MARSHALL AVE DONCASTER MONTREAL, CANADA

WE ISSUE OUR IRREVOCABLE DOCUMENTARY CREDIT NUMBER：TH2003
IN FAVOUR OF：SUZHOU KNITWEAR AND MANUFACTURED GOODS IMPORT AND EXPORT TRADE CORPORATION
321, ZHOUGSHAN ROAD SUZHOU, CHINA
BY ORDER OF：YI YANG TRADING CORPORATION
88 MARSHALL AVE
DONCASTER VIC 3108
CANADA
FOR AN AMOUNT OF USD 89,705.50
DATE OF EXPIRY：15NOV.21
PALCE：IN BENEFICIARY'S COUNTRY
AVAILABLE WITH ANY BANK
BY NEGOTIATION OF BENEFICIARY'S DRAFT DRAWN ON US
AT SIGHT IN MONTREAL
THIS CREDIT IS TRANSFERABLE
AGAINST DELIVERY OF THE FOLLOWING DOCUMENTS
+COMMERCIAL INVOICES IN 5 COPIES
+CANADA CUSTOMS INVOICES IN 6 COPIES
+FULL SET OF NEGOTIABLE INSURANCE POLICY OR CERTIFICATE BLANK ENDORSED FOR 110 PERCENT OF INVOICE VALUE COVERING ALL RISKS
+FULL SET OF ORIGINAL MARINE BILLS OF LADING CLEAN ON BOARD PLUS 2 NON-NEGOTIABLE COPIES MADE OUR OR ENDORSED TO ORDER OF NATIONAL PARIS BANK 24 MARSHALL AVE DONCASTER MONTREAL, CANADA.
+SPECIFICATION LIST OF WEIGHTS AND MEASURES IN 4 COPIES COVERING SHIPMENT OF COTTON TEATOWELS AS PER S/C ST303.
FOR 1-300 SIZE 10 INCHES * 10 INCHES 16,000 DOZ. AT USD 1.31/DOZ. 301-600 SIZE 20 INCHES 6,000 DOZ. AT USD 2.51/DOZ. AND 601-900 SIZE 30 INCHES * 30 INCHES 11,350 DOZ. AT USD 4.73/DOZ.
CIF MONTREAL
FROM CHINESE PORT TO MONTREAL PORT
NOT LATER THAN 31, OCT. 21
PARTIAL SHIPMENTS：ALLOWED
TRANSSHIPMENT：ALLOWED
SPECIAL INSTRUCTIONS

+ALL CHARGES IF ANY RELATED TO SETTLEMENTS ARE FOR ACCOUNT OF BENEFICIARY +IN CASE OF PRESENTATION OF DOCUMENTS WITH DISCREPANCY (IES) A CHARGE OF USD 55.00 THIS CREDIT IS SUBJECT TO UCP FOR DOCUMENTARY CREDITS2007 RECISION ICC PUBLICATION 600 AND IS THE OPERATIVE INSTRUMENT

根据信用证要求填写出口收汇核销单（编号：72C173229）

出口单位：苏州毛织品进出口贸易公司

单位编码：195762654

商品中文名称：全棉抹布

商品总包装数量：367 捆

本批货物于 2021 年 10 月 18 日报关，报关单编号为 DS9110006，预计 20 天收汇。

【样单 2-32】

出口收汇核销单 存根 （沪）编号：72C173229
出口单位： 苏州毛织品进出口贸易公司
单位编码：195762654
出口币种总价：USD89,705.50
收汇方式：L/C AT SIGHT
预计收款日期：2021 年 11 月 07 日
报关日期：2021 年 10 月 18 日
备注：
此单报关有效期截止到

（出口单位盖章）

出口收汇核销单 监制章 （沪）编号：72C173229				
出口单位： 苏州毛织品进出口贸易公司				
单位编码：195762654				
银行签注栏	类别	币种金额	日期	盖章
海关签注栏：				
外汇局签注栏 年 月 日（盖章）				

（出口单位盖章）

出口收汇核销单 监制章 （沪）编号：72C173229		
出口单位： 苏州毛织品进出口贸易公司		
单位编码：195762654		
货物名称	数量	币种总价
全棉抹布	367 捆	USD 89,705.50
报关单编号：DS9110006		
外汇局签注栏 年 月 日（盖章）		

未经核销此联不得撕开

任务二：制作出口许可证

相关知识

制作出口许可证操作指示

中华人民共和国出口货物许可证

EXPORT LICENCE OF THE PEOPLE'S REPUBLIC OF CHINA **A 类**

申领许可证单位 编码 Exporter 出口公司名称与编码，编码应按外经贸部授权的发证机关编订的代码填写。	出口许可证编号 License No. 由发证机关编排。

续表

<table>
<tr><td colspan="3">发货单位
Consignee 通常为出口公司名称及其编码。</td><td colspan="3">许可证有效期
Validity 实行“一批一证”制的商品，其有效期自发证之日起最长3个月；其他情况为6个月。</td></tr>
<tr><td colspan="3">贸易方式
Terms of trade 贸易方式有一般贸易、补偿贸易、外商投资企业出口等；应与报关单一致。</td><td colspan="3">输往国家（地区）
Country of destination 最终目的地所在国。</td></tr>
<tr><td colspan="3">合同号
Contract No. 原油、成品油与非贸易项下出口可不填合同号；展品出运时填外经贸部批准办展的文件号。</td><td colspan="3">收款方式
Terms of payment 收款方式有信用证、托收、汇付等。</td></tr>
<tr><td colspan="3">出运口岸
Port of shipment 填写装运港。</td><td colspan="3">运输方式
Means of transport 运输方式有江海运输、铁路运输、航空运输等。</td></tr>
<tr><td colspan="6">唛头——包装件数
Marks & numbers——number of packages 出口货物的唛头</td></tr>
<tr><td colspan="3">商品名称
Discription for commodity 按出口许可证管理商品目录的标准名称填写。</td><td colspan="3">商品编码
Commodity No. 注明HS编码。</td></tr>
<tr><td>商品规格、型号
Specification</td><td>单位
Unit</td><td>数量
Quantity</td><td>单价（ ）
Unit price</td><td>总值（ ）
Amount</td><td>总值折美元（ ）
Amount in USD</td></tr>
<tr><td>具体品种、规格，同一编码商品规格型号超过4种时，应另行填写出口许可证。</td><td>计量单位。</td><td>允许保留一位小数。计量单位为“批”的，此栏均为“1”。</td><td>计量单位为“批”的，此栏则为总金额。</td><td>数量与单价的乘积。</td><td>总值折美元，系统自动完成折算。</td></tr>
<tr><td></td><td></td><td></td><td></td><td></td><td></td></tr>
<tr><td></td><td></td><td></td><td></td><td></td><td></td></tr>
<tr><td>总计 Total</td><td></td><td>记总</td><td>记总</td><td>记总</td><td>记总</td></tr>
<tr><td colspan="3">备注
Supplementary details
实行非“一批一证”的商品，在此栏注明“非一批一证”。</td><td colspan="3">发证机关盖章
Issuing Authority's Stamp

发证日期
Signature Date</td></tr>
</table>

商务部监制　　　　本证不得涂改，不得转让

工作任务

根据任务一的信用证【样单2-31】以及补充资料，制作出口许可证。

补充资料：

根据信用证有关内容缮制出口许可证一份。唛头、件数等内容应与该信用证的要求相符。

单位中文名称：苏州毛织品进出口贸易公司

单位编码：195762654

出口许可证编码：2002122433

合同编号：ST303

商品中文名称：全棉抹布

商品编码：888.666

许可证有效期：2021 年 12 月 24 日

【样单 2-33】

中华人民共和国出口货物许可证

EXPORT LICENCE OF THE PEOPLE'S REPUBLIC OF CHINA　　A 类

申领许可证单位　　编码　195762654 Exporter 苏州毛织品进出口贸易公司	出口许可证编号 License No. 2002122433
发货单位 Consignee 苏州毛织品进出口贸易公司	许可证有效期 Validity 2021-12-24
贸易方式 Terms of trade 一般贸易	输往国家（地区） Country of destination 加拿大
合同号 Contract No. ST303	收款方式 Terms of payment L/C
出运口岸 Port of shipment 上海	运输方式 Means of transport 江海
唛头——包装件数 Marks & numbers——number of packages　N/M	
商品名称 Discription for commodity 全棉抹布	商品编码 Commodity No.　888.666

商品规格、型号 Specification	单位 Unit	数量 Quantity	单价 Unit price	总值 Amount	总值折/美元 Amount in USD
10" 10"	DOZ	16,000	USD1.31	USD20,960.00	20,960.00
20" 20"	DOZ	6,000	USD2.51	USD15,060.00	15,060.00
30" 30"	DOZ	11,350	USD4.73	USD53,685.50	53,685.50
总计 Total	DOZ	33,350		USD89,705.50	89,705.50

续表

备注 Supplementary details	发证机关盖章 Issuing Authority's Stamp 发证日期 Signature Date

商务部监制　　　　　　　　　　　　本证不得涂改，不得转让

能力训练

根据模块一中的信用证【样单 1-3】和合同【样单 1-4】，参考模块二中已做好的发票【2-6】和装箱单【2-7】，以及下列补充资料制作出口收汇核销单和出口许可证。

（1）根据信用证要求填写出口收汇核销单（编号：62C134527）。

（2）出口单位：南京唐朝纺织服装有限公司。

（3）单位编码：186762632。

（4）商品中文名称：女士全棉运动上衣。

（5）商品总包装数量：85 箱。

（6）报关单编号：619110013。

（7）出口许可证编码：2011122234。

（8）许可证有效期：2021 年 4 月 24 日。

【样单 2-34】

出口收汇核销单 存根 （沪）编号：72C173229
出口单位： 苏州毛织品进出口贸易公司
单位编码：195762654
出口币种总价：USD89, 705. 50
收汇方式：L/C AT SIGHT
预计收款日期：2021 年 11 月 07 日
报关日期：2021 年 10 月 18 日
备注：
此单报关有效期截至

（出口单位盖章）

出口收汇核销单 监制章 （沪）编号：72C173229				
出口单位： 苏州毛织品进出口贸易公司				
单位编码：195762654				
银行签注栏	类别	币种 金额	日期	盖章
海关签注栏：				
外汇局签注栏 年　　月　　日（盖章）				

（出口单位盖章）

出口收汇核销单 监制章 （沪）编号：72C173229		
出口单位： 苏州毛织品进出口贸易公司		
单位编码：195762654		
货物名称	数量	币种总价
全棉抹布	367 捆	USD 89, 705. 50
报关单编号：DS9110006		
外汇局签注栏 年　　月　　日（盖章）		

未经核销此联不得撕开

【样单 2-35】

中华人民共和国出口货物许可证

EXPORT LICENCE OF THE PEOPLE'S REPUBLIC OF CHINA　　A 类

申领许可证单位　　编码 Exporter	出口许可证编号 License No.
发货单位 Consignee	许可证有效期 Validity
贸易方式 Terms of trade	输往国家（地区） Country of destination
合同号 Contract No.	收款方式 Terms of payment
出运口岸 Port of shipment	运输方式 Means of transport
唛头——包装件数 Marks & numbers——number of packages	
商品名称 Discription for commodity	商品编码 Commodity No.

商品规格、型号 Specification	单位 Unit	数量 Quantity	单价 Unit price	总值 Amount	总值折/美元 Amount in USD
总计 Total					

备注 Supplementary details	发证机关盖章 Issuing Authority's Stamp 发证日期 Signature Date

商务部监制　　　　本证不得涂改，不得转让

项目九：交单前制作其他结汇单据

项目目标

根据信用证的要求，制作信用证中要求的其他议付单据，如汇票，受益人证明，船公司证明。

学习情境十

装船完毕之后，刘华要根据信用证的要求制作全套的议付单据，目前还有以下单据没有制作：汇票、受益人证明。现在，刘华要根据信用证的要求制作以上单据。

价值引领

汇票是一种常用的结汇单据，也是重要的金融单据，正确缮制汇票，有利于安全收汇。受益人证明、船公司证明关乎合同的正常履行，也关乎顺利结汇。受益人要认真、细心地缮制汇票，保障自己的权益。对于受益人证明、船公司证明等，受益人在审证时要注意是否能够提供，如遇软条款，要提出修改信用证，如能据实提供，则应准确、及时提供，以便顺利结汇。

任务一：汇票

相关知识

制作汇票操作指示

BILL OF EXCHANGE

Drawn under 填开证行名称 L/C NO. 填信用证号

Dated 填开证日期 Payable with interest@ 不填 %

NO. 汇票号码，一般填写发票号码 Exchange for 小写金额 Shanghai 出票日期 (Date)

At 付款期限 Of this FIRST of Exchange (Second of Exchange being Unpaid)

Pay to the order of 收款人

大写金额

Value received for 数量 of 商品名称

To: 付款人

出票人

(Authorized Signature)

注：

（1）汇票金额：汇票的金额和币值，必须准确无误，金额不得模棱两可，并应注意以下几点：

①当用托收方法时，汇票金额和发票金额一般均应一致。信用证项下，如没有特别规定，其金额应与发票金额一致。

②如信用证规定汇票金额为发票金额的比例，例如 97%，那么发票金额应为 100%，汇票金额为 97%，其差额 3% 一般为应付的佣金。

③如信用证规定部分信用证付款，部分托收，应分做两套汇票：信用证下的按信用证允许的金额支取，以银行为付款人；托收部分的以客户为付款人，发票金额是两套汇票金额的相加之和。

④汇票的金额小写和大写必须一致。汇票金额不得涂改，不允许加盖校正章。汇票的小写金额，由货币符号和阿拉伯数字组成，汇票的大写金额，由货币名称和文字或数字组成，例如，U. S. DOLLARS ONE THOUSAND AND FIVE AND CENTS THIRTY ONLY 或 U. S. DOLLARS ONE THOUSAND AND FIVE POINT THREE ZERO ONLY。

⑤零头的写法除了用“cents”外，还可以用“point”或“××%（××/100）”表示。

例如：USD819. 75，其中 0. 75 有以下几种写法：

a. US Dollars…cents seventy-five only.

b. US Dollars…point seventy-five only.

c. US Dollars…and 75%（75/100）only.

（2）出票地点及出票日期。出票地点一般应是出口商所在地，出票日期一般填交单日，该日期不能早于随附单据的签发日期，例如发票的制单日。信用证项下，出票日期不得迟于信用证或规定的交单期限，无论如何，不得迟于信用证的有效期。日期需用英文，不能全用阿拉伯数字。一般由议付银行议付时代填。出票地点通常已印好，为议付地点。

（3）付款期限，是汇票的重要项目，凡没有列明付款期限的汇票，根据票据法应视为无效。按照不同的付款期限，一般可采用下列方式缮制：

①即期付款，在汇票上的付款期限处，加打“×”或“_____”。

如 AT××× SIGHT，AT _____ SIGHT.

②远期付款，在汇票上的付款期限处，加打远期天数和起算期。

例如：“At 30 days after date ”（出票后 30 天付款）

“At 45 days after sight”（见票后 45 天付款）

“At 60 days after B/L date”（提单日后 60 天付款）。

③定期付款：应填上将来具体的付款到期日，如 At 31 Dec. 2003 fixed，并将汇票上的“SIGHT”划去。

（4）收款人，又称受款人，按国际习惯，信用证项下汇票的受款人，如信用证没有特别规定，应以议付行为受款人。无证托收的汇票，一般应以托收行（出口地银行）为受款人，在“Pay to the order of…”之后的横线上填写。

例如：“Pay to the order of Bank of China，Shanghai Branch”

A. 来证规定“限制议付”，则填限制银行。

例如：…negotiations are restricted to Bank of China only

此时填写：Pay to the order of Bank of China

B. 来证没有规定“限制议付”，则打任何一家议付行都可。

例如：“Draft for negotiation with any bank in Beneficiary's country.”

这是不限制收款人、不限制议付行的一种来证内容，是最常见的一种规定收款人的方法。收款人可以在自己的国家选择任何一个合适的银行作为议付行。

在填写汇票时，应将选择好的银行名称、地址直接填入这个栏目。例如选择中国银行山东分行作为收款人，应在收款人的栏目中写：Bank of China Shandong Branch.

（5）付款人，亦称受票人（Drawee）。在汇票中“To”之后的横线上填写付款人的名称和地址。付款人名称必须填写完整，托收的汇票，还必须填写完整的地址。

信用证项下汇票的付款人为开证行或其指定另一家银行。应详细填写付款行名称、地址。

信用证未作规定时，付款人仍为开证行。其常见的语句为：draft drawn on ** bank, Value on us, issued on ourselves. 在填写汇票付款人时，应把相应的银行名称、地址填上，切不可只填 us/ourselves.

托收项下，除非合同另有规定，应填写合同的买方。

（6）出票人，在汇票的右下角，一般由信用证的受益人（出口商）签章。按照我国的习惯，这一栏通常打上出口公司的全称，并由公司的经理或经办人签字盖章，也可以盖上出口公司包括有经理签字模的印章。

工作任务

根据合同【样单1-1】和信用证【样单2-2】，以及商业发票【样单2-4】和装箱单【样单2-5】，制作汇票。

【样单2-36】

BILL OF EXCHANGE

Drawn under ALRAJHI BANKING AND INVESTMENT CORPORATION RIYADH L/C NO. 0011LC123756

Dated APR. 8,2021 Payable with interest@ %

NO. 2021SDT001 Exchange for USD13,260.00 Shanghai (Date)

At ****** Of this FIRST of Exchange (Second of Exchange being Unpaid)

Pay to the order of BANK OF CHINA,SHANGHAI BRANCH

USD THIRTEEN THOUSAND TWO HUNDRED AND SIXTY ONLY.

Value received FOR 1,700 CARTONS OF CANNED MUSHROOM

To: RJHISARI ALRAJHI BANKING AND INVESTMENT CORPORATION RIYADH

LINJIANG TRADING CO., LTD.

(Authorized Signature)

任务二：制作受益人证明

相关知识

制作受益人证明指导图

<table>
<tr><td colspan="4" align="center">出口商公司名称和地址</td></tr>
<tr><td colspan="4" align="center">单据名称</td></tr>
<tr><td>To：</td><td>抬头</td><td>Invoice No.：
Date：</td><td>如实填写
受益人证明日期，参考信用证填写。</td></tr>
<tr><td colspan="4">证明内容，按信用证规定的内容填写，通常为“WE HEREBY CERTIFY THAT…”</td></tr>
<tr><td colspan="4" align="right">签署：注明出口商全称，由经办人签字盖章</td></tr>
</table>

注：

（1）受益人证明书的种类。

①寄单证明：根据信用证的规定，在货物装运前后的一定期限内，由发货人邮寄给信用证规定的收货人全套或部分副本单据，并出具给单证明书，或将寄单证明内容列明在发票内，作为向银行议付的单证。

②履约证明：发货人按照信用证规定证明所交货物的正确凭证。因此该证明书可以直接作为银行议付的单据。

（2）单据名称，一般标明“BENEFICIARY'S CERTIFICATE” （受益人证明）或“BENE-FICIARY'S STATEMENT”（受益人声明）。

（3）抬头，通常做成 TO：WHOM IT MAY CONCERN。

工作任务

根据合同【样单 1-1】和信用证【样单 2-2】，以及商业发票【样单 2-4】和装箱单【样单 2-5】，制作受益人证明。

【样单 2-37】

LINJIANG TRADING CO. , LTD.
HUARONG MANSION RM2901 NO. 85 GUANJIAQIAO,
NANJING 210005, CHINA

BENEFICIARY CERTIFICATE

To: WHOM IT MAY CONCERN

Invoice No. : 202SDT001
Date: APR. 28, 2021

WE HEREBY CERTIFY THAT THE PRODUCTION DATE OF THE GOODS NOT TO BE EARLIER THAN HALF MONTH AT TIME OF SHIPMENT.

LINJIANG TRADING CO. , LTD.

能力训练

根据模块一中的信用证【样单 1-3】和合同【样单 1-4】，参考模块二中已做好的发票【2-6】和装箱单【2-7】，制作汇票和受益人证明。

【样单 2-38】

BILL OF EXCHANGE

Drawn under ________________ L/C NO. ________
Dated ________________ Payable with interest@ ________ % ________
NO. ________ Exchange for ________ Shanghai ________ (Date)
At ________________ Of this FIRST of Exchange (Second of Exchange being Unpaid)
Pay to the order of
____
Value received ________________________________
To:
____

(Authorized Signature)

【样单 2-39】

To:	Invoice No. : Date:

模块评估

1. 模块课程评价表

模块内容________ 班级_______ 学号_______ 姓名_______ _______年___月___日

1. 你认为本模块最有价值的内容是：
2. 本堂课上教师使用的教学方法是否对学习有帮助，你对此有何建议？
3. 你是否有计划地组织学习？是否在朝学习目标努力？
4. 下列问题我需要得到进一步的了解和帮助：
教师签名 学生签名

2. 基本能力测评表

核心能力	评价指标	测评结果	备注
自我管理能力	1. 培养自己的责任心 2. 掌握时间管理技能 3. 将自己所学的知识运用到工作中		
交流能力	1. 知道如何尊重他人的观点、价值和信仰等 2. 能与其他人有效沟通 3. 在团队合作中表现积极 4. 能正确获取并反馈信息		
解决问题的能力	1. 学会搜集、使用信息资源 2. 能发现并解决常规及特殊问题		
创新能力	1. 面对问题，能提出有价值的观点或解决办法 2. 使用不同的思维方式		
其他			
教师评语 教师签字			
成绩		学生签字	

模块三 综合模拟——不同结算方式下的出口议付单据制作

学习情境十一

经过一个多月的学习，刘华基本能够独立开展工作，以下是刘华在工作中面临的需根据不同结算方式制作单据的工作任务，如果你是刘华，请根据你所掌握的资料和要求，制作单据。

价值引领

"单据填写无小事"，工作中我们一定要有专业专注、细致谨慎、严格把关的工作态度，谨防出现不必要的贸易争端，规避各种结算风险。

项目一：L/C 方式下制全套议付单据

项目目标

能够根据要求制作信用证方式下的全套议付单据。

请根据下列信用证和相关资料，制作相关单据。

ISSUE OF A DOCUMENTARY CREDIT

ISSUING BANK	51A:	THE ROYAL BANK, TOKYO
SEQUENCE OF TOTAL	*27:	1/1
FORM OF DOC. CREDIT	*40A:	IRREVOCABLE
DOC. CREDIT NUMBER	*20:	JST-AB12

DATE OF ISSUE	31C:	20030405
EXPIRY	*31D:	DATE 20040615 PLACE CHINA
APPLICANT	*50:	WAV GENEAL TRADING CO., LTD 5-18 ISUKI-CHOHAKI, OSAKA, JAPAN
BENEFICIARY	*59:	DESUN TRADING CO, LTD 224 JINLIN ROAD, NANJING, CHINA
AMOUNT	*32B:	CURRENCY USD AMOUNT 10300.00
AVAILABLE WITH/BY	*41:	BANK OF CHINA BY NEGOTIATION
DRAFTS AT...	42C:	DRAFTS AT SIGHT FOR FULL INVOICE VALUE
DRAWEE	42A:	THE ROYAL BANK, TOKYO
PARTIAL SHIPMTS	43P:	ALLOWED
TRANSSHIPMENT	43T:	ALLOWED
PORT OF LOADING	44E:	NANJING PORT, CHINA
PORT OF DISCHARGE	44F:	OSAKA PORT, JAPAN
LATEST SHIPMENT	44C:	20030531
GOODS DESCRIPT.	45A:	

LADIES GARMENTS AS PER S/C NO. SHL553

PACKING: 10PCS/CTN

ART NO.	QUANTITY	UNIT PRICE
STYLE NO. ROCOCO	1000 PCS	USD 5.50
STYLE NO. ROMANTICO	1000 PCS	USD 4.80

CIF OSAKA

SHIPPING MARK: ITOCHU/OSAKA/NO, 1-200

DOCS REQUIRED 46A:

* 3/3 SET OF ORIGINAL CLEAN ON BOARD OCEAN BILLS OF LADING MADE OUT TO ORDER OF SHIPPER AND BLANK ENDORSED AND MARKED "FREIGHT PREPAID" NOTIFY APPLICANT (WITH FULL NAME AND ADDRESS).
* ORIGINAL SIGNED COMMERCIAL INVOICE IN 5 FOLD.
* INSURANCE POLICY OR CERTIFICATE IN 2 FOLD ENDORSED IN BLANK, FOR 110PCT OF THE INVOICE VALUE COVERING THE INSTITUTE CARGO CLAUSES (A), THE INSTITUTE WAR CLAUSES, INSURANCE CLAIMS TO BE PAYABLE IN JAPAN IN THE CURRENCY OF THE DRAFTS.
* CERTIFICATE OF ORIGIN GSP FORM A IN 1 ORIGINAL AND 1 COPY.
* PACKING LIST IN 5 FOLD.

ADDITIONAL COND. 47A:

1. T. T. REIMBURSEMENT IS PROHIBITED
2. THE GOODS TO BE PACKED IN EXPORT STRONG COLORED CARTONS.
3. SHIPPING MARKS:
   ITOCHU
   OSAKA
   NO, 1-200

DETAILS OF CHARGES 71B: ALL BANKING CHARGES OUTSIDE JAPAN INCLUDING REIMBURSE-

		MENT COMMISSION, ARE FOR ACCOUNT OF BENEFICIARY.
PRESENTATION PERIOD	48:	DOCUMENTS TO BE PRESENTED WITHIN 10 DAYS AFTER THE DATE OF SHIPMENT, BUT WITHIN THE VALIDITY OF THE CREDIT.
CONFIRMATION	*49:	WITHOUT
INSTRUCTIONS	78:	THE NEGOTIATION BANK MUST FORWARD THE DRAFTS AND ALL DOCUMENTS BY REGISTERED AIRMAIL DIRECT TO U. S. IN TWO CONSECUTIVE LOTS, UPON RECEIPT OF THE DRAFTS AND DOCUMENTS IN ORDER, WE WILL REMIT THE PROCEEDS AS INSTRUCTED BY THE NEGOTIATING BANK.

商品资料：

（1）包装：10PCS PER CARTON。

（2）单位毛重：15.40KGS/CTN。

（3）单位净重：13.00KGS/CTN。

（4）单位尺码：60×40×50 CM/CTN。

其他资料：

（1）发票号码：SH25586，汇票号同发票号。

（2）发票日期：2021-4-20。

（3）船名：DAFENG V3336。

（4）提单号码：SH223545。

（5）提单日期：2021-5-15。

（6）汇票出票日期：2021-5-20。

（7）产地证日期地点：NANJING，JIANGSU，APR. 20, 2021。

请思考

根据此信用证的要求，思考需要制作哪些单据。

需要制作的单据有：

1. 商业发票【样单 3-1】

COMMERCIAL INVOICE

To			Invoice No.	
			Invoice Date	
			S/C No.	
			S/C Date	
From			To	
Letter of Credit No.			Date	
Marks and Numbers	Number and Kind of Package Description of Goods	Quantity	Unit Price	Amount
		Total		
SAY TOTAL				

2. 装箱单【样单3-2】

PACKING LIST						
To			Invoice No.			
			Invoice Date			
From			To			
Marks and Numbers	Number and Kind of Package Description of Goods	Quantity	Package	G. W	N. W	Meas.
Total						
SAY TOTAL						

3. 海运提单【样单 3-3】

<table>
<tr><td>Shipper</td><td rowspan="3">B/L NO.

PIL
PACIFIC INTERNATION LINES (PTE) LTD.
(Incorporated in Singapore)
COMBINED TRANSPORT BILL OF LADING
Received in apparent good order and condition except as otherwise noted the total number of container or other packages or units enumerated below for transportation from the place of receipt to the place of delivery subject to the terms hereof. One of the signed Bills of Lading must be surrendered duly endorsed in exchange for the Goods or delivery order. On presentation of this document (duly) Endorsed to the Carrier by or on behalf of the Holder, the rights and liabilities arising in accordance with the terms hereof shall (without prejudice to any rule of common law or statute rendering them binding on the Merchant) become binding in all respects between the Carrier and the Holder as though the contract evidenced hereby had been made between them.
SEE TERMS ON ORIGINAL B/L</td></tr>
<tr><td>Consignee</td></tr>
<tr><td>Notify Party</td></tr>
</table>

Vessel and Voyage Number	Port of Loading	Port of Discharge
Place of Receipt	Place of Delivery	Number of Original B/L

PARTICULARS AS DECLARED BY SHIPPER-CARRIER NOT RESPONSIBLE

Container Nos/Seal Nos. Marks and/Numbers	No. of Container / Packages / Description of Goods	Gross Weight (kgs)	Measurement (m^3)

<table>
<tr><td rowspan="4">FREIGHT & CHARGES</td><td>Number of Containers/Packages</td></tr>
<tr><td>Shipped on Board Date</td></tr>
<tr><td>Place and Date of Issue</td></tr>
<tr><td>In Witness Whereof this number of Original Bills of Lading stated Above all of the tenor and date one of which being accomplished the others to stand void.

for PACIFIC INTERNATIONAL LINES (PTE) LTD. as Carrier</td></tr>
</table>

4. 普惠制产地证【样单3-4】

ORIGIN

1. Goods Consigned From (Exporter's business name, address, country)

Reference No.

GENERALIZED SYSTEM OF PREFERENCES CERTIFICATE OF ORIGIN

(Combined declaration and certificate)

FORM A

Issued in THE PEOPLE'S REPUBLIC OF CHINA
(country)

See Notes overleaf

2. Goods consigned to (Consignee's name, address, country)

3 Means of Transport and Route (as far as known)

4. For Official Use

5. Item Number	6. Marks and Numbers of Packages	7. Number and Kind of Packages; Description of Goods	8. Origin Criterion	9. Gross Weight or Other Quantity	10. Number and Date of Invoices

11. Certification

It is hereby certified, on the basis of control carried out, that the declaration by the exporter is correct.

Place and date, signature and stamp of certifying authority

12. Declaration by the exporter

The undersigned hereby declares that the above details and statements are correct, that all the goods were

produced in CHINA
(country)

and that they comply with the origin requirements specified for those goods in the Generalized System of Preferences for goods exported to

Place and date, signature and stamp of authorized signatory

5. 保险单【样单 3-5】

中保财产保险有限公司

The People's Insurance (Property) Company of China, Ltd.

发票号码　　　　　　　　　　　　保险单号次

Invoice No.　　　　　　　　　　　　Policy No.

海洋货物运输保险单

MARINE CARGO TRANSPORTATION INSURANCE POLICY

被保险人：

Insured：

中保财产保险有限公司（以下简称本公司）根据被保险人的要求，及其所缴付约定的保险费，按照本保险单承担险别和背面所载条款与下列特别条款承保下列货物运输保险，特签发本保险单。

This policy of Insurance witnesses that the People's Insurance Company of China, Ltd. (hereinafter called "The Company"), at the request of the Insured and in consideration of the agreed premium paid by the Insured, undertakes to insure the undermentioned goods in transportation subject to conditions of the Policy as per the Clauses printed overleaf and other special clauses attached hereon.

保险货物项目 Descriptions of Goods	包装 Packing	单位 Unit	数量 Quantity	保险金额 Amount Insured

承保险别　　　　　　　　　　　　货物标记

Conditions　　　　　　　　　　　　Marks of Goods

总保险金额：

Total Amount Insured: ____________________

保费　　　　　　　　载运输工具　　　　　　　　开航日期

Premium ____________　Per conveyance S. S ____________　Slg. on or abt ____________

起运港　　　　　　　　目的港

From ____________　To ____________

所保货物，如发生本保险单项下可能引起索赔的损失或损坏，应立即通知本公司下述代理人查勘。如有索赔，应向本公司提交保险单正本（本保险单共有　　份正本）及有关文件。如一份正本已用于索赔，其余正本则自动失效。

In the event of loss or damage which may result in acclaim under this Policy, immediate notice must be given to the Company's Agent as mentioned here under. Claims, if any, one of the Original Policy which has been issued in __________ original (s) together with the relevant documents shall be surrendered to the Company. If one of the Original Policy has been accomplished, the others to be void.

赔款偿付地点

Claim payable at

日期　　　　　　　　在

Date ____________　at ____________

地址

Address ____________

6. 汇票【样单3-6】

BILL OF EXCHANGE			
Drawn under ________		L/C NO. ________	
Dated ________		Payable with interest@ ________	% ________
NO. ________	Exchange for ________	Shanghai ________	(Date)
At ________		Of this FIRST of Exchange (Second of Exchange being Unpaid)	
Pay to the order of ________			
Value received ________			
To: ________			
			(Authorized Signature)

项目二：T/T 方式下制全套议付单据

项目目标

根据要求，制作电汇方式下的全套议付单据。

请根据如下资料制作商业发票、装箱单、汇票。

（1）客户名称地址：AL. BALOUSHI TRADING EST JEDDAH。

（2）付款方式：20% T/T BEFORE SHIPMENT AND 80% D/P AT SIGHT。

（3）装运信息：指定 APL 承运，装期：2021. 04. 29；起运港：NINGBO，目的港：JEDDAH。

（4）价格条款：CFR JEDDAH。

（5）唛头：ROYAL

05AR225031

JEDDAH

C/N：1-460。

（6）货物描述：P. P INJECTION CASES 14”/22”/27”/31” 230SET @ USD42. 00/SET

USD9, 660. 00

P. P INJECTION CASES 14”/19”/27”/31” 230SET @ USD41. 00/SET

USD9, 430. 00

（中文品名：注塑箱四件套）。

（7）装箱资料：

箱号	货号	包装	件数	毛重（KGS）	净重（KGS）	体积（m^3）
1-230	ZL0322+BC05	CTNS	230	18. 5/4, 255	16. 5/3, 795	34
1-230	ZL0319+BC01	CTNS	230	18. 5/4, 255	16. 5/3, 795	34

（8）合同号：05AR225031　　签订日期：2021 年 3 月 30 日。

（9）商业发票号：AC05AR031。

1. 商业发票【样单 3-7】

<table>
<tr><td colspan="6"></td></tr>
<tr><td colspan="6">COMMERCIAL INVOICE</td></tr>
<tr><td rowspan="4">To</td><td colspan="2" rowspan="4"></td><td>Invoice No.</td><td colspan="2"></td></tr>
<tr><td>Invoice Date</td><td colspan="2"></td></tr>
<tr><td>S/C No.</td><td colspan="2"></td></tr>
<tr><td>S/C Date</td><td colspan="2"></td></tr>
<tr><td>From</td><td colspan="2"></td><td>To</td><td colspan="2"></td></tr>
<tr><td>Letter of Credit No.</td><td colspan="2"></td><td>Date</td><td colspan="2"></td></tr>
<tr><td></td><td colspan="2"></td><td></td><td colspan="2"></td></tr>
<tr><td>Marks and Numbers</td><td>Number and Kind of Package
Description of Goods</td><td>Quantity</td><td>Unit Price</td><td colspan="2">Amount</td></tr>
<tr><td rowspan="2"></td><td colspan="5"></td></tr>
<tr><td></td><td></td><td></td><td colspan="2"></td></tr>
<tr><td colspan="2">Total</td><td colspan="2"></td><td colspan="2"></td></tr>
<tr><td>SAY TOTAL</td><td colspan="5"></td></tr>
<tr><td colspan="6"></td></tr>
</table>

2. 装箱单【样单3-8】

PACKING LIST

To		Invoice No.	
		Invoice Date	

From		To	

Marks and Numbers	Number and Kind of Package Description of Goods	Quantity	Package	G. W	N. W	Meas.
Total						
SAY TOTAL						

3. 汇票【样单3-9】

BILL OF EXCHANGE			
Drawn under		L/C NO.	
Dated		Payable with interest@	%
NO.	Exchange for	Shanghai	(Date)
At		Of this FIRST of Exchange (Second of Exchange being Unpaid)	
Pay to the order of			
Value received			
To:			
			(Authorized Signature)

项目三：托收方式下制全套议付单据

项目目标

根据要求，制作托收方式下的全套议付单据。

根据以下合同和相关资料，制作相关单据。

售货确认书 SALES CONFIRMATION			
Seller	ZHONGCHENG INTERNATIONAL TRADE CO. , LTD. 20, HANZHONG RD. , NANJING, P. R OF CHINA	编号 NO.	05SUG0012
		日期 DATE	FEB. 6, 2021
Buyer	GREEN TRADE CO. , LTD. 22 MARK STREET, OSLO, NORWAY		
下列签字双方同意按以下条款达成交易 The undersigned Sellers and Buyers have agreed to close the following transactions according to the terms and conditions stipulated below			
1 品名及规格 Commodity & Specification	2 数量 Quantity	3 单价 Unit Price	4 金额 Amount
		CIF OSLO	

续表

HAND TOOLS ART NO. 1018 ART NO. 1019 GOODS ARE OF CHINESE ORIGIN	5, 000SETS 5, 000SETS 10, 000SETS	USD4. 00/SET USD3. 00/SET	USD20, 000. 00 USD15, 000. 00 USD35, 000. 00
TOTAL AMOUNT: SAY US DOLLARS THIRTY FIVE THOUSAND ONLY			
5. 装运期限 Time of Shipment	NOT LATER THAN APR. 30, 2021. PARTIAL SHIPMENT ALLOWED.		
6. 装运口岸 Port of Loading	CHINA PORT		
7. 目的口岸 Port of Destination	PORT OF DISCHARGE: OSLO NORWAY		
8. 付款方式 Payment	BY D/P AT 30 DAYS AFTER B/L DATE		
9. 保险 Insurance	TO BE EFFECTED BY THE SELLER AT 110% OF THE INVOICE VALUE COVERING ALL RISK AND WAR RISK AS PER PICC CLAUSES.		
10. 单据 Documents	+SIGNED INVOICE IN 3 COPIES. + FULL SET OF CLEAN ON BOARD B/L ISSUED BY APL SHIPPING CO. +DETAILED PACKING LIST +INSURANCE POLICY		
Buyer: MARY	Seller: LI LING		

相关资料:

(1) 发票号: ET335。

(2) 制作发票和装箱单的日期: 2021. 04. 10。

(3) 报检单位联系人: 张敏 电话: 67678333。

(4) 船名: SPRING V. 011, 开船日: 2021. 04. 15。

(5) 集装箱数量和编号: 3×40', APLU 1234501, 1234502, 1234503。

(6) 商品编码: 8204. 1100

包装情况:

Style 1018 10 套装一纸箱　每箱毛重 12 公斤　净重 10 公斤　体积 0. 2m^3/箱

Style 1019 8 套装一纸箱　每箱毛重 10 公斤　净重 8 公斤　体积 0. 1m^3/箱

假定此货物属法定检验范围

报检随附单据为合同、发票、装箱单

托收银行: 中国银行江苏分行

船唛: GREEN

05SUG0012
OSLO
CTN. 1/1125。

请思考

根据上述合同信息，思考需要制作哪些单据。

需要制作的单据有：

1. 商业发票【样单 3-10】

COMMERCIAL INVOICE				
To			Invoice No.	
			Invoice Date	
			S/C No.	
			S/C Date	
From		To		
Letter of Credit No.		Date		
Marks and Numbers	Number and Kind of Package Description of Goods	Quantity	Unit Price	Amount
Total				
SAY TOTAL				

2. 装箱单【样单3-11】

PACKING LIST

To		Invoice No.	
		Invoice Date	
From		To	

Marks and Numbers	Number and Kind of Package Description of Goods	Quantity	Package	G. W	N. W	Meas.
Total						

SAY TOTAL	

3. 海运提单【样单 3-12】

<table>
<tr><td>Shipper</td><td rowspan="3">B/L NO.

PACIFIC INTERNATION LINES (PTE) LTD
(Incorporated in Singapore)
COMBINED TRANSPORT BILL OF LADING
Received in apparent good order and condition except as otherwise noted the total number of container or other packages or units enumerated below for transportation from the place of receipt to the place of delivery subject to the terms hereof. One of the signed Bills of Lading must be surrendered duly endorsed in exchange for the Goods or delivery order. On presentation of this document (duly) Endorsed to the Carrier by or on behalf of the Holder, the rights and liabilities arising in accordance with the terms hereof shall (without prejudice to any rule of common law or statute rendering them binding on the Merchant) become binding in all respects between the Carrier and the Holder as though the contract evidenced hereby had been made between them.
SEE TERMS ON ORIGINAL B/L</td></tr>
<tr><td>Consignee</td></tr>
<tr><td>Notify Party</td></tr>
</table>

Vessel and Voyage Number	Port of Loading	Port of Discharge
Place of Receipt	Place of Delivery	Number of Original B/L

PARTICULARS AS DECLARED BY SHIPPER-CARRIER NOT RESPONSIBLE

Container Nos/Seal Nos. Marks and/Numbers	No. of Container / Packages / Description of Goods	Gross Weight (kgs)	Measurement (m^3)

<table>
<tr><td rowspan="4">FREIGHT & CHARGES</td><td>Number of Containers/Packages</td></tr>
<tr><td>Shipped on Board Date</td></tr>
<tr><td>Place and Date of Issue</td></tr>
<tr><td>In Witness Whereof this number of Original Bills of Lading stated Above all of the tenor and date one of which being accomplished the others to stand void.

for PACIFIC INTERNATIONAL LINES (PTE) LTD. as Carrier</td></tr>
</table>

4. 保险单【样单 3-13】

中保财产保险有限公司

The People's Insurance (Property) Company of China, Ltd.

发票号码 保险单号次

Invoice No. Policy No.

海洋货物运输保险单

MARINE CARGO TRANSPORTATION INSURANCE POLICY

被保险人：

Insured：

中保财产保险有限公司（以下简称本公司）根据被保险人的要求，及其所缴付约定的保险费，按照本保险单承担险别和背面所载条款与下列特别条款承保下列货物运输保险，特签发本保险单。

This policy of Insurance witnesses that the People's Insurance (Property) Company of China, Ltd. (hereinafter called "The Company"), at the request of the Insured and in consideration of the agreed premium paid by the Insured, undertakes to insure the undermentioned goods in transportation subject to conditions of the Policy as per the Clauses printed overleaf and other special clauses attached hereon.

保险货物项目 Descriptions of Goods	包装 单位 数量 Packing Unit Quantity	保险金额 Amount Insured

承保险别 货物标记

Conditions Marks of Goods

总保险金额：

Total Amount Insured: ____________________

保费 载运输工具 开航日期

Premium ________ Per conveyance S. S ________ Slg. on or abt ________

起运港 目的港

From ____________________ To ____________________

所保货物，如发生本保险单项下可能引起索赔的损失或损坏，应立即通知本公司下述代理人查勘。如有索赔，应向本公司提交保险单正本（本保险单共有　　份正本）及有关文件。如一份正本已用于索赔，其余正本则自动失效。

In the event of loss or damage which may result in acclaim under this Policy, immediate notice must be given to the Company's Agent as mentioned here under. Claims, if any, one of the Original Policy which has been issued in　　　original (s) together with the relevant documents shall be surrendered to the Company. If one of the Original Policy has been accomplished, the others to be void.

赔款偿付地点

Claim payable at

日期 在

Date ____________________ at ____________________

地址：

Address: ____________________

5. 汇票【样单3-14】

BILL OF EXCHANGE

Drawn under ______________________ L/C NO. ____________

Dated ______________ Payable with interest@ ____________ % ____________

NO. ________ Exchange for ____________ Shanghai ________________ (Date)

At ______________________ Of this FIRST of Exchange (Second of Exchange being Unpaid)

Pay to the order of

____

Value received ____

To:

____

(Authorized Signature)

模块评估

1. 模块课程评价表

模块内容________ 班级______ 学号______ 姓名______ ______年___月___日

1. 你认为本模块最有价值的内容是：
2. 本堂课上教师使用的教学方法是否对学习有帮助，你对此有何建议。
3. 你是否有计划地组织学习？是否在朝学习目标努力？
4. 下列问题我需要得到进一步的了解和帮助：
教师签名 学生签名

2. 基本能力测评表

核心能力	评价指标	测评结果	备注
自我管理能力	1. 培养自己的责任心 2. 掌握时间管理技能 3. 将自己所学的知识运用到工作中		
交流能力	1. 知道如何尊重他人的观点、价值和信仰等 2. 能与其他人有效沟通 3. 在团队合作中表现积极 4. 能正确获取并反馈信息		
解决问题的能力	1. 学会搜集、使用信息资源 2. 能发现并解决常规及特殊问题		
创新能力	1. 面对问题，能提出有价值的观点或解决办法 2. 使用不同的思维方式		
其他			
教师评语 教师签字			
成绩		学生签字	

模块四 制作进口单据

学习情境十二

广东国际进出口贸易公司与 A. B. C. TRADING CO. LTD. 签订了编号为 AB44001 的合同，作为单证员的刘华，要根据合同，制作开证申请书，货物运到之后还要制作一系列单据。

价值引领

作为外贸业务人员，应熟悉相关的法律法规，做到“遵守程序、业务规范、办事诚信”，合理合法地办理货物、物品、运输工具等的进出境手续。

项目一：制作开证申请书

项目目标

根据合同和相关资料，制作开证申请书。

相关知识

制作开证申请书指导。

IRREVOCABLE DOCUMENTARY CREDIT APPLICATION

TO:		Date:
☐ Issue by airmail　☐ With brief advice by teletransmission ☐ Issue by express delivery ☐ Issue by teletransmission (which shall be the operative instrument)		Credit No. Date and place of expiry
Applicant		Beneficiary (Full name and address)
Advising Bank		Amount
Partial shipments ☐ allowed　☐ not allowed	Transshipment ☐ allowed　☐ not allowed	Credit available with By ☐ sight payment　☐ acceptance ☐ negotiation ☐ deferred payment at against the documents detailed herein ☐ and beneficiary's draft (s) for ____% of invoice value at ____________ sight drawn on
Loading on board/dispatch/taking in charge at/from not later than For transportation to:		
☐ FOB　☐ CFR　☐ CIF ☐ or other terms		

Documents required: (marked with X)

1. (　) Signed commercial invoice in____copies indicating L/C No. and Contract No.
2. (　) Full set of clean on board Bills of Lading made out to order and blank endorsed, marked "freight [　] to collect / [　] prepaid [　] showing freight amount" notifying ____________________
______.

   (　) Airway bills/cargo receipt/copy of railway bills issued by ____________________ showing "freight [　] to collect/ [　] prepaid [　] indicating freight amount" and consigned to ________________.
3. (　) Insurance Policy/Certificate in ______ copies for ______ % of the invoice value showing claims payable in ________________ in currency of the draft, blank endorsed, covering All Risks, War Risks and ____________________________________.
4. (　) Packing List/Weight Memo in ________ copies indicating quantity, gross and weights of each package.
5. (　) Certificate of Quantity/Weight in ________ copies issued by ______________.
6. (　) Certificate of Quality in ______ copies issued by [　] manufacturer/ [　] public recognized surveyor __________________.
7. (　) Certificate of Origin in ______ copies.
8. (　) Beneficiary's certified copy of fax / telex dispatched to the applicant within ________ days after shipment advising L/C No. , name of vessel, date of shipment, name, quantity, weight and value of goods.

Other documents, if any

续表

Description of goods: Additional instructions: 1. ( ) All banking charges outside the opening bank are for beneficiary's account. 2. ( ) Documents must be presented within ______ days after date of issuance of the transport documents but within the validity of this credit. 3. ( ) Third party as shipper is not acceptable, Short Form/Blank back B/L is not acceptable. 4. ( ) Both quantity and credit amount ________ % more or less are allowed. 5. ( ) All documents must be sent to issuing bank by courier/speed post in one lot. ( ) Other terms, if any

注：

进口方与出口方签订国际贸易货物进出口合同并确认以信用证为结算方式后，即由进口方向有关银行申请开立信用证。开证申请是整个进口信用证处理实务的第一个环节，进口方应根据合同规定的时间或在规定的装船前一定时间内申请开证，并填制开证申请书，开证行根据有关规定收取开证押金和开证费用后开出信用证。

开证申请人（进口方）在向开证行申请开证时必须填制开证申请书。开证申请书是开证申请人对开证行的付款指示，也是开证申请人与开证行之间的一种书面契约，它规定了开证申请人与开证行的责任。在这一契约中，开证行只是开证申请人的付款代理人。

开证申请书主要依据贸易合同中的有关主要条款填制，申请人填制后附合同副本一并提交银行，供银行参考、核对。但信用证一经开立则独立于合同，因而在填写开证申请时应审慎查核合同的主要条款，并将其列入申请书中。

一般情况下，开证申请书都由开证银行事先印就，以便申请人直接填制。开证申请书通常为一式两联，申请人除填写正面内容外，还须签具背面的“开证申请人承诺书”。

TO

致____________________行。

填写开证行名称。

Date

申请开证日期，如050428。

Issue by airmail

以信件的形式开立信用证。

选择此种方式，开证行以航邮将信用证寄给通知行。

With brief advice by teletransmission

以简电开证形式开立信用证。

选择此种方式，开证行将信用证主要内容发电预先通知受益人，银行承担必须使其生效的责任，但简电本身并非信用证的有效文本，不能凭以议付或付款，银行随后寄出的“证实书”才是正式的信用证。

Issue by express delivery

以信件的形式开立信用证。

选择此种方式，开证行以快递将信用证寄给通知行。

Issue by teletransmission (which shall be the operative instrument)

以全电开证形式开立信用证。

选择此种方式，开证行将信用证的全部内容加注密押后发出，该电讯文本为有效的信用证正本。如今大多用“全电开证”的方式开立信用证。

Credit No.

信用证号码，由银行填写。

Date and place of expiry

信用证有效期及地点，地点填受益人所在国家。

如 050815 IN THE BENEFICIARY'S COUNTRY.

Applicant

填写开证申请人名称及地址。

开证申请人（Applicant）又称开证人（Opener），指向银行提出申请开立信用证的人，一般为进口人，就是买卖合同的买方。开证申请人为信用证交易的发起人。

Beneficiary (Full name and address)

填写受益人全称和详细地址。

受益人指信用证上所指定的有权使用该信用证的人。一般为出口人，也就是买卖合同的卖方。

Advising Bank

填写通知行名址。

如果该信用证需要通过收报行以外的另一家银行转递、通知或加具保兑后给受益人，该项目内填写该银行。

Amount

填写信用证金额，分别用数字小写和文字大写。以小写输入时须包括币种与金额。

如 USD89 600

U. S. DOLLARS EIGHTY NINE THOUSAND SIX HUNDRED ONLY。

Parital shipments

分批装运条款。填写跟单信用证项下是否允许分批装运。

Transshipment

转运条款。填写跟单信用证项下是否允许货物转运。

Loading on board/dispatch/taking in charge at/from

填写装运港。

not later than

填写最后装运期，如 050610。

For transportation to

填写目的港。

价格条款

根据合同内容选择或填写价格条款。

Credit available with

填写此信用证可由__________银行即期付款、承兑、议付、延期付款，即押汇银行

（出口地银行）名称。

如果该信用证为自由议付信用证，银行可用“ANY BANK IN...（地名/国名）”表示。

如果该信用证为自由议付信用证，而且对议付地点也无限制，可用“ANY BANK”表示。

Sight Payment

勾选此项，表示开具即期付款信用证。

即期付款信用证指受益人（出口商）根据开证行的指示开立即期汇票或无须汇票仅凭运输单据即可向指定银行提示请求付款的信用证。

Acceptance

勾选此项，表示开具承兑信用证。

承兑信用证指信用证规定开证行对受益人开立以开证行为付款人或以其他银行为付款人的远期汇票，在审单无误后，应承兑汇票并于到期日付款的信用证。

Negotiation

勾选此项，表示开具议付信用证。

议付信用证指开证行承诺延伸至第三当事人，即议付行，第三当事人拥有议付或购买受益人提交信用证规定的汇票/单据权利行为的信用证。如果信用证不限制某银行议付，可由受益人（出口商）选择任何愿意议付的银行，提交汇票、单据给所选银行请求议付的信用证称为自由议付信用证，反之为限制性议付信用证。

Deferred Payment at

勾选此项，表示开具延期付款信用证。

如果开具这类信用证，需要写明延期多少天付款，例如：at 60 days from payment confirmation（60 天承兑付款）、at 60 days from B/L date（提单日期后 60 天付款）等。

延期付款信用证指不需汇票，仅凭受益人提交的单据，审核相符，指定银行承担延期付款责任，延长至到期日付款。该信用证能够为欧洲地区进口商避免向政府交纳印花税，从而免开具汇票。

against the documents detailed herein

and beneficiary's draft（s）for ______% of invoice value

at ______ sight

drawn on

连同下列单据：

受益人按发票金额______%，作成限制为______天，付款人为____________的汇票。注意延期付款信用证不需要选择连同此单据。

“at　　sight”为付款期限。如果是即期，需要在“at　　sight”之间填“＊＊＊＊”或“_____”，不能留空。远期有几种情况：at ×× days after date（出票后××天），at ×× days after sight（见票后××天）或 at ×× days after date of B/L（提单日后××天）等。如果是远期，要注意两种表达方式的不同：一种是见票后××天（at ×× days after sight），一种是提单日后××天（at ×× days after B/L date）。这两种表达方式在付款时间上是不同的，“见单后××天”是指从银行见到申请人提示的单据时间算起，而“提单日后××天”是指从提单上的出具日开始计算的××天，所以如果能尽量争取到以“见单后××天”的条件成交，等于又争取了几天迟付款的时间。

"drawn on"为指定付款人。注意汇票的付款人应为开证行或指定的付款行。

如：against the documents detailed herein

and beneficiary's draft（s）for 100% of invoice value

at　* *　sight

drawn on　THE CHARTERED BANK

Documents required：(marked with ××)

信用证需要提交的单据（用"××"标明）。

根据国际商会《UCP600》，信用证业务是纯单据业务，与实际货物无关，所以信用证申请书上应按合同要求明确写出所应出具的单据，包括单据的种类，每种单据所表示的内容，正、副本份数，出单人等。一般要求提示的单据有提单（或空运单、收货单）、发票、箱单、重量证明、保险单、数量证明、质量证明、产地证、装船通知、商检证明以及其他申请人要求的证明等。

注意：如果是以 CFR 或 CIF 成交，就要要求对方出具的提单为"运费已付"（Freight Prepaid），如果是以 FOB 成交，就要要求对方出具的提单为"运费到付"（Freight Collect）。如果按 CIF 成交，申请人应要求受益人提供保险单，且注意保险险别，赔付地应要求在到货港，以便出现问题方便解决。汇票的付款人应为开证行或指定的付款行，不可规定为开证申请人，否则会被视作额外单据，例如：

（1）经签字的商业发票一式____份，标明信用证号__________和合同号__________。

（2）全套清洁已装船海运提单，作成空白抬头、空白背书，注明"运费［　］待付/［　］已付"，［　］标明运费金额，并通知________________。

空运提单收货人为____________，注明"运费［　］待付/［　］已付"，［　］标明运费金额，并通知____________。

（3）保险单/保险凭证一式________份，按发票金额的________%投保，注明赔付地在____________，以汇票同种货币支付，空白背书，投保一切险、战争险和__________。

（4）装箱单/重量证明一式________份，注明每一包装的数量、毛重和净重。

（5）数量/重量证一式________份，由____________出具。

（6）品质证一式______份，由［　］制造商/［　］公众认可的检验机构__________出具。

（7）产地证一式________份，由____________出具。

（8）受益人以传真/电传方式通知申请人装船证明副本，该证明须在装船后______日内发出，并通知该信用证号、船名、装运日以及货物的名称、数量、重量和金额。

other documents, if any

其他单据。

description of goods

货物描述。

如01005 CANNED SWEET CORN, 3060G×6TINS/CTN

QUANTITY：800 CARTON

PRICE：USD14/CTN

additional instructions

附加条款，对以上各条款未述之情况的补充和说明，且包括对银行的要求等。

(1) 开证行以外的所有银行费用由受益人担保。
(2) 所需单据须在运输单据出具日后________天内提交，但不得超过信用证有效期。
(3) 第三方为托运人不可接受，简式/背面空白提单不可接受。
(4) 数量及信用证金额允许有____% 的增减。
(5) 所有单据须指定___________船公司。

other terms, if any
其他条款。

工作任务

根据以下合同及补充资料，制作开证申请书。

【样单 4-1】

CONTRACT

Sellers	Contract No.	AB44001
A. B. C. TRADING CO., LTD. P. O. BOX8935, NEW TERMINAL, LATA. VISTA, OTTAWA, CANADA	Date	Feb. 12, 2021
	Signed at	GUANGZHOU
Buyers		
GUANGDONG FOREIGN TRADE IMP. AND EXP. GRANDTON 267 TIANHE ROAD GUANGZHOU, CHINA TEL: 86-20-31872589		

兹经买卖双方同意按下列条款成交
The undersigned sellers and buyers have agreed to close the following transactions according to the terms and conditions stipulated below

货号 Art. No.	品名及规格 Description	数量 Quantity	单价 Unit Price	金额 Amount
	AIR CONDITIONER (BREAK BRAND)			FOBC2 TORONTO
ART NO. P97811	KF-23GW	500PCS	USD 1, 000. 00	USD 500, 000. 00
ART NO. P97801	KF-25GW	500PCS	USD 1, 000. 00	USD 500, 000. 00
		1, 000PCS		USD 1, 000, 000. 00

数量及总值允许 5% 的增减，由卖方决定。
With 5% more or less both in amount and quantity allowed at the seller's option.

续表

总值 Total Value：USD 1 000 000. 00（U. S. DOLLARS ONE MILLION ONLY）
包装 Packing：1 PC PER CARTON
装运期 Time of Shipment：APR. 30,2021
装运口岸和目的地 Loading port & Destination：FROM TORONTO TO GUANGZHOU
保险由卖方按发票全部金额 110% 投保至　　　为止的　　　险。 Insurance：To be effected by sellers for 110% of full invoice value covering　　　up to　　　only.
付款条件：买方须于 2021 年 3 月 10 日前将不可撤销的即期信用证开到卖方，议付有效期延至上列装运期后 15 天在中国到期，该信用证中必须注明允许分运及装运。 Terms of payment：By Irrevocable，and Divisible Letter of Credit to be available by sight draft to reach the sellers before MAR. 10，1997 and to remain valid for negotiation in China until the 15th day after the foresaid Time of Shipment. The L/C must specify that transshipment and partial shipments are allowed.
装船标记 Shipment Mark：A. B. C. /GUANGZHOU/NOSI-1000/MADE IN CANADA
开立信用证时请注明成交确认书号码。 When opening L/C，please mention our contract number.
备注 Remarks：THE CREDIT IS SUBJECT TO《UCP600》（2020 REVISION）

THE SELLER：	THE BUYER：

补充资料：

申请日期：2021 年 2 月 20 日

【样单 4-2】

IRREVOCABLE DOCUMENTARY CREDIT APPLICATION

TO：BANK OF CHINA，GUANGZHOU BRANCH	Date：FEB. 20,2021
☐ Issue by airmail　　☐ With brief advice by teletransmission ☐ Issue by express delivery ☒ Issue by teletransmission（which shall be the operative instrument）	Credit No. Date and place of expiry MAY 15,2021 IN CHINA
Applicant GUANGDONG FOREIGN TRADE IMP. AND EXP. GRANDTON 267 TIANHE ROAD GUANGZHOU，CHINA	Beneficiary（Full name and address） A. B. C. TRADING CO.，LTD. P. O. BOX8935，NEW TERMINAL，LATA. VISTA，OTTAWA， CANADA

续表

<table>
<tr><td colspan="2">Advising Bank</td><td>Amount
USD 1, 000, 000. 00
U. S. DOLLAR ONE MILLION ONLY</td></tr>
<tr><td>Partial Shipments
☒ allowed ☐ not allowed</td><td>Transshipment
☒ allowed ☐ not allowed</td><td rowspan="3">Credit available with
ANY BANK
☐ by sight payment ☐ by acceptance
☒ by negotiation
☐ by deferred payment at
against the documents detailed herein
☒ and beneficiary's draft (s) for 100% of invoice value
at * * sight
drawn on</td></tr>
<tr><td colspan="2">Loading on board/dispatch/taking in charge at/from
TORONTO
not later than APR. 30, 2021
For transportation to GUANGZHOU PORT</td></tr>
<tr><td colspan="2">☒ FOB ☐ CFR ☐ CIF
☐ or other terms</td></tr>
<tr><td colspan="3">Documents Required: (marked with ×)
1. (×) Signed commercial invoice in 3 copies indicating L/C No. and Contract No.
2. (×) Full set of clean on board Bills of Lading made out to order and blank endorsed, marked "freight [×] to collect / [ ] prepaid [ ] showing freight amount" notifying THE APPLICANT WITH FULL NAME AND ADDRESS.
( ) Airway bills/cargo receipt/copy of railway bills issued by ______ showing "freight [ ] to collect/ [ ] prepaid [ ] indicating freight amount" and consigned to ______.
3. ( ) Insurance Policy/Certificate in ______ copies for ______ % of the invoice value showing claims payable in ______ in currency of the draft, blank endorsed, covering All Risks, War Risks and ______.
4. (×) Packing List/Weight Memo in 3 copies indicating quantity, gross and weights of each package.
5. ( ) Certificate of Quantity/Weight in ______ copies issued by ______.
6. ( ) Certificate of Quality in ______ copies issued by [ ] manufacturer/ [ ] public recognized surveyor ______.
7. (×) Certificate of Origin in 2 copies.
8. (×) Beneficiary's certificate copy of fax / telex dispatched to the applicant within 1 days after shipment advising L/C No., name of vessel, date of shipment, name, quantity, weight and value of goods.

Other Documents, if any

Description of Goods:
MEN'S DENIM UTILITY SHORT
COLOR: MEDDEST SANDBLAS
FABRIC CONTENT: 100% COTTON
QUANTITY: 2, 000 CARTONS
PRICE TERM: FOB NEW YORK</td></tr>
</table>

续表

COUNTRY OF ORIGIN AND MANUFACTURERS：UNITED STATES OF AMERICA，VICTORY FACTORY Additional instructions： 1. （×） All banking charges outside the opening bank are for beneficiary's account. 2. （×） Documents must be presented within 10 days after date of issuance of the transport documents but within the validity of this credit. 3. （　） Third party as shipper is not acceptable，Short Form/Blank back B/L is not acceptable. 4. （　） Both quantity and credit amount ______ % more or less are allowed. 5. （×） All documents must be sent to issuing bank by courier/speed post in one lot. （　） Other terms，if any

项目二：制作入境货物报检单

项目目标

能够根据合同和相关资料，制作入境货物报检单。

相关知识

制作入境货物报检单指导。

中华人民共和国出入境检验检疫
入境货物报检单

报检单位（加盖公章）：　　　　　　　　　　　　　　　＊编号

报检单位登记号：　　　　　联系人：　　　　电话：　　　　报检日期：　　年　　月　　日

收货人	（中文）					
	（外文）					
发货人	（中文）					
	（外文）					
货物名称（中/外文）	H. S. 编码	原产国（地区）	数/重量	货物总值	包装种类及件数	
运输工具名称号码			合同号			
贸易方式		贸易国家（地区）		提单/运单号		
到货日期		启运国家（地区）		许可证/审批号		
卸毕日期		启运口岸		入境口岸		

续表

<table>
<tr><td>索赔有效期至</td><td></td><td>经停口岸</td><td></td><td>目的地</td><td></td></tr>
<tr><td>集装箱规格、数量及号码</td><td colspan="5"></td></tr>
<tr><td colspan="2" rowspan="2">合同、信用证订立的特殊条款以及其他要求</td><td rowspan="2"></td><td>货物存放地点</td><td colspan="2"></td></tr>
<tr><td>用　　途</td><td colspan="2"></td></tr>
<tr><td colspan="2">随附单据（划"√"或补填）</td><td>标记及号码</td><td colspan="2">＊外商投资财产（划"√"）</td><td>□是　□否</td></tr>
<tr><td rowspan="4">□合同
□发票
□提/运单
□兽医卫生证书
□植物检疫证书
□动物检疫证书
□卫生证书
□原产地证
□许可/审批文件</td><td rowspan="4">□到货通知
□装箱单
□质保书
□理货清单
□磅码单
□验收报告
□
□
□</td><td rowspan="4"></td><td colspan="3">＊检验检疫费</td></tr>
<tr><td>总金额
（人民币元）</td><td colspan="2"></td></tr>
<tr><td>计费人</td><td colspan="2"></td></tr>
<tr><td>收费人</td><td colspan="2"></td></tr>
<tr><td colspan="3" rowspan="3">报检人郑重声明：
本人被授权报验。
上列填写内容正确属实。
签名：</td><td colspan="3">领取证单</td></tr>
<tr><td>日期</td><td colspan="2"></td></tr>
<tr><td>签名</td><td colspan="2"></td></tr>
</table>

注：有"＊"号栏由出入境检验检疫机关填写　　◆国家质检总局制

注：

报检单位（加盖公章）栏：填写报检单位全称并加盖公章（已做报检专用章备案的企业可加盖报检专用章）。

报检单位登记号：填写报检单位在检验检疫机构注册登记的10位数代码。

联系人：填写报检单位联系人姓名。

电话：填写联系人电话。

报检日期：此栏不需填写，自动显示检验检疫机构电子平台系统日期。

编号：此栏不需填写，由系统自动生成15位数报检流水号。

收货人：填报对外签订并执行进出口贸易合同的中国境内企业或单位全称及注册号，包括自行从境外进口货物的单位或外贸代理单位。对于未经注册登记的特殊单位，应向检验检疫机构申请特殊号办理。

企业性质：根据收货人的企业性质，在对应的□内打"√"。

发货人：填写外贸合同中的发货人，英文名应录入。

货物名称：录入HS编码条目名或报检货物的实际名称及规格（需与发票上所列货物的规格和名称一致）。

货物名称应具体列明，不得填写笼统的商品类别，如玩具应如实填报塑料玩具或电动玩具等。

废旧物品应在品名后标注“废”或“旧”等字样。

货物品名应按“含检验检疫类别的货物、无检验检疫类别的废旧货物、无检验检疫类别的普通货物”的顺序列明。（注：法检商品一份报检单最多只能申报 20 个品名，多于 20 个品名的需分单申报）。

HS 编码：填报货物对应的商品 10 位数编码，以当年海关公布的商品税则编码分类为准。

原产国（地区）：填报进口货物的生产、开采或加工制造的国家（地区），相同品名的进口货物原产国不同应分别填报原产国（地区）。

数/重量：根据 HS 编码对应的法定第一计量单位（即 HS 标准量）填写数量或重量，依实际情况也可同时输入数量和重量（法定计量单位应以《中华人民共和国海关统计商品目录》中的计量单位为准）。根据 HS 归类规则，货物零部件按整机归类的，法定计量单位是非重量的，其对应的法定数量按 0.1 申报。

货物总值：填报本报检批货物的总值及币种，应与发票上的货物总值及币种一致。同一批次多品名货物应分别列明各自的货值及币种（如申报货物总值和国际、国内市场价格有较大差异，检验检疫机构保留核价的权利）。

包装种类及数量：填写货物运输的包装种类及数量，并注明包装材质。填写“其他”的注明实际包装种类，并在“辅助包装”栏内注明“有木”或“无木”。

运输工具名称号码：填写货物入境的运输工具的名称及号码。选择船舶、飞机、汽车、火车等（不包括国内运输）。海运货物报检时录入运输工具号码，格式为：交通工具名称/航次。若报检时未能确定运输工具编号的，可只填写运输工具类别。

贸易方式：填写货物进口的贸易方式，如一般贸易、来料加工、进料加工、展览品等，贸易方式应与报关单相符（如系统中无对应的贸易方式，应根据实际贸易情况填写“其他贸易性货物”或“其他非贸易性货物”）。

贸易国别（地区）：填报合同关系人所在国别。以合同提示为准，需与报关单一致。

提运单号：进口货物提单或运单的编号，一份报检单只允许填报一个提运单号。江海运输的填报进口提货单号；铁路运输的填报运单号；空运的应在该栏内填报总运单号，分运单号应填报在“运输工具名称号码”栏运输工具之后（无分运单的可不填）；汽车陆路运输的填报运输车辆的国内行驶车牌号；邮政运输的填报邮政包裹单号。

启运国家（地区）：填报进口货物起始发出的国家（地区），对发生运输中转的货物，如中转地未发生任何商业性交易，则启运国家（地区）不变。如中转地发生商业性交易，则以中转地为启运国家（地区）填报。

许可证/审批号：该栏涉及的许可证/审批号类型包括：进口动植物及产品的检疫审批、进口电池产品备案书、装运前检验证书、进口旧机电产品备案书、进口旧机电免装运前检验证明书、CCC 证书或 CCC 免办证明等。对于须凭许可证、审批号等报检的货物应在该栏内填报相应的凭证编号。如进口旧机电：申报时须在该栏勾选“进口旧机电产品备案书”项并录入相应的备案书编号；再如实施国家强制性认证制的产品：申报时须在该栏勾选“CCC 证书或 CCC 免办证明”项并录入相应的证书号或免办号（有关 CCC 证书、免办证明或不需 CCC 认证的情况详见 www.shciq.gov.cn 网站专题信息→认证监管→CCC 入境验证→CCC 入境验证商品报检指南）。对于无对应类别选项的，勾选“进口其他证书”并录入证书编号。

到货日期：填报货物到达国境口岸的日期。

卸毕日期：填写货物全部卸离运载工具的实际日期。

合同号：填写外贸合同、订单的全部字头和号码。

启运口岸：填写装运货物的交通工具直运至我国的启运口岸。

入境口岸：填写装运货物的交通工具入境时首次停靠的口岸。

索赔期：填写外贸合同中的规定日期。

经停口岸：填写货物启运后到达目的地前中途曾经停靠或发生装卸货的口岸名称。

目的地：填写货物的境内使用、销售地或最终运抵地。

集装箱规格、数量及号码：若以集装箱运输应填写集装箱的规格、数量及号码。当一个报检批有两种或以上规格时，应按不同规格分别录入。

合同订立物特殊条款以及其他要求：填写在外贸合同中特别订立的有关质量、卫生等条款或报检单位对本批货物检验检疫的特别要求。

货物存放地点：填写货物实施现场采样或监督查验时的实际存放地点。

用途：填写货物用途，动植物及其产品报检时应按实际用途录入，如种用、食用、奶用、观赏或演艺、伴侣、实验、药用、饲用、加工等。

随附单据：根据所附报检资料在列表中选择，并在所提供单据对应的“□”上打“√”，若选项中没有相应单据应自行补填。

标记及号码：标记唛码中除图形以外的文字、数字，应与合同、发票等外贸单据保持一致。若没有标记号码应录入“N/M”，该栏内不得填报任何无关内容。

外商投资财产：由检验检疫工作人员填写。

检验检疫计费：由检验检疫工作人员填写。

报检人郑重声明：报检人员必须亲笔签名。

领取单证：报检人在领取证单时填写领证日期并签名。

工作任务

2021 年 3 月 15 日，广东国际进出口贸易公司（单位登记号：5124785269，联系人：李平）收到提单号为 SOC092588 的进口货物到货通知，计划 3 月 20 日卸货。公司于 3 月 19 日填制入境货物报检单，随附合同、发票箱单及提单向检验机关申请检验。进口商品为 AIR CONDITIONER（BREAK BRAND）（BREAK 牌空调），海关编码 84151021，用于外贸自营内销。本次运输的船名航次为 Volendam Voy. 0932，用 3 个 40 尺集装箱装运，现存放于广州市第二码头。

【样单 4-3】

中华人民共和国出入境检验检疫
入境货物报检单

报检单位（加盖公章）：广东国际进出口贸易公司　　　　*编　　号________

报检单位登记号：5124785269　　联系人：李平　　电话：020-31872589　　报检日期：2021 年 3 月 19 日

收货人	（中文）广东国际进出口贸易公司	企业性质（划“√”）	□合资　□合作　□外资
	（外文）GUANGDONG FOREIGN TRADE IMP. AND EXP. GRANDTON		
发货人	（中文）//		
	（外文）A. B. C. TRADING CO., LTD.		

货物名称（中/外文）	H. S. 编码	原产国（地区）	数/重量	货物总值	包装种类及数量
BREAK 牌空调 AIR CONDITIONER (BREAK BRAND) ART NO. P97811 KF-23GW ART NO. P97801 KF-25GW	84151021	加拿大	500 台 500 台	USD 1,000,000.00	1,000 箱

运输工具名称号码	Volendam Voy. 0932	合同号	AB44001

贸易方式	一般贸易	贸易国别（地区）	加拿大	提单/运单号	SOC092588
到货日期	21-03-15	启运国家（地区）	加拿大	许可证/审批号	
卸货日期	21-03-20	启运口岸	多伦多	入境口岸	广州
索赔有效期至		经停口岸		目的地	广州
集装箱规格、数量及号码	40 尺 * 3				
合同、信用证订立的检验检疫条款或特殊要求		货物存放地点	广州市第二码头		
		用途	外贸自营内销		

随附单据（划“√”或补填）		标记及号码	*外商投资资产（划“√”）	□是□否
☑合同 ☑发票 ☑提/运单 □兽医卫生证书 □植物检疫证书 □动物检疫证书 □卫生证书 □原产地证 □许可/审批文件	□到货通知 ☑装箱单 □质保书 □理货清单 □磅码单 □验收报告 □ □ □	A. B. C. GUANGZHOU NOSI-1000 MADE IN CANADA	*检验检疫费	
			总金额（人民币元）	
			计费人	
			收费人	

续表

报检人郑重声明： 1. 本人被授权报检。 2. 上列填写内容正确属实。 签名：李平	领 取 证 单	
	日期	
	签名	

注：有“＊”号栏由出入境检验检疫机关填写　　◆国家出入境检验检疫局制

［1-2（2000. 1. 1）］

项目三：制作入境货物报关单

项目目标

能够根据合同和相关资料，制作入境货物报关单。

相关知识

制作入境货物报关单指导

中华人民共和国海关进口货物报关单

预录入编号：不填　　海关编号：不填　　页码/页数：

进口口岸 实际进境口岸海关名+4位海关代码	备案号 手册（BCDE）纸质手册、电子手账册/征免税证明Z特定减免税、国家减免税/原产地代码及编号Y	进口日期 装载该货物的运输工具申报进境日期，一般可不填	申报日期 海关接受货物报关的日期，例如20110811 不得早于进口日期
经营单位 对外签订并执行合同的境内单位中文名+10位单位代码	运输方式 1. 水路运输 2. 航空运输	运输工具名称 1. 船名/航次 2. 航班号	提运单号 1. 提单号（B/L NO.） 2. 如果是航空运输，则填总运单号-分运单号
收货单位 境内最终消费使用单位中文名+10位单位代码	贸易方式 由备案号决定	征免性质 由备案号、贸易方式决定	征税比例 不填
许可证号 限制进口、两用物项进口、废物进口等需要填写	起运国（地区） 直接运到我国或中转未发生交易运到我国	装货港 进口货物进境前最后一个境外装运港	境内目的地 进口货物在境内的最终消费使用地

续表

批准文号 进口不填	成交方式 1. CIF 2. CFR 3. FOB	运费 1. 不填 2. 不填 3. 要填	保费 1. 不填 2. 要填 3. 要填	杂费 折扣、佣金或手续费，如果要扣除的应在前面加负号。 502/-1000/3 如发票单独列出才需要填写
合同协议号 CONTRACT NO.	件数 除集装箱外的货物最大外包装数量	包装种类 除集装箱外的货物最大外包装材料	毛重（公斤） GROSS WEIGHT 或 G/W	净重（公斤） 都在装箱单找 NET WEIGHT 或 N/W

集装箱号 不能空非集装箱 填 0 CONTAINER NO./SIZE/TARE WEIGHT 只能填一个，有多的填在备注中	随附单据 出入境通关单（A/B）、自动进口许可证（7/O/V）、原产地证书（Y）、关税配额许可证（e） 只能填一个，有多的填在备注中	用途 由备案号、贸易方式决定

标记唛码及备注

MARKS

备注：1. 多的集装箱号

2. 随附单据

项号	商品编号	商品名称、规格型号	数量及单位	原产国（地区）	单价	总价	币制	征免
依次填商品项目，例如：1	进口货物的商品编码	第一行：中文商品名称；第二行：规格型号。必要时加注原文	第一行：法定第一计量单位；第二行：法定第二计量单位，依次填写	产地（地区）代码，无法确认的填报“国别不详”代码 701	单位价格	商品总价	成交币种	征免由备案号、贸易方式决定，一般填写照章征免

后面的内容一般不填

税费征收情况

录入员 录入单位	兹声明以上申报无讹并承担法律责任	海关审单批注及放行日期（签章） 审单 审价
报关员 申报单位（签章） 单位地址 邮编 电话 填制日期		征税 统计 查验 放行

工作任务

2021 年 3 月 15 日，广东国际进出口贸易公司（单位登记号：5124785269，联系人：李平）收到提单号为 SOC092588 的进口货物到货通知，计划 3 月 20 日卸货。公司于 3 月 23 日填制入境货物报关单，随附合同、发票箱单及提单向检验机关申请检验。进口商品为 AIR CONDITIONER（BREAK BRAND）（BREAK 牌空调），海关编码 84151021，用于外贸自营内销。本次运输的船名航次为 Volendam Voy. 0932，用 3 个 40 尺集装箱装运，现存放于广州市第二码头。

【样单 4-4】

中华人民共和国海关进口货物报关单

预录入编号：619110002　　　　海关编号：

<table>
<tr><td colspan="3">进口口岸　广州海关 5101</td><td colspan="2">备案号</td><td colspan="2">进口日期
2021-03-15</td><td colspan="2">申报日期
2021-03-23</td></tr>
<tr><td colspan="3">经营单位　广东国际进出口贸易公司
4201003830</td><td>运输方式
江海运输</td><td colspan="3">运输工具名称
Volendam Voy. 0932</td><td colspan="2">提运单号
SOCO02596</td></tr>
<tr><td colspan="3">收货单位　广东国际进出口贸易公司
4201003830</td><td colspan="2">贸易方式
一般贸易 0110</td><td colspan="2">征免性质
一般征税（101）</td><td colspan="2">征税比例</td></tr>
<tr><td colspan="2">许可证号</td><td colspan="2">起运国（地区）
加拿大（501）</td><td colspan="3">装货港
多伦多（1303）</td><td colspan="2">境内目的地</td></tr>
<tr><td colspan="2">批准文号</td><td>成交方式
FOB</td><td colspan="2">运费（美元）
费额　543.00</td><td colspan="3">保费（美元）
费额　139.00</td><td>杂费
//</td></tr>
<tr><td colspan="2">合同协议号　AB44001</td><td colspan="2">件数
1 000</td><td colspan="2">包装种类
纸箱</td><td colspan="2">毛重（公斤）
1 300</td><td>净重（公斤）
1 100</td></tr>
<tr><td colspan="2">集装箱号　FCIU8275823</td><td colspan="5">随附单据</td><td colspan="2">用途
外贸自营内销</td></tr>
<tr><td colspan="9">标记唛码及备注
A. B. C.　　　　集装箱号　FCIU8275824　FCIU8275825
GUANGZHOU
NOSI-1000
MADE IN CANADA</td></tr>
</table>

项号	商品编号	商品名称、规格型号	数量及单位	原产国（地区）	单价	总价	币制	征免
1	84151021	BREAK 牌空调	1 000 件	加拿大（501）	1 000	1 000 000.00	USD 美元	照章征税

续表

<table>
<tr><td colspan="3"></td></tr>
<tr><td colspan="3">税费征收情况</td></tr>
<tr><td>录入员　录入单位</td><td>兹声明以上申报无讹并承担法律责任</td><td>海关审单批注及放行日期（签章）
审单　　审价</td></tr>
<tr><td colspan="2" rowspan="2">报关员
申报单位（签章）
单位地址
邮编　　电话　　填制日期</td><td>征税　　统计</td></tr>
<tr><td>查验　　放行</td></tr>
</table>

项目四：制作进口付汇核销单

项目目标

能够根据合同和相关资料，制作进口付汇核销单。

相关知识

制作进口付汇核销单指导

贸易进口付汇核销单（代申报单）

印单局代码：　　　　　　　　　　　　　　　　核销单编号：

<table>
<tr><td>单位代码</td><td>单位名称</td><td>所在地外汇局名称</td></tr>
<tr><td>付汇银行名称</td><td>收汇人国别</td><td></td></tr>
<tr><td>收款人是否在保税区：是□否□</td><td colspan="2">交易附言</td></tr>
<tr><td colspan="3">对外付汇币种　　　　对外付汇总额
其中：购汇金额　　　　现汇金额　　　　其他方式金额
人民币账号　　　　外汇账号</td></tr>
<tr><td colspan="3">付汇性质
□正常付汇
□不在名录　　□90 天以上信用证　　□90 天以上托收　　□异地付汇
□90 天以上到货　　□转口贸易
备案表编号</td></tr>
</table>

续表

<table>
<tr><td colspan="2">预计到货日期</td><td colspan="2">进口批件号</td><td>合同/发票号</td></tr>
<tr><td colspan="5">结算方式</td></tr>
<tr><td colspan="5">信用证 90 天以内□　90 天以上□　承兑日期　/ /　付汇日期　/ /　期限　天</td></tr>
<tr><td colspan="5">托收　90 天以内□　90 天以上□　承兑日期　/ /　付汇日期　/ /　期限　天</td></tr>
<tr><td rowspan="7">汇
款</td><td colspan="4">预付货款□　货到付汇（凭报关单付汇）□　付汇日期　/ /</td></tr>
<tr><td>报关单号</td><td>报关日期　/ /</td><td>报关单币种</td><td>金额</td></tr>
<tr><td>报关单号</td><td>报关日期　/ /</td><td>报关单币种</td><td>金额</td></tr>
<tr><td>报关单号</td><td>报关日期　/ /</td><td>报关单币种</td><td>金额</td></tr>
<tr><td>报关单号</td><td>报关日期　/ /</td><td>报关单币种</td><td>金额</td></tr>
<tr><td>报关单号</td><td>报关日期　/ /</td><td>报关单币种</td><td>金额</td></tr>
<tr><td colspan="4">（若报关单填写不完，可另附纸。）</td></tr>
<tr><td colspan="5">其他□　付汇日期　/ /</td></tr>
<tr><td colspan="5">以下由付汇银行填写
申报号码：□□□□□□□□□□□□□□□□□□□□□□
业务编号：　审核日期：　/ /　（付汇银行签章）</td></tr>
</table>

进口单位签章

注：

“贸易进口付汇核销单（代申报单）”（以下简称进口核销单）指由国家外汇管理局监制、保管和发放，进口单位和银行填写，银行凭之为进口单位办理贸易进口项下的进口售付汇和核销的凭证。每份进口核销单只能办理一笔售付汇手续。

根据《国际收支统计申报办法实施细则》，进口核销单既用于贸易项下进口售付汇核销，又用于国际收支申报统计。

在填写进口核销单时，应注意各项内容与售付汇情况是否一致。

印单局代码：为印制本核销单的 6 位外汇局代码。

核销单编号：由各印制本核销单的外汇局自行编制。

单位代码：应根据国家技术监督局颁发的组织机构代码填写。

所在地外汇局名称：指付汇单位所在地外汇局名称。

付汇银行名称：通常为进口地银行。

收汇人国别：指该笔对外付款的实际收款人常驻国家，即出口国家，如 China。

交易编码：应根据本笔对外付汇交易的性质对应国家外汇管理局国际收支交易编码表填写。

0101　一般贸易

0102　国家间、国际组织无偿援助和赠送的物资

0103　华侨、港澳台同胞、外籍华人捐赠物资

0104　补偿贸易

0105　来料加工装配贸易

0106　进料加工装配贸易

0107　寄售代销贸易
0108　边境小额贸易
0109　来料加工装配进口的设备
0111　租赁贸易
0112　免税外汇商品
0113　出料加工贸易
0114　易货贸易
0115　外商投资企业进口供加工内销的料、件
0116　其他
0201　预付货款

交易附言：是付款人对该笔对外付款用途的描述，可不填。

对外付汇币种、报关单币种：应按币种的英文缩写填写，如 USD。

对外付汇总额、购汇金额、现汇金额、其他方式金额、汇款中报关单“金额”：应用阿拉伯数字填写。

人民币账号、外汇账号：如所付款项系从现汇账户中支出，则在“外汇账号”栏填写该现汇账户的账号；如所付款项系从银行购得的外汇，则在“人民币账号”栏填写其用于购汇的人民币账户的账号。

付汇性质：应选择适当的付汇性质打√。其中，“正常付汇”指除不在名录、90 天以上信用证、90 天以上托收、异地付汇、90 天以上到货、转口贸易、境外工程使用物资、真实性审查以外无须办理进口付汇备案业务的付款业务；“90 天以上信用证”及“90 天以上托收”均指付汇日期距承兑日期在 90 天以上的对外付汇业务；除“正常付汇”之外的各付汇性质在标注√时，均须对应填写备案表编号。

结算方式：应选择适当的结算方式打√。其中，90 天以内信用证、90 天以内托收的付汇日期距该笔付汇的承兑日期均小于 90 天且含 90 天；90 天以上信用证、90 天以上托收的付汇日期距该笔付汇的承兑日期均大于 90 天；结算方式为“货到付汇”时，应同时填写对应“报关单号”“报关日期”“报关单币种”“金额”。

申报号码：共 22 位，第 1 至第 6 位为地区标识码，第 7 至第 10 位为银行标识码，第 11 和第 12 位为金融机构顺序号，第 13 至第 18 位为该笔贸易进口付汇的付汇日期或该笔对外付汇的申报日期，最后 4 位为银行营业部门的当日业务流水码。

其他各栏：均应按栏目提示对应填写。

工作任务

根据合同【样单 4-1】和下列信息，填制进口付汇核销单。

补充资料：

（1）印单局代码：320000。
（2）核销单编号：00492425。
（3）单位代码：13438589-8。
（4）所在地外汇局名称 ：省外汇局。
（5）付汇银行名称 ：中行广东省分行。

（6）交易编码：0101。

（7）收款人是否在保税区：否。

（8）进口批件号：20313768。

（9）付汇日期：2021 年 4 月 5 日。

【样单 4-5】

贸易进口付汇核销单（代申报单）

印单局代码：320000　　　　核销单编号：00492425

单位代码　13438589-8		单位名称 广东国际进出口贸易公司		所在地外汇局名称 省外汇局
付汇银行名称　中行广东省分行		收汇人国别　加拿大		交易编码 0 1 0 1
收款人是否在保税区：是□否☑		交易附言		
对外付汇币种/美元　　对外付汇总额 1 000 000. 00 其中：购汇金额 1 000 000. 00　　现汇金额　　其他方式金额 人民币账号　　外汇账号				
付汇性质 ☑正常付汇 □不在名录　□90 天以上信用证　□90 天以上托收　□异地付汇 □90 天以上到货　□转口贸易 备案表编号				
预计到货日期 2021/03/20		进口批件号 20313768		合同/发票号 AB44001
结算方式				
信用证 90 天以内☑　90 天以上□　承兑日期　/ /　付汇日期　21/04/05　期限　天				
托收　90 天以内□　90 天以上□　承兑日期　/ /　付汇日期　/ /　期限　天				
汇款	预付货款□　货到付汇（凭报关单付汇）□　付汇日期　/ /			
	报关单号	报关日期/　/	报关单币种	金额
	报关单号	报关日期/　/	报关单币种	金额
	报关单号	报关日期/　/	报关单币种	金额
	报关单号	报关日期/　/	报关单币种	金额
	报关单号	报关日期/　/	报关单币种	金额
	（若报关单填写不完，可另附纸。）			
其他 □　付汇日期　/ /				
以下由付汇银行填写 申报号码：□□□□□□□□□□□□□□□□□□□□□□ 业务编号：　　审核日期：　/ /　（付汇银行签章）				

进口单位签章

能力训练

根据以下资料，制作开证申请书、进口报关单、进口报检单、进口付汇核销单。

PAYMENT: BY IRREVOCABLE FREELY NEGOTIABLE L/C AGAINST SIGHT DRAFTS FOR 100PCT OF INVOICE VALUE AND THE DOCUMENTS DETAILED HEREUNDER.

DOCUMETNS:

1. INVOICES IN TRIPLICATE
2. PACKING LIST IN TRIPLICATE
3. FULL SET OF CLEAN ON BOARD BILLS OF LADING MADE OUT TO ORDER AND BLANK ENDORSED NOTIFYING THE APPLICANT WITH FULL NAME AND ADDRESS MARKED FREIGHT COLLECT.
4. CERTIFICATE OF ORIGIN IN DUPLICATE
5. BENEFICIARY'S CERTIFIED COPY OF FAX TO THE APPLICANT WITHIN 1 DAY AFTER SHIPMENT ADVISING GOODS NAME OF VESSEL, INVOICE VALUE, DATE OF SHIPMENT, QUANTITY AND WEIGHT.

OTHER TERMS AND CONDITIONS:

1. L/C TO BE ISSUED BY TELETRANSMISSION.
2. THE BUYER SHALL BEAR ALL BANKING CHARGES INCURRED INSIDE THE ISSUING BANK.
3. ALL DOCUMENTS MUST BE MAILED IN ONE LOT TO THE ISSUING BANK BY COURIER SERVICE.
4. PRESENTATION PERIOD: WITHIN 10 DAYS AFTER THE DATE OF SHIPMENT.

2021 年 8 月 12 日，上海朗明商贸有限公司（单位登记号：52304125596）填制入境货物报检单，随附合同、发票、装箱单、许可证、提单等申请报检。

相关资料如下：

卖方：EAST AGENT COMPANY（东方代理公司）

买方：SHANGHAI LANGMING TRADING CO. , LTD.（上海朗明商贸有限公司）

电话：021-58693215，联系人：王明

合同号：03TG28711

提单号：SOC002596

进口许可证号：CT88661125839

品名：H6-59940BS GOLF CAPS（高尔夫球帽）

H. S. 编码：59019091

数量：1 800 打

包装：每 50 打装一纸箱

单价：USD8. 10/打

集装箱：20' * 1

唛头：V. H

SHANGHAI

C/NO. 1-36

MADE IN JAPAN

商品用途：外贸自营内销

装运港：大阪

目的港：上海

到货日期：2021 年 8 月 9 日

卸货日期：2021 年 8 月 13 日

索赔时效：两年

货物存放地点：上海市康元街 119 号

2021 年 8 月 11 日，上海朗明商贸有限公司（单位海关代码：3201586932）填制进口货物报关单，委托代理公司向上海海关（口岸代码：2200）申报。

相关资料如下：

预录入编号：819110002

贸易方式：一般贸易，代码 0110

运输方式：江海运输

征免性质：一般征税，代码（101）

币制：USD 美元

征免方式：照章征税

毛重：13kgs

净重：11kgs

单价：USD 8.10 CFR SHANGHAI

总价：14 580.00 美元

出口国：日本，代码：116

装运港：大阪，代码：1303

船名：Veendam

航次：DY105-08

集装箱号：FCIU8275823

保费费额：USD 139.000

进口日期：2021 年 8 月 9 日

印单局代码：450000

核销单编号：07492457

单位代码：43438589-9

所在地外汇局名称 ：上海市外汇局

付汇银行名称 ：中国银行上海分行

交易编码：0101

收款人是否在保税区：否

进口批件号：51313768

付汇日期：2021 年 9 月 5 日

【样单 4-6】

IRREVOCABLE DOCUMENTARY CREDIT APPLICATION

TO	Date
☐ Issue by airmail　☐ With brief advice by teletransmission ☐ Issue by express delivery ☐ Issue by teletransmission (which shall be the operative instrument)	Credit No. Date and place of expiry
Applicant	Beneficiary (Full name and address)
Advising Bank	Amount
Partial shipments ☐ allowed　☐ not allowed Transshipment ☐ allowed　☐ not allowed	Credit available with ☐ by sight payment　☐ by acceptance ☐ by negotiation ☐ by deferred payment at ______ against the documents detailed herein ☐ and beneficiary's draft (s) for ____% of invoice value at ________ sight drawn on
Loading on board/dispatch/taking in charge at/from not later than For transportation to	
☐ FOB　☐ CFR　☐ CIF ☐ or other terms	

Documents required: (marked with ×)

1. (　) Signed commercial invoice in ____ copies indicating L/C No. and Contract No.
2. (　) Full set of clean on board Bills of Lading made out to order and blank endorsed, marked "freight [　] to collect / [　] prepaid [　] showing freight amount" notifying ________________.
   (　) Airway bills/cargo receipt/copy of railway bills issued by ____________ showing "freight [　] to collect/ [　] prepaid [　] indicating freight amount" and consigned to ________.
3. (　) Insurance Policy/Certificate in ______ copies for ______ % of the invoice value showing claims payable in ____________ in currency of the draft, blank endorsed, covering All Risks, War Risks and ____ ________________.
4. (　) Packing List/Weight Memo in ____ copies indicating quantity, gross and weights of each package.
5. (　) Certificate of Quantity/Weight in ________ copies issued by ____________.
6. (　) Certificate of Quality in ______ copies issued by [　] manufacturer/ [　] public recognized surveyor ____________.
7. (　) Certificate of Origin in ____ copies.
8. (　) Beneficiary's certificate copy of fax / telex dispatched to the applicant within ______ days after shipment advising L/C No. , name of vessel, date of shipment, name, quantity, weight and value of goods.

续表

Other documents, if any

Description of goods:

Additional instructions:

1. ( ) All banking charges outside the opening bank are for beneficiary's account.
2. ( ) Documents must be presented within ____ days after date of issuance of the transport documents but within the validity of this credit.
3. ( ) Third party as shipper is not acceptable, Short Form/Blank back B/L is not acceptable.
4. ( ) Both quantity and credit amount ______% more or less are allowed.
5. ( ) All documents must be sent to issuing bank by courier/speed post in one lot.

( ) Other terms, if any

【样单 4-7】

中华人民共和国海关进口货物报关单

预录入编号：　　　　　　　　海关编号：

进口口岸	备案号	进口日期	申报日期	
经营单位	运输方式	运输工具名称	提运单号	
收货单位	贸易方式	征免性质	征税比例	
许可证号	起运国（地区）	装货港	境内目的地	
批准文号	成交方式	运费（美元）	保费（美元）	杂费
合同协议号	件数	包装种类	毛重（公斤）	净重（公斤）
集装箱号	随附单据	用途		
标记唛码及备注				
项号 商品编号 商品名称、规格型号 数量及单位 原产国（地区） 单价 总价 币制 征免				

续表

<table>
<tr><td colspan="3"></td></tr>
<tr><td colspan="3"></td></tr>
<tr><td colspan="3"></td></tr>
<tr><td colspan="3"></td></tr>
<tr><td colspan="3">税费征收情况</td></tr>
<tr><td>录入员　录入单位</td><td>兹声明以上申报无讹并承担法律责任</td><td rowspan="2">海关审单批注及放行日期（签章）
审单　审价</td></tr>
<tr><td colspan="2" rowspan="3">报关员
申报单位（签章）
单位地址
邮编　电话　填制日期</td></tr>
<tr><td>征税　统计</td></tr>
<tr><td>查验　放行</td></tr>
</table>

【样单 4-8】

中华人民共和国出入境检验检疫
入境货物报检单

报检单位（加盖公章）：　　　　　　　　　　　　　　　　　*编号

报检单位登记号：　　　　　联系人：　　　　电话：　　　　报检日期：　　年　月　日

<table>
<tr><td rowspan="2">收货人</td><td colspan="6">（中文）</td></tr>
<tr><td colspan="6">（外文）</td></tr>
<tr><td rowspan="2">发货人</td><td colspan="6">（中文）</td></tr>
<tr><td colspan="6">（外文）</td></tr>
<tr><td colspan="2">货物名称（中/外文）</td><td>H. S. 编码</td><td>原产国（地区）</td><td>数/重量</td><td>货物总值</td><td>包装种类及件数</td></tr>
<tr><td colspan="2"></td><td></td><td></td><td></td><td></td><td></td></tr>
</table>

运输工具名称号码				合同号	
贸易方式		贸易国家（地区）		提单/运单号	
到货日期		启运国家（地区）		许可证/审批号	
卸毕日期		启运口岸		入境口岸	
索赔有效期至		经停口岸		目的地	
集装箱规格、数量及号码					

续表

<table>
<tr><td colspan="2">合同、信用证订立的特殊条款以及其他要求</td><td colspan="2"></td><td colspan="2">货物存放地点</td><td></td></tr>
<tr><td colspan="2"></td><td colspan="2"></td><td colspan="2">用途</td><td></td></tr>
<tr><td colspan="2">随附单据（划“√”或补填）</td><td>标记及号码</td><td colspan="3">＊外商投资财产（划“√”）</td><td>□是 □否</td></tr>
<tr><td rowspan="4">□合同
□发票
□提/运单
□兽医卫生证书
□植物检疫证书
□动物检疫证书
□卫生证书
□原产地证
□许可/审批文件</td><td rowspan="4">□到货通知
□装箱单
□质保书
□理货清单
□磅码单
□验收报告
□
□
□</td><td rowspan="4"></td><td colspan="4">＊检验检疫费</td></tr>
<tr><td colspan="2">总金额
（人民币元）</td><td colspan="2"></td></tr>
<tr><td colspan="2">计费人</td><td colspan="2"></td></tr>
<tr><td colspan="2">收费人</td><td colspan="2"></td></tr>
<tr><td colspan="3" rowspan="3">报检人郑重声明：
1. 本人被授权报验。
2. 上列填写内容正确属实。
签名：________</td><td colspan="4">领取证单</td></tr>
<tr><td colspan="2">日期</td><td colspan="2"></td></tr>
<tr><td colspan="2">签名</td><td colspan="2"></td></tr>
</table>

注：有“＊”号栏由出入境检验检疫机关填写　　　　◆国家质检总局制

【样单 4-9】

贸易进口付汇核销单（代申报单）

印单局代码：　　　　　　　　　　　　　　　　核销单编号：

<table>
<tr><td>单位代码</td><td>单位名称</td><td>所在地外汇局名称</td></tr>
<tr><td>付汇银行名称</td><td>收汇人国别</td><td>交易编码□□□□</td></tr>
<tr><td>收款人是否在保税区：是□否□</td><td colspan="2">交易附言</td></tr>
<tr><td colspan="3">对外付汇币种　　　　　　对外付汇总额
其中：购汇金额　　　　　现汇金额　　　　　其他方式金额
　　　人民币账号　　　　外汇账号</td></tr>
<tr><td colspan="3">付汇性质
□正常付汇
□不在名录　　□90 天以上信用证　　□90 天以上托收　　□异地付汇
□90 天以上到货　　□转口贸易
备案表编号</td></tr>
<tr><td>预计到货日期</td><td>进口批件号</td><td>合同/发票号</td></tr>
<tr><td colspan="3">结算方式</td></tr>
<tr><td colspan="3">信用证 90 天以内□　90 天以上□　承兑日期　/　/　付汇日期　/　/　期限　天</td></tr>
<tr><td colspan="3">托收　90 天以内□　90 天以上□　承兑日期　/　/　付汇日期　/　/　期限　天</td></tr>
</table>

续表

<table>
<tr><td rowspan="7">汇

款</td><td>预付货款□　　货到付汇（凭报关单付汇）□　　付汇日期　　/　　/</td></tr>
<tr><td>报关单号　　报关日期/　　/　　报关单币种　　金额</td></tr>
<tr><td>报关单号　　报关日期/　　/　　报关单币种　　金额</td></tr>
<tr><td>报关单号　　报关日期/　　/　　报关单币种　　金额</td></tr>
<tr><td>报关单号　　报关日期/　　/　　报关单币种　　金额</td></tr>
<tr><td>报关单号　　报关日期/　　/　　报关单币种　　金额</td></tr>
<tr><td>（若报关单填写不完，可另附纸。）</td></tr>
<tr><td colspan="2">其他□　付汇日期　　/　　/</td></tr>
<tr><td colspan="2">以下由付汇银行填写
申报号码：□□□□□□□□□□□□□□□□□□□□□□
业务编号：　　　　审核日期：　/　/　　　（付汇银行签章）</td></tr>
</table>

进口单位签章

模块评估

1. 模块课程评价表

模块内容________ 班级________ 学号________ 姓名________ ________年__月__日

1. 你认为本模块最有价值的内容是：
2. 本堂课上教师使用的教学方法是否对学习有帮助，你对此有何建议。
3. 你是否有计划地组织学习？是否在朝学习目标努力？
4. 下列问题我需要得到进一步的了解和帮助：
教师签名 学生签名

2. 基本能力测评表

核心能力	评价指标	测评结果	备注
自我管理能力	1. 培养自己的责任心 2. 掌握时间管理技能 3. 将自己所学的知识运用到工作中		
交流能力	1. 知道如何尊重他人的观点、价值和信仰等 2. 能与其他人有效沟通 3. 在团队合作中表现积极 4. 能正确获取并反馈信息		
解决问题的能力	1. 学会搜集、使用信息资源 2. 能发现并解决常规及特殊问题		
创新能力	1. 面对问题，能提出有价值的观点或解决办法 2. 使用不同的思维方式		
其他			
教师评语 教师签字			
成绩		学生签字	

附　录

附录1　国际贸易词汇表

简称	描述
HS	HS是国际商品统一分类和编码制度（Harmonized System）的缩写。HS Code为税则号，又称海关编码，全球各国前6位海关编码基本相同。HS也是环商国际集团有限公司（HS International Group Ltd.）的缩写
ImpExp	ImpExp是进出口英文名称（Import Export）的缩写。ImpExp. com是进出口数据网英文网站域名和网址
JKCK	JKCK是进出口中文拼音（Jin Kou Chu Kou）的缩写。JKCK. com是进出口数据网中文网站域名和网址
CD	CD是海关数据（Customs Data）的缩写。海关数据又称海关进出口数据，含进出口企业名称和海关编码，一般按海关编码或企业名称查询。海关数据分海关进口数据和海关出口数据。
CCD	CCD为中国海关数据（China Customs Data）的缩写。中国海关数据又称中国海关进出口数据，含中国进出口企业名称和海关编码，按8位海关编码查询
BD	BD是提单数据（Bills Data）的缩写。提单数据又称提单进出口数据，或进出口提单数据。提单数据含收货人（进口商）和发货人（出口商），一般按产品名称关键词或企业名称查询。提单数据分为提单进口数据和提单出口数据
USBID	USBID为美国提单进口数据（US Bills Import Data）的缩写
USBED	USBED为美国提单出口数据（US Bills Export Data）的缩写
CSD	CSD为中国进出口统计数据（China Statistics Data）的缩写
TF	TF为贸易流向数据（Trade Flow）的缩写，又称进出口贸易流向数据，是一种按国别分类统计的进出口数据，一般按前6位海关编码查询
EI	EI是进出口企业名录（Exporters & Importers）的缩写

续表

简称	描述
Incoterm	Incoterm 是国际商业条款（International Commercial Term）的缩写
CIF	CIF 是 cost，insurance and freignt 的缩写，成本、保险费加运费是指卖方负责按通常条件租船订舱、支付到目的港的运费，并在规定的装运港和规定的期限内将货物装上船，装船后及时通知买方
CFR	CFR 是 cost and freight 的缩写，成本加运费是指装运货物越过船舷，卖方即完成交货
FOB	FOB 是 free on board 的缩写，船上交货是指卖方必须在合同规定的日期或期间内在指定的装运港将货物交到买方指定的船上，并负担货物越过船舷为止的一切费用和货物灭失或损坏的风险。仅适用于海运或内河运输
CIP	CIP 是 carriage and insurance paid to 的缩写，运费、保险费付至是指卖方除了须承担在 CPT 术语下同样的义务外，还须对货物在运输途中灭失或损坏的买方风险取得货物保险，订立保险合同并支付保险费
EXW	EXW 是 ex works 的缩写，工厂交货是指卖方在商品的生产地或所在地将货物提供给买方时，即履行了交货义务。适合于各种运输
FCA	FCA 是 free carrier 的缩写，货交承运人是指卖方只要将货物在合同规定的期限内，在指定地点交由买方指定的承运人，并办理了出口报关手续，即完成了交货。适用于铁路、公路、空运、海运、内河运输或联合运输
FAS	FAS 是 free alongside ship 的缩写，船边交货（一指定装运港）是指卖方在装运港将货物交到港口码头或驳船上的船边，即完成了交货。这是指买方必须自该时刻起负担一切费用和货物灭失或损坏的一切风险
CPT	CPT 是 carriage paid to 的缩写，运费付至是指卖方向其指定的承运人交货（货交承运人），但卖方还必须支付将货物运至目的地的运费。即买方承担交货之后一切风险和其他费用

数据来源：根据海关数据网信息整理

附录 2　跟单信用证统一惯例关于电子交单的附则（eUCP）（版本 2.0）

预先考虑事项

受益人或其代表向指定银行、保兑行（如有）或开证行仅以电子记录或电子记录与纸质单据混合的交单方式，在 eUCP 的范畴之外。

开证行向申请人仅以电子记录或电子记录与纸质单据混合的交单方式，在 eUCP 的范畴之外。

UCP 600 中的定义，如 eUCP 未重新定义或修改，将继续适用。

在同意开立、通知、保兑、修改或转让 eUCP 信用证前，银行应确保自己能够审核在该信用证项下要求提交的电子记录。

第 e1 条 《跟单信用证统一惯例(UCP600)关于电子交单附则》(“eUCP”)的范围

a. eUCP 是对《跟单信用证统一惯例》（2007 年修订本，国际商会第 600 号出版物）（“UCP”）的补充，以适应电子记录的单独提交或与纸质单据联合提交。

b. 当信用证表明受 eUCP 约束（“eUCP 信用证”）时，eUCP 适用。

c. 本文本版本号为 2.0。eUCP 信用证必须表明适用的版本，否则即受开证日最新的有效版本约束；或如果因受益人接受的修改而使信用证受 eUCP 约束，则受在该修改日期的有效版本约束。

d. eUCP 信用证必须表明开证行的实体地址。此外，信用证还必须表明任何指定银行的实体地址，以及保兑行（如有）的实体地址（如与指定银行的不同），如开证行开证时已知悉该实体地址。如果信用证中未表明任何指定银行及/或保兑行的实体地址，则该银行必须在不迟于通知或保兑信用证之时向受益人表明其实体地址；或者，在信用证可在任一银行兑用的情况下，如另一家非通知行或保兑行的银行愿意按指定承付或议付，则在其同意按指定行事之时向受益人表明其实体地址。

第 e2 条 eUCP 与 UCP 的关系

a. eUCP 信用证也受 UCP 约束，而无须将 UCP 明确纳入信用证。

b. 当 eUCP 适用时，如其与适用 UCP 产生不同结果，应以 eUCP 规定为准。

c. 如果 eUCP 信用证允许受益人在提交纸质单据或电子记录两者之间进行选择，而其选择了只提交纸质单据，则该笔交单仅适用 UCP。如果 eUCP 信用证只允许提交纸质单据，则仅适用 UCP。

第 e3 条 定义

a. UCP 使用的下列用语，为了将 UCP 适用于 eUCP 信用证项下提交的电子记录的目的，解释为：

ⅰ. “在其表面看来（appear on their face）”以及类似用语适用于审核电子记录的数据内容。

ⅱ. “单据（document）”应包括电子记录。

ⅲ. 电子记录的“交单地点（place for presentation）”意指一个数据处理系统的电子地址。

ⅳ. “交单人（presenter）”意指受益人，或代表其向指定银行、保兑行（如有）或直接向开证行实施交单行为的任何人。

ⅴ. “签署（sign）”及类似用语应包括电子签字。

ⅵ. “添加的（superimposed）”“批注（notation）”或“盖印戳的（stamped）”意指在电子记录中其增补特征明显的数据内容。

b. 在 eUCP 中使用的下列用语应具有以下含义：

ⅰ. “数据变损（data corruption）”意指因任何数据的失真或丢失而致使无法全部或部分读取已提交的电子记录。

ⅱ. “数据处理系统（data processing system）”意指全部或部分用于处理和操作数据、发起指令或响应数据信息或性能的计算机化或电子化或任何其他自动化的方法。

ⅲ. “电子记录（electronic record）”意指，以电子方式创建、生成、发送、传播、收到或储存的数据，包括（适当时）逻辑上相关或另外链接在一起以便成为电子记录一部分的所有信息，而无论这些信息是否同时生成，并且：

• 其发送人的表面身份、其包含的数据的表面来源及其是否保持完整和未被更改，可以被证实；并且

• 能够根据 eUCP 信用证条款审核其相符性。

ⅳ. “电子签字（electronic signature）”意指附加于或与一份电子记录有逻辑关联的数据处理，由签字人实施或采用，用以表明签字人身份及其对电子记录的证实。

ⅴ. “格式（format）”意指表达电子记录的数据组织形式或电子记录提到的数据组织形式。

ⅵ. “纸质单据（paper document）”意指纸面形式的单据。

ⅶ. “收到（received）”意指电子记录以系统可接受的形式、根据 eUCP 信用证中指明的交单地点进入数据处理系统的时间。此系统生成的任何对收到的确认并不意味着该电子记录已在 eUCP 信用证下被查看、审核、接受或拒绝。

ⅷ. “再次提交（re-present）”或“再次提交的（re-presented）”意指替代或更换已经提交的电子记录。

第 e4 条　电子记录和纸质单据与货物、服务或履约行为

银行不处理电子记录或纸质单据可能涉及的货物、服务或履约行为。

第 e5 条　格式

eUCP 信用证必须注明每份电子记录的格式。如未注明，则电子记录可以任何格式提交。

第 e6 条　交单

a. ⅰ. eUCP 信用证必须注明提交电子记录的地点。

ⅱ. 如 eUCP 信用证要求或允许提交电子记录和纸质单据，除必须注明提交电子记录的地点外，还必须注明提交纸质单据的地点。

b. 电子记录可以分别提交，并且无需同时提交。

c. ⅰ. 如一份或多份电子记录被单独提交或与纸质单据混合提交，交单人有责任向指定银行、保兑行（如有）或开证行（如直接向开证行交单）提供表明交单结束的通知。该结束通知的收到将作为交单已经完毕并且交单的审核期限将开始的通知。

ⅱ. 结束通知可以电子记录或纸质单据方式做出，且必须注明其所关联的 eUCP 信用证。

ⅲ. 如果未收到结束通知，将视为未曾交单。

ⅳ. 指定银行无论是否按指定行事，当其向保兑行或开证行转发或提供其获取的电子记录时，无需发送结束通知。

d. ⅰ. 在 eUCP 信用证下提交的每份电子记录必须注明其据以交单的 eUCP 信用证。注明方式可以是在电子记录本身中或是在所附加的或添加的元数据中或是在随附的交单面函中明确提及。

ⅱ. 任何未如此注明的电子记录交单可被视为未曾收到。

e. ⅰ. 如果将接收交单的银行在营业中，但在规定的截止日及/或最迟交单日（视何种情形适用），其系统不能接收传来的电子记录，则视为歇业，截止日及/或最迟交单日应

延展至银行能够接收电子记录的下一个银行工作日。

ⅱ. 在此情况下，指定银行必须在其面函中向保兑行（如有）或开证行声明，电子记录是在根据第 e6（e）（i）条顺延的期限内提交的。

ⅲ. 如果尚待提交的电子记录只剩下结束通知，则可以用电讯方式或纸质单据提交，并被视为及时，只要其在该银行能够接收电子记录之前发出。

f. 不能被证实的电子记录将被视为未曾提交。

第 e7 条　审核

a. ⅰ. 审单时限自指定银行、保兑行（如有）或开证行（如直接向开证行交单）收到交单结束通知后的下一个银行工作日起算。

ⅱ. 如果交单时间或交单结束通知的时限根据第 e6（e）（i）条规定顺延，单据审核时限自接受交单的银行在交单地点能够接收结束通知后的下一个银行工作日起算。

b. ⅰ. 如果电子记录包含一个外部系统的超级链接，或指明电子记录可参照一外部系统审核，则超级链接中的或该外部系统中的电子记录应被视为构成电子记录不可分割的一部分予以审核。

ⅱ. 在审核时，如该外部系统不能提供所需电子记录的读取条件，则构成不符点，第 e7（d）（ii）条规定的情形除外。

c. 按指定行事的指定银行、保兑行（如有）或开证行无法审核 eUCP 信用证所要求格式的电子记录，或当未要求格式时，无法审核提交的电子记录，这一情形不构成拒付的依据。

d. ⅰ. 无论是否按指定承付或议付，指定银行转递电子记录的行为表明其已确信电子记录的表面真实性。

ⅱ. 如果指定银行确定交单相符并将该电子记录转发或提供给保兑行或开证行，无论指定银行是否已经承付或议付，开证行或保兑行必须承付或议付，或偿付该指定银行，即使指定的超级链接或外部系统不允许开证行或保兑行审核已由指定银行提供给开证行或保兑行或由保兑行提供给开证行的一份或多份电子记录。

第 e8 条　拒付通知

如果按指定行事的指定银行、保兑行（如有）或开证行对包含电子记录的交单发出了拒付通知，在发出拒付通知后 30 个日历日内未收到被通知方关于电子记录的处理指示，银行应退还被通知方以前尚未退还的任何纸质单据，但可以其认为合适的任何方式处理电子记录而不承担任何责任。

第 e9 条　正本与副本

要求提供一份或多份电子记录正本或副本时，提交一份电子记录即满足要求。

第 e10 条　出具日期

电子记录必须表明其出具日期。

第 e11 条　运输

如果证明运输的电子记录没有表明货物装运或发送或接管或已被收妥待运日期，电子记录的发出日期将被视为货物装运或发送或接管或已被收妥待运日期。但如果电子记录载有证明货物装运或发送或接管或已被收妥待运日期的批注时，该批注日期将被视为货物装运或发送或接管或已被收妥待运日期。显示附加数据内容的该批注无需另行签字或以其他方式证实。

第 e12 条　电子记录数据损坏

a. 如果指定银行（无论是否按指定行事）、保兑行（如有）或开证行收到的电子记录看似受到了数据损坏的影响，银行可通知交单人，也可要求再次提交电子记录。

b. 如果银行要求再次提交电子记录：

ⅰ. 则审单时限中止，待电子记录再次提交时恢复；并且

ⅱ. 如果指定银行不是保兑行，则必须将其关于再次提交电子记录的要求知会开证行和任何保兑行，并告知时限中止；但是

ⅲ. 如果该电子记录未在 30 个日历日内，或截止日及/或最迟交单日当天或之前（以日期先到者为准）再次提交，该银行可以将该电子记录视为未提交过。

第 e13 条　根据 eUCP 提交电子记录时的额外免责

a. 除通过使用数据处理系统接收、证实和识别电子记录即可发现者外，银行审核电子记录的表面真实性的行为并不使其对发送人身份、信息来源、完整性或未被更改性承担责任。

b. 银行对除其自身之外的数据处理系统无法运行所产生的后果概不负责。

第 e14 条　不可抗力

对由于天灾、暴动、骚乱、叛乱、战争、恐怖主义行为、网络攻击或任何罢工、停工或包括设备、软件或通信网络故障等任何其他的银行无法控制的原因导致的营业中断的后果，包括但不限于无法访问数据处理系统，或者设备、软件或通信网络故障，银行概不负责。

附录 3　ICC 跟单信用证统一惯例（UCP600）

第一条　UCP 的适用范围

《跟单信用证统一惯例——国际商会第 600 号出版物》（简称“UCP”）乃一套规则，适用于所有在其文本中明确表明受本惯例约束的跟单信用证（下称信用证）（在其可适用的范围内，包括备用信用证）。除非信用证明确修改或排除，本惯例各条文对信用证所有当事人均具有约束力。

第二条　定义

就本惯例而言：

通知行　指应开证行的要求通知信用证的银行。

申请人　指要求开立信用证的一方。

银行工作日　指银行在其履行受本惯例约束的行为的地点通常开业的一天。

受益人　指接受信用证并享受其利益的一方。

相符交单　指与信用证条款、本惯例的相关适用条款以及国际标准银行实务一致的交单。

保兑　指保兑行在开证行承诺之外做出的承付或议付相符交单的确定承诺。

保兑行　指根据开证行的授权或要求对信用证加具保兑的银行。

信用证　指一项不可撤销的安排，无论其名称或描述如何，该项安排构成开证行对相符交单予以承付的确定承诺。

承付　指：

a. 如果信用证为即期付款信用证，则即期付款。

b. 如果信用证为延期付款信用证，则承诺延期付款并在承诺到期日付款。

c. 如果信用证为承兑信用证，则承兑受益人开出的汇票并在汇票到期日付款。

开证行　指应申请人要求或者代表自己开出信用证的银行。

议付　指指定银行在相符交单下，在其应获偿付的银行工作日当天或之前向受益人预付或者同意预付款项，从而购买汇票（其付款人为指定银行以外的其他银行）及/或单据的行为。

指定银行　指信用证可在其处兑用的银行，如信用证可在任一银行兑用，则任何银行均为指定银行。

交单　指向开证行或指定银行提交信用证项下单据的行为，或指按此方式提交的单据。

交单人　指实施交单行为的受益人、银行或其他人。

第三条　解释

就本惯例而言：

如情形适用，单数词形包含复数含义，复数词形包含单数含义。

信用证是不可撤销的，即使未如此表明。

单据签字可用手签、摹样签字、穿孔签字、印戳、符号或任何其他机械或电子的证实方法为之。

诸如单据须履行法定手续、签证、证明等类似要求，可由单据上任何看似满足该要求的签字、标记、印戳或标签来满足。

一家银行在不同国家的分支机构被视为不同的银行。

用诸如“第一流的”“著名的”“合格的”“独立的”“正式的”“有资格的”或“本地的”等词语描述单据的出单人时，允许除受益人之外的任何人出具该单据。

除非要求在单据中使用，否则诸如“迅速地”“立刻地”或“尽快地”等词语将被不予理会。

“在或大概在（on or about）”或类似用语将被视为规定事件发生在指定日期的前后五个日历日之间，起讫日期计算在内。

“至（to）”“直至（until，till）”“从……开始（from）”及“在……之间（between）”等词用于确定发运日期时包含提及的日期，使用“在……之前（before）”及“在……之后（after）”时则不包含提及的日期。

“从……开始（from）”及“在……之后（after）”等词用于确定到期日时不包含提及的日期。

“前半月”及“后半月”分别指一个月的第一日到第十五日及第十六日到该月的最后一日，起讫日期计算在内。

一个月的“开始（beginning）”“中间（middle）”及“末尾（end）”分别指第一

到第十日、第十一日到第二十日及第二十一日到该月的最后一日，起讫日期计算在内。

第四条 信用证与合同

a. 就其性质而言，信用证与可能作为其开立基础的销售合同或其他合同是相互独立的交易，即使信用证中含有对此类合同的任何援引，银行也与该合同无关，且不受其约束。因此，银行关于承付、议付或履行信用证项下其他义务的承诺，不受申请人基于其与开证行或与受益人之间的关系而产生的任何请求或抗辩的影响。

受益人在任何情况下不得利用银行之间或申请人与开证行之间的合同关系。

b. 开证行应劝阻申请人试图将基础合同、形式发票等文件作为信用证组成部分的做法。

第五条 单据与货物、服务或履约行为

银行处理的是单据，而不是单据可能涉及的货物、服务或履约行为。

第六条 兑用方式、截止日和交单地点

a. 信用证必须规定可在其处兑用的银行，或是否可在任一银行兑用。规定在指定银行兑用的信用证同时也可以在开证行兑用。

b. 信用证必须规定其是以即期付款、延期付款、承兑还是议付的方式兑用。

c. 信用证不得开成凭以申请人为付款人的汇票兑用。

d. ⅰ. 信用证必须规定一个交单的截止日。规定的承付或议付的截止日将被视为交单的截止日。

ⅱ. 可在其处兑用信用证的银行所在地即为交单地点。可在任一银行兑用的信用证其交单地点为任一银行所在地。除规定的交单地点外，开证行所在地也是交单地点。

e. 除非如第二十九条 a 款规定的情形，否则受益人或者代表受益人的交单应在截止日当天或之前完成。

第七条 开证行责任

a. 只要规定的单据提交给指定银行或开证行，并且构成相符交单，则开证行必须承付，如果信用证为以下情形之一：

ⅰ. 信用证规定由开证行即期付款、延期付款或承兑；

ⅱ. 信用证规定由指定银行即期付款但其未付款；

ⅲ. 信用证规定由指定银行延期付款但其未承诺延期付款，或虽已承诺延期付款，但未在到期日付款；

ⅳ. 信用证规定由指定银行承兑，但其未承兑以其为付款人的汇票，或虽承兑了汇票，但未在到期日付款；

ⅴ. 信用证规定由指定银行议付但其未议付。

b. 开证行自开立信用证之时起即不可撤销地承担承付责任。

c. 指定银行承付或议付相符交单并将单据转给开证行之后，开证行即承担偿付该指定银行的责任。对承兑或延期付款信用证下相符交单金额的偿付应在到期日办理，无论指定银行是否在到期日之前预付或购买了单据。开证行偿付指定银行的责任独立于开证行对受益人的责任。

第八条 保兑行责任

a. 只要规定的单据提交给保兑行，或提交给其他任何指定银行，并且构成相符交单，保兑行必须：

ⅰ. 承付，如果信用证为以下情形之一：

a）信用证规定由保兑行即期付款、延期付款或承兑；

b）信用证规定由另一指定银行即期付款，但其未付款；

c）信用证规定由另一指定银行延期付款，但其未承诺延期付款，或虽已承诺延期付款但未在到期日付款；

d）信用证规定由另一指定银行承兑，但其未承兑以其为付款人的汇票，或虽已承兑汇票但未在到期日付款；

e）信用证规定由另一指定银行议付，但其未议付。

ⅱ. 无追索权地议付，如果信用证规定由保兑行议付。

b. 保兑行自对信用证加具保兑之时起即不可撤销地承担承付或议付的责任。

c. 其他指定银行承付或议付相符交单并将单据转往保兑行之后，保兑行即承担偿付该指定银行的责任。对承兑或延期付款信用证下相符交单金额的偿付应在到期日办理，无论指定银行是否在到期日之前预付或购买了单据。保兑行偿付指定银行的责任独立于保兑行对受益人的责任。

d. 如果开证行授权或要求一银行对信用证加具保兑，而其并不准备照办，则其必须毫不延误地通知开证行，并可通知此信用证而不加保兑。

第九条　信用证及其修改的通知

a. 信用证及其任何修改可以经由通知行通知给受益人。非保兑行的通知行通知信用证及修改时不承担承付或议付的责任。

b. 通知行通知信用证或修改的行为表示其已确信信用证或修改的表面真实性，而且其通知准确地反映了其收到的信用证或修改的条款。

c. 通知行可以通过另一银行（“第二通知行”）向受益人通知信用证及修改。第二通知行通知信用证或修改的行为表明其已确信收到的通知的表面真实性，并且其通知准确地反映了收到的信用证或修改的条款。

d. 经由通知行或第二通知行通知信用证的银行必须经由同一银行通知其后的任何修改。

e. 如一银行被要求通知信用证或修改但其决定不予通知，则应毫不延误地告知自其处收到信用证、修改或通知的银行。

f. 如一银行被要求通知信用证或修改，但其不能确信信用证、修改或通知的表面真实性，则应毫不延误地通知从其处收到指示的银行。如果通知行或第二通知行决定仍然通知信用证或修改，则应告知受益人或第二通知行其不能确信信用证、修改或通知的表面真实性。

第十条　修改

a. 除第三十八条另有规定者外，未经开证行、保兑行（如有的话）及受益人同意，信用证既不得修改，也不得撤销。

b. 开证行自发出修改之时起，即不可撤销地受其约束。保兑行可将其保兑扩展至修改，并自通知该修改之时，即不可撤销地受其约束。但是，保兑行可以选择将修改通知受益人而不对其加具保兑。若然如此，其必须毫不延误地将此告知开证行，并在其给受益人的通知中告知受益人。

c. 在受益人告知通知修改的银行其接受该修改之前，原信用证（或含有先前被接受的修改的信用证）的条款对受益人仍然有效。受益人应提供接受或拒绝修改的通知。如果受益人未能给予通知，当交单与信用证以及尚未表示接受的修改的要求一致时，即视为受益人已作出接受修改的通知，并且从此时起，该信用证被修改。

d. 通知修改的银行应将任何接受或拒绝的通知转告发出修改的银行。

e. 对同一修改的内容不允许部分接受，部分接受将被视为拒绝修改的通知。

f. 修改中关于除非受益人在某一时间内拒绝修改否则修改生效的规定应被不予理会。

第十一条 电讯传输的和预先通知的信用证和修改

a. 以经证实的电讯方式发出的信用证或信用证修改即被视为有效的信用证或修改文据，任何后续的邮寄确认书应被不予理会。

如电讯声明“详情后告”（或类似用语）或声明以邮寄确认书为有效信用证或修改，则该电讯不被视为有效信用证或修改。开证行必须随即不迟延地开立有效信用证或修改，其条款不得与该电讯矛盾。

b. 开证行只有在准备开立有效信用证或作出有效修改时，才可以发出关于开立或修改信用证的初步通知（预先通知）。开证行作出该预先通知，即不可撤销地保证不迟延地开立或修改信用证，且其条款不能与预先通知相矛盾。

第十二条 指定

a. 除非指定银行为保兑行，对于承付或议付的授权并不赋予指定银行承付或议付的义务，除非该指定银行明确表示同意并且告知受益人。

b. 开证行指定一银行承兑汇票或做出延期付款承诺，即为授权该指定银行预付或购买其已承兑的汇票或已做出的延期付款承诺。

c. 非保兑行的指定银行收到或审核并转递单据的行为并不使其承担承付或议付的责任，也不构成其承付或议付的行为。

第十三条 银行之间的偿付安排

a. 如果信用证规定指定银行（“索偿行”）向另一方（“偿付行”）获取偿付时，必须同时规定该偿付是否按信用证开立时有效的 ICC 银行间偿付规则进行。

b. 如果信用证没有规定偿付遵守 ICC 银行间偿付规则，则按照以下规定：

ⅰ. 开证行必须给予偿付行有关偿付的授权，授权应符合信用证关于兑用方式的规定，且不应设定截止日。

ⅱ. 开证行不应要求索偿行向偿付行提供与信用证条款相符的证明。

ⅲ. 如果偿付行未按信用证条款见索即偿，开证行将承担利息损失以及产生的任何其他费用。

ⅳ. 偿付行的费用应由开证行承担。然而，如果此项费用由受益人承担，开证行有责任在信用证及偿付授权中注明。如果偿付行的费用由受益人承担，该费用应在偿付时从付给索偿行的金额中扣取。如果偿付未发生，偿付行的费用仍由开证行负担。

c. 如果偿付行未能见索即偿，开证行不能免除偿付责任。

第十四条 单据审核标准

a. 按指定行事的指定银行、保兑行（如果有的话）及开证行须审核交单，并仅基于单据本身确定其是否在表面上构成相符交单。

b. 按指定行事的指定银行、保兑行（如有的话）及开证行各有从交单次日起的至多五个银行工作日用以确定交单是否相符。这一期限不因在交单日当天或之后信用证截止日或最迟交单日届至而受到缩减或影响。

c. 如果单据中包含一份或多份受第十九、二十、二十一、二十二、二十三、二十四或二十五条规制的正本运输单据，则须由受益人或其代表在不迟于本惯例所指的发运日之后的二十一个日历日内交单，但是在任何情况下都不得迟于信用证的截止日。

d. 单据中的数据，在与信用证、单据本身以及国际标准银行实务参照解读时，无须与该单据本身中的数据、其他要求的单据或信用证中的数据等同一致，但不得矛盾。

e. 除商业发票外，其他单据中的货物、服务或履约行为的描述，如果有的话，可使用与信用证中的描述不矛盾的概括性用语。

f. 如果信用证要求提交运输单据、保险单据或者商业发票之外的单据，却未规定出单人或其数据内容，则只要提交的单据内容看似满足所要求单据的功能，且其他方面符合第十四条 d 款，银行将接受该单据。

g. 提交的非信用证所要求的单据将被不予理会，并可被退还给交单人。

h. 如果信用证含有一项条件，但未规定用以表明该条件得到满足的单据，银行将视为未作规定并不予理会。

i. 单据日期可以早于信用证的开立日期，但不得晚于交单日期。

j. 当受益人和申请人的地址出现在任何规定的单据中时，无须与信用证或其他规定单据中所载相同，但必须与信用证中规定的相应地址同在一国。联络细节（传真、电话、电子邮件及类似细节）作为受益人和申请人地址的一部分时将被不予理会。然而，如果申请人的地址和联络细节为第十九、二十、二十一、二十二、二十三、二十四或二十五条规定的运输单据上的收货人或通知方细节的一部分时，应与信用证规定的相同。

k. 在任何单据中注明的托运人或发货人无须为信用证的受益人。

l. 运输单据可以由任何人出具，无须为承运人、船东、船长或租船人，只要其符合第十九、二十、二十一、二十二、二十三或二十四条的要求。

第十五条　相符交单

a. 当开证行确定交单相符时，必须承付。

b. 当保兑行确定交单相符时，必须承付或者议付并将单据转递给开证行。

c. 当指定银行确定交单相符并承付或议付时，必须将单据转递给保兑行或开证行。

第十六条　不符单据、放弃及通知

a. 当按照指定行事的指定银行、保兑行（如有的话）或者开证行确定交单不符时，可以拒绝承付或议付。

b. 当开证行确定交单不符时，可以自行决定联系申请人放弃不符点。然而这并不能延长第十四条 b 款所指的期限。

c. 当按照指定行事的指定银行、保兑行（如有的话）或开证行决定拒绝承付或议付时，必须给予交单人一份单独的拒付通知。

该通知必须声明：

ⅰ. 银行拒绝承付或议付；及

ⅱ. 银行拒绝承付或者议付所依据的每一个不符点；及

ⅲ. a）银行留存单据听候交单人的进一步指示；或者

b）开证行留存单据直到其从申请人处接到放弃不符点的通知并同意接受该放弃，或者其同意接受对不符点的放弃之前从交单人处收到其进一步指示；或者

c）银行将退回单据；或者

d）银行将按之前从交单人处获得的指示处理。

d. 第十六条 c 款要求的通知必须以电讯方式，如不可能，则以其他快捷方式，在不迟于自交单之翌日起第五个银行工作日结束前发出。

e. 按照指定行事的指定银行、保兑行（如有的话）或开证行在按照第十六条 c 款ⅲ项 a）或 b）发出了通知之后，可以在任何时候将单据退还交单人。

f. 如果开证行或保兑行未能按照本条行事，则无权宣称交单不符。

g. 当开证行拒绝承付或保兑行拒绝承付或者议付，并且按照本条发出了拒付通知后，有权要求返还已偿付的款项及利息。

第十七条　正本单据及副本

a. 信用证规定的每一种单据须至少提交一份正本。

b. 银行应将任何带有看似出单人的原始签名、标记、印戳或标签的单据视为正本单据，除非单据本身表明其非正本。

c. 除非单据本身另有说明，在以下情况下，银行也将其视为正本单据：

ⅰ. 单据看似由出单人手写、打字、穿孔或盖章；或者

ⅱ. 单据看似使用出单人的原始信纸出具；或者

ⅲ. 单据声明其为正本单据，除非该声明看似不适用于提交的单据。

d. 如果信用证要求提交单据的副本，提交正本或副本均可。

e. 如果信用证使用诸如"一式两份（in duplicate）""两份（in two fold）""两套（in two copies）"等用语要求提交多份单据，则提交至少一份正本，其余使用副本即可满足要求，除非单据本身另有说明。

第十八条　商业发票

a. 商业发票：

ⅰ. 必须看似由受益人出具（第三十八条规定的情形除外）；

ⅱ. 必须出具成以申请人为抬头（第三十八条 g 款规定的情形除外）；

ⅲ. 必须与信用证的货币相同；且

ⅳ. 无须签名。

b. 按指定行事的指定银行、保兑行（如有的话）或开证行可以接受金额大于信用证允许金额的商业发票，其决定对有关各方均有约束力，只要该银行对超过信用证允许金额的部分未作承付或者议付。

c. 商业发票上的货物、服务或履约行为的描述应该与信用证中的描述一致。

第十九条　涵盖至少两种不同运输方式的运输单据

a. 涵盖至少两种不同运输方式的运输单据（多式或联合运输单据），无论名称如何，必须看似：

ⅰ. 表明承运人名称并由以下人员签署：

* 承运人或其具名代理人，或

* 船长或其具名代理人。

承运人、船长或代理人的任何签字，必须标明其承运人、船长或代理人的身份。

代理人签字必须标明其系代表承运人还是船长签字。

ⅱ. 通过以下方式表明货物已经在信用证规定的地点发送、接管或已装运。

* 事先印就的文字；或者

* 表明货物已经被发送、接管或装运日期的印戳或批注。

运输单据的出具日期将被视为发送、接管或装运的日期，也即发运的日期。然而如单据以印戳或批注的方式表明了发送、接管或装运日期，该日期将被视为发运日期。

ⅲ. 表明信用证规定的发送、接管或发运地点，以及最终目的地，即使：

a）该运输单据另外还载明了一个不同的发送、接管或发运地点或最终目的地；或者，

b）该运输单据载有“预期的”或类似的关于船只、装货港或卸货港的限定语。

ⅳ. 为唯一的正本运输单据，或者，如果出具为多份正本，则为运输单据中表明的全套单据。

ⅴ. 载有承运条款和条件，或提示承运条款和条件参见别处（简式/背面空白的运输单据）。银行将不审核承运条款和条件的内容。

ⅵ. 未表明受租船合同约束。

b. 就本条而言，转运指在从信用证规定的发送、接管或者发运地点至最终目的地的运输过程中从某一运输工具上卸下货物并装上另一运输工具的行为（无论其是否为不同的运输方式）。

c. ⅰ. 运输单据可以表明货物将要或可能被转运，只要全程运输由同一运输单据涵盖。

ⅱ. 即使信用证禁止转运，注明将要或者可能发生转运的运输单据仍可接受。

第二十条　提单

a. 提单，无论名称如何，必须看似：

ⅰ. 表明承运人名称，并由下列人员签署：

* 承运人或其具名代理人，或者

* 船长或其具名代理人。

承运人、船长或代理人的任何签字必须表明其承运人、船长或代理人的身份。

代理人的任何签字必须标明其系代表承运人还是船长签字。

ⅱ. 通过以下方式表明货物已在信用证规定的装货港装上具名船只：

* 预先印就的文字，或

* 已装船批注注明货物的装运日期。

提单的出具日期将被视为发运日期，除非提单载有表明发运日期的已装船批注，此时已装船批注中显示的日期将被视为发运日期。

如果提单载有“预期船只”或类似的关于船名的限定语，则需以已装船批注明确发运日期以及实际船名。

ⅲ. 表明货物从信用证规定的装货港发运至卸货港。

如果提单没有表明信用证规定的装货港为装货港，或者其载有“预期的”或类似的关于装货港的限定语，则需以已装船批注表明信用证规定的装货港、发运日期以及实际船名。即使提单以事先印就的文字表明了货物已装载或装运于具名船只，本规定仍适用。

ⅳ. 为唯一的正本提单，或如果以多份正本出具，为提单中表明的全套正本。

ⅴ. 载有承运条款和条件，或提示承运条款和条件参见别处（简式/背面空白的提单）。银行将不审核承运条款和条件的内容。

ⅵ. 未表明受租船合同约束。

b. 就本条而言，转运系指在信用证规定的装货港到卸货港之间的运输过程中，将货物从一船卸下并再装上另一船的行为。

c. ⅰ. 提单可以表明货物将要或可能被转运，只要全程运输由同一提单涵盖。

ⅱ即使信用证禁止转运，注明将要或可能发生转运的提单仍可接受，只要其表明货物由集装箱、拖车或子船运输。

d. 提单中声明承运人保留转运权利的条款将被不予理会。

第二十一条　不可转让的海运单

a. 不可转让的海运单，无论名称如何，必须看似：

ⅰ. 表明承运人名称并由下列人员签署：

* 承运人或其具名代理人，或者

* 船长或其具名代理人。

承运人、船长或代理人的任何签字必须标明其承运人、船长或代理人的身份。

代理人签字必须标明其系代表承运人还是船长签字。

ⅱ. 通过以下方式表明货物已在信用证规定的装货港装上具名船只：

* 预先印就的文字，或者

* 已装船批注表明货物的装运日期。

不可转让海运单的出具日期将被视为发运日期，除非其上带有已装船批注注明发运日期，此时已装船批注注明的日期将被视为发运日期。

如果不可转让海运单载有“预期船只”或类似的关于船名的限定语，则需要以已装船批注表明发运日期和实际船名。

ⅲ. 表明货物从信用证规定的装货港发运至卸货港。

如果不可转让海运单未以信用证规定的装货港为装货港，或者如果其载有“预期的”或类似的关于装货港的限定语，则需要以已装船批注表明信用证规定的装货港、发运日期和船名。即使不可转让海运单以预先印就的文字表明货物已由具名船只装载或装运，本规定也适用。

ⅳ. 为唯一的正本不可转让海运单，或如果以多份正本出具，为海运单上注明的全套正本。

ⅴ. 载有承运条款和条件，或提示承运条款和条件参见别处（简式/背面空白的海运单）。银行将不审核承运条款和条件的内容。

ⅵ. 未注明受租船合同约束。

b. 就本条而言，转运系指在信用证规定的装货港到卸货港之间的运输过程中，将货物从一船卸下并装上另一船的行为。

c. ⅰ. 不可转让海运单可以注明货物将要或可能被转运，只要全程运输由同一海运单涵盖。

ⅱ. 即使信用证禁止转运，注明转运将要或可能发生的不可转让的海运单仍可接受，只要其表明货物装于集装箱、拖船或子船中运输。

d. 不可转让的海运单中声明承运人保留转运权利的条款将被不予理会。

第二十二条　租船合同提单

a. 表明其受租船合同约束的提单（租船合同提单），无论名称如何，必须看似：

ⅰ. 由以下人员签署：

* 船长或其具名代理人，或
* 船东或其具名代理人，或
* 租船人或其具名代理人。

船长、船东、租船人或代理人的任何签字必须标明其船长、船东、租船人或代理人的身份。

代理人签字必须表明其系代表船长、船东还是租船人签字。

代理人代表船东或租船人签字时必须注明船东或租船人的名称。

ⅱ. 通过以下方式表明货物已在信用证规定的装货港装上具名船只：

* 预先印就的文字，或者
* 已装船批注注明货物的装运日期。

租船合同提单的出具日期将被视为发运日期，除非租船合同提单载有已装船批注注明发运日期，此时已装船批注上注明的日期将被视为发运日期。

ⅲ. 表明货物从信用证规定的装货港发运至卸货港。卸货港也可显示为信用证规定的港口范围或地理区域。

ⅳ. 为唯一的正本租船合同提单，或如以多份正本出具，为租船合同提单注明的全套正本。

b. 银行将不审核租船合同，即使信用证要求提交租船合同。

第二十三条　空运单据

a. 空运单据，无论名称如何，必须看似：

ⅰ. 表明承运人名称，并由以下人员签署：

* 承运人，或
* 承运人的具名代理人。

承运人或其代理人的任何签字必须标明其承运人或代理人的身份。

代理人签字必须表明其系代表承运人签字。

ⅱ. 表明货物已被收妥待运。

ⅲ. 表明出具日期。该日期将被视为发运日期，除非空运单据载有专门批注注明实际发运日期，此时批注中的日期将被视为发运日期。

空运单据中其他与航班号和航班日期相关的信息将不被用来确定发运日期。

ⅳ. 表明信用证规定的起飞机场和目的地机场。

ⅴ. 为开给发货人或托运人的正本，即使信用证规定提交全套正本。

ⅵ. 载有承运条款和条件，或提示条款和条件参见别处。银行将不审核承运条款和条件的内容。

b. 就本条而言，转运是指在信用证规定的起飞机场到目的地机场的运输过程中，将货物从一飞机卸下再装上另一飞机的行为。

c. ⅰ. 空运单据可以注明货物将要或可能转运，只要全程运输由同一空运单据涵盖。

ⅱ. 即使信用证禁止转运，注明将要或可能发生转运的空运单据仍可接受。

第二十四条　公路、铁路或内陆水运单据

a. 公路、铁路或内陆水运单据，无论名称如何，必须看似：

ⅰ. 表明承运人名称，并且

＊由承运人或其具名代理人签署，或者

＊由承运人或其具名代理人以签字、印戳或批注表明货物收讫。

承运人或其具名代理人的收货签字、印戳或批注必须标明其承运人或代理人的身份。

代理人的收货签字、印戳或批注必须标明代理人系代表承运人签字或行事。

如果铁路运输单据没有指明承运人，可以接受铁路运输公司的任何签字或印戳作为承运人签署单据的证据。

ⅱ. 表明货物在信用证规定地点的发运日期，或者收讫待运或待发送的日期。运输单据的出具日期将被视为发运日期，除非运输单据上盖有带日期的收货印戳，或注明了收货日期或发运日期。

ⅲ. 表明信用证规定的发运地及目的地。

b. ⅰ. 公路运输单据必须看似为开给发货人或托运人的正本，或没有任何标记表明单据开给何人。

ⅱ. 注明“第二联”的铁路运输单据将被作为正本接受。

ⅲ. 无论是否注明正本字样，铁路或内陆水运单据都被作为正本接受。

c. 如运输单据上未注明出具的正本数量，提交的份数即视为全套正本。

d. 就本条而言，转运是指在信用证规定的发运、发送或运送的地点到目的地之间的运输过程中，在同一运输方式中从一运输工具卸下再装上另一运输工具的行为。

e. ⅰ. 只要全程运输由同一运输单据涵盖，公路、铁路或内陆水运单据可以注明货物将要或可能被转运。

ⅱ. 即使信用证禁止转运，注明将要或可能发生转运的公路、铁路或内陆水运单据仍可接受。

第二十五条　快递收据、邮政收据或投邮证明

a. 证明货物收讫待运的快递收据，无论名称如何，必须看似：

ⅰ. 表明快递机构的名称，并在信用证规定的货物发运地点由该具名快递机构盖章或签字；并且

ⅱ. 表明取件或收件的日期或类似词语。该日期将被视为发运日期。

b. 如果要求显示快递费用付讫或预付，快递机构出具的表明快递费由收货人以外的一方支付的运输单据可以满足该项要求。

c. 证明货物收讫待运的邮政收据或投邮证明，无论名称如何，必须看似在信用证规定的货物发运地点盖章或签署并注明日期。该日期将被视为发运日期。

第二十六条　“货装舱面”“托运人装载和计数”“内容据托运人报称”及运费之外的费用

a. 运输单据不得表明货物装于或者将装于舱面。声明货物可能被装于舱面的运输单据条款可以接受。

b. 载有诸如“托运人装载和计数”或“内容据托运人报称”条款的运输单据可以接受。

c. 运输单据上可以以印戳或其他方式提及运费之外的费用。

第二十七条　清洁运输单据

银行只接受清洁运输单据。清洁运输单据指未载有明确宣称货物或包装有缺陷的条款或批注的运输单据。“清洁”一词并不需要在运输单据上出现，即使信用证要求运输单据

为“清洁已装船”的。

第二十八条 保险单据及保险范围

a. 保险单据，例如保险单或预约保险项下的保险证明书或者声明书，必须看似由保险公司或承保人或其代理人或代表出具并签署。

代理人或代表的签字必须表明其系代表保险公司或承保人签字。

b. 如果保险单据表明其以多份正本出具，所有正本均须提交。

c. 暂保单将不被接受。

d. 可以接受保险单代替预约保险项下的保险证明书或声明书。

e. 保险单据日期不得晚于发运日期，除非保险单据表明保险责任不迟于发运日生效。

f. ⅰ. 保险单据必须表明投保金额并以与信用证相同的货币表示。

ⅱ. 信用证对于投保金额为货物价值、发票金额或类似金额的某一比例的要求，将被视为对最低保额的要求。

如果信用证对投保金额未做规定，投保金额须至少为货物的 CIF 或 CIP 价格的百分之一百一十。

如果从单据中不能确定 CIF 或者 CIP 价格，投保金额必须基于要求承付或议付的金额，或者基于发票上显示的货物总值来计算，两者之中取金额较高者。

ⅲ. 保险单据须表明承保的风险区间至少涵盖从信用证规定的货物接管地或发运地开始到卸货地或最终目的地为止。

g. 信用证应规定所需投保的险别及附加险（如有的话）。如果信用证使用诸如“通常风险”或“惯常风险”等含义不确切的用语，则无论是否有漏保之风险。保险单据将被照样接受。

h. 当信用证规定投保“一切险”时，如保险单据载有任何“一切险”批注或条款，无论是否有“一切险”标题，均将被接受，即使其声明任何风险除外。

i. 保险单据可以援引任何除外条款。

j. 保险单据可以注明受免赔率或免赔额（减除额）约束。

第二十九条 截止日或最迟交单日的顺延

a. 如果信用证的截止日或最迟交单日适逢接受交单的银行非因第三十六条所述原因而歇业，则截止日或最迟交单日，视何者适用，将顺延至其重新开业的第一个银行工作日。

b. 如果在顺延后的第一个银行工作日交单，指定银行必须在其致开证行或保兑行的面函中声明交单是在根据第二十九条 a 款顺延的期限内提交的。

c. 最迟发运日不因第二十九条 a 款规定的原因而顺延。

第三十条 信用证金额、数量与单价的伸缩度

a.“约”或“大约”用于信用证金额或信用证规定的数量或单价时，应解释为允许有关金额或数量或单价有不超过百分之十的增减幅度。

b. 在信用证未以包装单位件数或货物自身件数的方式规定货物数量时，货物数量允许有百分之五的增减幅度，只要总支取金额不超过信用证金额。

c. 如果信用证规定了货物数量，而该数量已全部发运，及如果信用证规定了单价，而该单价又未降低，或当第三十条 b 款不适用时，则即使不允许部分装运，也允许支取的金额有百分之五的减幅。若信用证规定有特定的增减幅度或使用第三十条 a 款提到的用语限定数量，则该减幅不适用。

第三十一条　部分支款或部分发运

a. 允许部分支款或部分发运。

b. 表明使用同一运输工具并经由同次航程运输的数套运输单据在同一次提交时，只要显示相同目的地，将不视为部分发运，即使运输单据上表明的发运日期不同或装货港、接管地或发送地点不同。如果交单由数套运输单据构成，其中最晚的一个发运日将被视为发运日。

含有一套或数套运输单据的交单，如果表明在同一种运输方式下经由数件运输工具运输，即使运输工具在同一天出发运往同一目的地，仍将被视为部分发运。

c. 含有一份以上快递收据、邮政收据或投邮证明的交单，如果单据看似由同一快递或邮政机构在同一地点和日期加盖印戳或签字并且表明同一目的地，将不视为部分发运。

第三十二条　分期支款或分期发运

如信用证规定在指定的时间段内分期支款或分期发运，任何一期未按信用证规定期限支取或发运时，信用证对该期及以后各期均告失效。

第三十三条　交单时间

银行在其营业时间外无接受交单的义务。

第三十四条　关于单据有效性的免责

银行对任何单据的形式、充分性、准确性、内容真实性、虚假性或法律效力，或对单据中规定或添加的一般或特殊条件，概不负责；银行对任何单据所代表的货物、服务或其他履约行为的描述、数量、重量、品质、状况、包装、交付、价值或其存在与否，或对发货人、承运人、货运代理人、收货人、货物的保险人或其他任何人的诚信与否、作为或不作为、清偿能力、履约或资信状况，也概不负责。

第三十五条　关于信息传递和翻译的免责

当报文、信件或单据按照信用证的要求传输或发送时，或当信用证未作指示，银行自行选择传送服务时，银行对报文传输或信件或单据的递送过程中发生的延误、中途遗失、残缺或其他错误产生的后果，概不负责。

如果指定银行确定交单相符并将单据发往开证行或保兑行，无论指定银行是否已经承付或议付，开证行或保兑行必须承付或议付，或偿付指定银行，即使单据在指定银行送往开证行或保兑行的途中，或保兑行送往开证行的途中丢失。

银行对技术术语的翻译或解释上的错误，不负责任，并可不加翻译地传送信用证条款。

第三十六条　不可抗力

银行对由于天灾、暴动、骚乱、叛乱、战争、恐怖主义行为或任何罢工、停工或其无法控制的任何其他原因导致的营业中断的后果，概不负责。

银行恢复营业时，对于在营业中断期间已逾期的信用证，不再进行承付或议付。

第三十七条　关于被指示方行为的免责

a. 为了执行申请人的指示，银行利用其他银行的服务，其费用和风险由申请人承担。

b. 即使银行自行选择了其他银行，如果发出的指示未被执行，开证行或通知行对此亦不负责。

c. 指示另一银行提供服务的银行有责任负担被指示方因执行指示而发生的任何佣金、手续费、成本或开支（费用）。

如果信用证规定费用由受益人负担，而该费用未能收取或从信用证款项中扣除，开证行依然承担支付此费用的责任。信用证或其修改不应规定向受益人的通知以通知行或第二通知行收到其费用为条件。

d. 外国法律和惯例加诸银行的一切义务和责任，申请人应受其约束，并就此对银行负补偿之责。

第三十八条　可转让信用证

a. 银行无办理信用证转让的义务，除非其明确同意。

b. 就本条而言：

可转让信用证系指特别注明“可转让（transferable）”字样的信用证。可转让信用证可应受益人（第一受益人）的要求转为全部或部分由另一受益人（第二受益人）兑用。

转让行系指办理信用证转让的指定银行，或当信用证规定可在任一银行兑用时，指开证行特别如此授权并实际办理转让的银行。开证行也可担任转让行。

已转让信用证指已由转让行转为可由第二受益人兑用的信用证。

c. 除非转让时另有约定，有关转让的所有费用（诸如佣金、手续费、成本或开支）须由第一受益人支付。

d. 只要信用证允许部分支款或部分发运，信用证可以分部分地转让给数名第二受益人。

已转让信用证不得应第二受益人的要求转让给任何其后受益人。第一受益人不视为其后受益人。

e. 任何转让要求须说明是否允许及在何条件下允许将修改通知第二受益人。已转让信用证须明确说明该项条件。

f. 如果信用证转让给数名第二受益人，其中一名或多名第二受益人对信用证修改的拒绝并不影响其他第二受益人接受修改。对接受者而言该已转让信用证即被相应修改，而对拒绝修改的第二受益人而言，该信用证未被修改。

g. 已转让信用证须准确转载原证条款，包括保兑（如果有的话），但下列项目除外：

——信用证金额，

——规定的任何单价，

——截止日期，

——交单期限，或

——最迟发运日或发运期间。

以上任何一项或全部均可减少或缩短。

必须投保的保险比例可以增加，以达到原信用证或本惯例规定的保险金额。

可用第一受益人的名称替换原证中的开证申请人名称。

如果原证特别要求开证申请人名称应在除发票以外的任何单据中出现时，已转让信用证必须反映该项要求。

h. 第一受益人有权以自己的发票和汇票（如有的话）替换第二受益人的发票和汇票，其金额不得超过原信用证的金额。经过替换后，第一受益人可在原信用证项下支取自己发票与第二受益人发票间的差价（如有的话）。

i. 如果第一受益人应提交其自己的发票和汇票（如有的话），但未能在第一次要求时照办，或第一受益人提交的发票导致了第二受益人的交单中本不存在的不符点，而其未能在第一次要求时修正，转让行有权将从第二受益人处收到的单据照交开证行，并不再对第一受益人承担责任。

j. 在要求转让时，第一受益人可以要求在信用证转让后的兑用地点，在原信用证的截止日之前（包括截止日），对第二受益人承付或议付。本规定并不损害第一受益人在第三十八条 h 款下的权利。

k. 第二受益人或代表第二受益人的交单必须交给转让行。

第三十九条　款项让渡

信用证未注明可转让，并不影响受益人根据所适用的法律规定，将该信用证项下其可能有权或可能将成为有权获得的款项让渡给他人的权利。本条只涉及款项的让渡，而不涉及在信用证项下进行履行行为的权利让渡。

数据来源：中国国际贸易促进委员会

参考文献

[1] 吴国新，李元旭．国际贸易实务［M］．北京：清华大学出版社，2002.

[2] 王莉，陈琳，刘琳，等．进出口业务单证操作手册［M］．广州：广东经济出版社，2005.

[3] 朱春兰．外贸单证实训［M］．浙江：浙江大学出版社，2010.

[4] 朱春兰．外贸单证实务［M］．大连：大连理工大学出版社，2010.